GRAND HOTELS *of the* JAZZ AGE

GRAND HOTELS *of the* JAZZ AGE

THE ARCHITECTURE OF SCHULTZE *&* WEAVER

Marianne Lamonaca and Jonathan Mogul, editors

The Wolfsonian–Florida International University
Miami Beach

Princeton Architectural Press
New York

Published by
Princeton Architectural Press
37 East Seventh Street
New York, New York 10003

For a free catalog of books, call 1.800.722.6657.
Visit our web site at www.papress.com.

Printed and bound in China
08 07 06 05 5 4 3 2 1 First edition

This publication is made possible by grants from the Cowles Charitable Trust, the Aaron I. Fleischman Foundation, and Furthermore: A program of the J. M. Kaplan Fund.

Frontispiece: Presentation drawing for the Sherry-Netherland Hotel, rendered by Chester Price, 1924

Editing: Nancy Eklund Later
Design: Jan Haux

Special thanks to: Nettie Aljian, Dorothy Ball, Nicola Bednarek, Janet Behning, Megan Carey, Penny (Yuen Pik) Chu, Russell Fernandez, Clare Jacobson, John King, Mark Lamster, Linda Lee, Katharine Myers, Lauren Nelson, Jane Sheinman, Scott Tennent, Jennifer Thompson, Paul Wagner, Joseph Weston, and Deb Wood of Princeton Architectural Press —Kevin C. Lippert, publisher

Library of Congress Cataloging-in-Publication Data

Grand hotels of the jazz age : the architecture of Schultze & Weaver
/ Marianne Lamonaca and Jonathan Mogul, eds.—1st ed.
p. cm.
Includes bibliographical references and index.
ISBN 1-56898-555-X (Princeton Architectural Press : alk. paper)
1. Schultze & Weaver—Themes, motives. 2. Schultze, Leonard, 1877–1951. 3. Weaver, S. Fullerton (Spencer Fullerton) d. 1939. 4. Resort architecture—United States. 5. Hotels—United States. 6. Architecture—United States—20th century. I. Schultze, Leonard, 1877–1951. II. Weaver, S. Fullerton (Spencer Fullerton) d. 1939. III. Lamonaca, Marianne. IV. Mogul, Jonathan, 1963– . V. Schultze & Weaver. VI. Wolfsonian–Florida International University.
NA737.S356A4 2005
728'.5'097309041—dc22

2005023444

Contents

DIRECTOR'S PREFACE

Cathy Leff

In 1994, Mitchell Wolfson, Jr., founder of The Wolfsonian, bought a compilation of material related to an architectural firm established in New York City in 1921 by Leonard Schultze and S. Fullerton Weaver. The Schultze & Weaver collection contains thousands of architectural plans and more than a hundred renderings of buildings as well as photographs, documents, and other items. The collection presents a remarkably rich picture of a firm that designed a great variety of buildings—large and small, public and private—over more than forty years.

Leonard Schultze, S. Fullerton Weaver, and their younger associate Lloyd Morgan do not rank among the pioneers of modern architecture, and they have largely escaped the attention of architectural historians. Still, as designers of office and apartment buildings, housing developments, schools, hospitals, and many other types of structures, they were significant participants in the building of several American metropolitan areas. For a decade they were also the country's foremost designers of a particular building type—the luxury hotel. Between 1921 and 1931, Schultze & Weaver designed fourteen hotels, many of which—including the Waldorf-Astoria, Sherry-Netherland, and Pierre in New York; the Breakers and Miami Biltmore in South Florida; and the Los Angeles Biltmore (now Millennium Biltmore)—remain among the grandest in America.

This book and the exhibition that it accompanies provide a close look at the Schultze & Weaver collection and explore the significance of this material. Our aim is to offer a detailed view of the luxury hotels Schultze & Weaver designed during the 1920s while placing these establishments in the context of longer trends of development stretching forward from the nineteenth century. The luxury hotel, as it emerges from these pages and from the walls of the exhibition, is a complex, even contradictory, institution, the history of which is embedded in patterns of social, cultural, and technological change in America.

This book consists of four essays, each of which offers a frame of reference for understanding the design of luxury hotels. The opening essay, by Jonathan Mogul, Wolfsonian research associate, surveys the nine Schultze & Weaver hotels that were built in South Florida and New York City, the two places where the architects were most active between 1921 and 1931. The second essay, by Robin F. Bachin, associate professor of history at the University of Miami, places Schultze & Weaver's

Florida hotels in the broader history of American beachfront resorts, particularly Atlantic City and Miami Beach, and explores the many connections between these resorts and the urban world from which they ostensibly offered an escape. The third essay shifts the focus north, to New York City. Keith D. Revell, associate professor of public administration at Florida International University, traces the different ways in which Schultze & Weaver responded to the urban context—especially its changing real estate conditions, regulatory codes, and social customs—in their designs for New York City hotels. The final essay, by Kenneth J. Lipartito, professor of history at Florida International University, considers the "hotel machine" as an embodiment of modern business and management practices, with examples drawn from Schultze & Weaver's last and largest hotel, the Waldorf-Astoria. The final section of the book contains brief illustrated essays about each of the fourteen hotels designed by Schultze & Weaver. These pieces are written by Marianne Lamonaca, the Wolfsonian's assistant director for exhibitions and curatorial affairs.

We are especially pleased that the exhibition and publication are the result of a collaborative effort between our own Florida International University and the University of Miami. I want to thank Marianne Lamonaca and Jonathan Mogul for taking the lead on this important project, as well as Robin F. Bachin, Kenneth Lipartito, and Keith D. Revell for contributing their scholarship to this book.

I want to especially thank Wolfsonian board member Charles Cowles and the Cowles Charitable Trust for providing significant support for this publication. We also thank the Aaron I. Fleischman Foundation and Furthermore: A Program of the J. M. Kaplan Fund for their generous funding of this project.

The Wolfsonian is grateful to Mitchell Wolfson, Jr., for acquiring this extraordinary collection and placing it in the public domain; FIU President Modesto A. Maidique, Executive Vice President and Provost Mark B. Rosenberg, and the university community for providing the supportive environment in which The Wolfsonian has been able to thrive; The Wolfsonian–FIU Advisory Board; the State of Florida Division of Cultural Affairs and Florida Arts Council, Miami-Dade County Department of Cultural Affairs and Board of County Commissioners, the City of Miami Beach and its Cultural Arts Council, Continental Airlines, and the Arthur F. and Alice E. Adams Foundation for providing ongoing support of our exhibitions and research programs; and the Wolfsonian's staff, who have been organizing, documenting, interpreting, and making this vast collection accessible to the public.

As a museum and research center, The Wolfsonian's focus is on how the design of all kinds of objects both reflects and acts upon the broader world. Our collection is international in scope, and our exhibitions, public programs, and publications invite visitors to think about their connections to people, places, and historical events that are remote from their own experience. At the same time, we have a strong commitment to casting light on our local community. In this sense, an exploration of American hotels is an especially fitting project for us to undertake. Based in Miami Beach, the Wolfsonian resides in a neighborhood and a region whose fates have been, and continue to be, strongly shaped by hotels. From this vantage point, it is powerfully clear that hotels are important institutions—as engines of economic development, as employers, as centers of social life, and as models of living spaces that offer a vision of life as it might be. We are proud to offer a book and exhibition that look at hotels from all of these perspectives.

ACKNOWLEDGMENTS

Many people worked diligently to create this book and the accompanying exhibition at the Wolfsonian–Florida International University. Robin F. Bachin, Kenneth Lipartito, and Keith D. Revell brought a richness of experience and intellectual curiosity to their essays. Sarah Schleuning and Lisa Li, our colleagues in the Curatorial Department, ferreted out dozens of photographs and checked a thousand facts. Lisa's extraordinary organizational skills, perseverance, and general good spirits formed a strong foundation that helped make the myriad tasks related to the project manageable.

The entire staff of the Wolfsonian has contributed to the project in various ways. A special thank you is extended to director Cathy Leff, who has been a tireless champion of our research on Schultze & Weaver. The Collections Department staff, Kim Bergen, Debbye Kirschtel-Taylor, and Amy Silverman, made the hotel materials accessible to all of the project researchers; Amy also spent long hours in our storage annex assisting with the photography of architectural materials. Together with the Exhibitions staff, Richard Miltner, Steve Forero-Paz, John Paul Noonan, and Kevin Vellake, they also handled the delicate task of shipping the Schultze & Weaver presentation drawings to the Northeast Document Conservation Center for conservation. Librarians Frank Luca and Nicholas Blaga generously coordinated a barrage of inter-library loans and located hard-to-find materials. Anya Domlesky, during her brief internship, helped a great deal with organizing and digitizing the illustrations. Silvia Ros photographed all of the objects from the museum's collection that are published here, as well as those from several South Florida collections, within an extraordinarily tight schedule. This rich visual presentation would not have been possible without her skill and hard work.

In the project's earliest planning phases, Wendy Kaplan, Amanda Badgett, Birgit Scaglione, and Aldo J. Regalado made important contributions. Seth Bramson, Vicki Gold Levi, Arva Moore Parks, and Frederic A. Sharf generously opened their collections to us and provided important research information, documents, and photographs. Many colleagues from near and far contributed to the project: John Duncan of V. & J. Duncan Antique Maps & Prints and William D. Stroud of Savannah, Georgia; Janet S. Parks of the Avery Architectural and Fine Arts Library, Columbia University; Ruth Grimm of the Bass Museum of Art; Susan

Gillis of the Boca Raton Historical Society; Piriya Metcalfe of the Chicago Historical Society; Mary Agnes Beach and Dona Lubin of the City of Coral Gables, Department of Historical Resources; Micki Blakely, Rachel Bradshaw, and Nicole Shuey of the Henry Morrison Flagler Museum; Rebecca A. Smith and Dawn Hugh of the Historical Museum of Southern Florida; Richard Marconi of the Historical Society of Palm Beach County; Marlene Armas-Zermeno of the Millennium Biltmore Hotel, Los Angeles; Robin Strong of the Montauk Library; Deborah Waters, Melanie Bower, and Marguerite Lavin of the Museum of the City of New York; Kristine Paulus, Eric Robinson, Joseph Ditta, Sandra Markham, Jenny Gotwals, and Jill Reichenbach of the New-York Historical Society; Stephan Saks of the New York Public Library; Mary Todd Glaser and Walter Newman of the Northeast Document Conservation Center; Joy Kestenbaum of Pratt Institute, Art & Architecture Department; N. Adam Watson of the Florida State Archives; Esperanza B. de Varona and Maria R. Estorino of the University of Miami, Cuban Heritage Collection; Schlomit Schwarzer and Lisa Diaz-Heimer of the University of Miami, Otto G. Richter Library; and Jim Blauvelt of the Waldorf-Astoria Hotel. We want to note, especially, the remarkable generosity shown by the staff of the Kyushu University Design Library in Kyushu, Japan. Megumi Ieda and her colleagues scanned dozens and dozens of photographs from the library's Lloyd Morgan Architectural Collection and made them available to us for use in this book.

At Princeton Architectural Press, Nancy Eklund Later has been an unflagging supporter of this book since she first saw our proposal. Her guidance, enthusiasm, and editorial input have been invaluable.

ESCAPE AND CONTINUITY

The Florida and New York Hotels of Schultze & Weaver

Jonathan Mogul

In 1921, Leonard Schultze left the New York architectural firm Warren & Wetmore, where he had spent nearly two decades, and started a firm of his own. Schultze's partner in this venture was S. Fullerton Weaver, a real estate developer and engineer. Schultze & Weaver and its successor firms went on to design buildings for more than four decades.

Schultze and Weaver chose a good time to start an architectural firm. With the end of World War I and the devastating influenza outbreak that followed it, the United States entered a period of rapid economic growth. An ebullient business outlook and ample resources combined to fuel a building boom that kept many American architects busy. Schultze & Weaver were no exception.

The work that Schultze & Weaver completed in their first decade reflects important features of this period of economic exuberance. The wealth created during the 1920s gave large numbers of people—if only temporarily, in many cases—the opportunity to engage in the kinds of conspicuous consumption and display once confined to a more exclusive elite. Schultze & Weaver designed many types of buildings during this period, ranging from private homes to office buildings, but a strikingly large part of their output consisted of facilities that catered to this growing "leisure class," including fourteen hotels and three private clubs.[1] Although the architects worked in a number of regions of the country (as well as in Canada and Cuba), they made their greatest impact during these years in two places: South Florida and New York City.

By 1931, when new economic conditions forced the firm to seek different kinds of projects, Schultze & Weaver had made a name for themselves as preeminent hotel architects. They had won commissions from some of the country's leading hotel executives and developers; they had designed several of the largest and most luxurious hotels in the country (such as the Los Angeles Biltmore, the Breakers in Palm Beach, and the Waldorf-Astoria in New York) [fig. 1]; and their projects had garnered significant attention in the architectural press. "Leonard Schultze and Fullerton Weaver probably know the hotel problem better than do any architects in this country," wrote one critic in 1931.[2]

The luxury hotel architect had to balance different sorts of demands. During the early twentieth century, what had been a business dominated by individual,

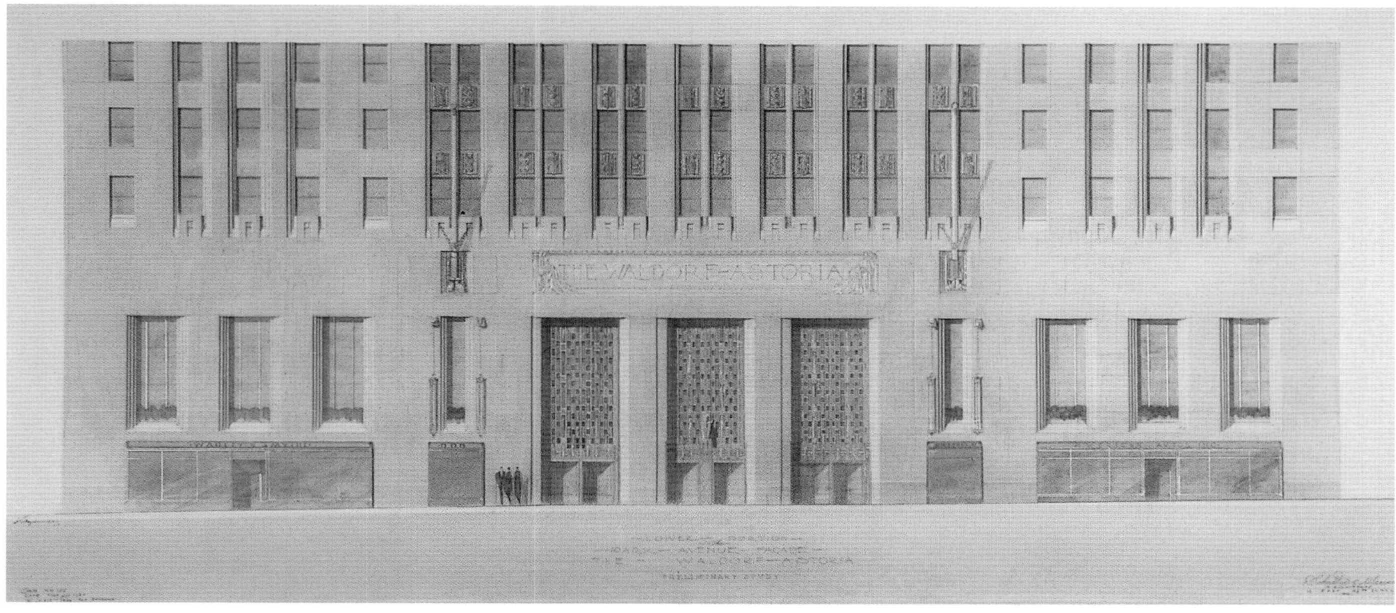

[fig. 1]
Park Avenue elevation, lower stories, Waldorf-Astoria Hotel, New York (Schultze & Weaver, 1931), presentation drawing, ca. 1930

often family-owned, hotels began to turn itself into a modern industry—the seventh largest industry in the country, in terms of employees and capital invested, according to one report from the late 1920s.[3] The characteristics of this change were consolidation of ownership and the creation of chains, professionalization of management, rationalization and standardization of operations, and increasing use of technology. The job of the architect within this industry was to design a building that would permit the business enterprise to operate profitably. The hotel architect needed to know, among other things, how to design for efficient circulation of employees between service areas and guest areas; how to maximize the revenue-producing portion of the building's volume without sacrificing service and comfort; how to organize quasi-industrial spaces, such as laundries and kitchens, for greatest efficiency; and how to integrate into the various parts of the building the infrastructure for such things as ventilation and climate control, communications, elevators, and plumbing.[4] Schultze, himself, was keenly aware of his responsibility for the hotel's efficiency and profitability. Like the designer of "any other commercial building," he wrote in a 1923 article, the hotel architect must "make the building a safe commercial investment."[5]

Efficiency, however, was far from the only responsibility of the hotel architect. A major client of Schultze & Weaver during the 1920s was John McEntee Bowman, president of the Bowman-Biltmore hotel chain and one of the country's leading hotel executives. Bowman wrote a short article in 1923 in which he declared that the chief responsibility of the hotel architect was to create "atmosphere—that intangible contribution to the well being and satisfaction of hotel guests." Atmosphere, as Bowman described it, was a product of "hotel exteriors and interiors which attract and hold interest, establish correct impressions, and create memories which insure recurring patronage and recommendation."[6]

The guests who paid for a room in a luxury hotel expected first-class service, fine food, a prime location, and a range of facilities in which to relax and mix with others of their class. The resorts and apartment hotels designed by Schultze & Weaver met these demands, but they offered a less tangible luxury, as well. By appropriating and combining a variety of architectural and ornamental styles, the architects designed atmospheres that affirmed the high social status of their inhabitants

[fig. 2]
Leonard Schultze, ca. 1931

and spoke to their desires for escape, for reassurance, and—eventually—for accommodation with modern trends. The atmospheres of Schultze & Weaver's Florida and New York hotels, then, are important documents of American luxury in the 1920s.

Architects as Insiders

Both Leonard Schultze and S. Fullerton Weaver were in their forties when they became partners in 1921. Both already had considerable experience and important contacts, and these assets put the new firm in a strong position to take advantage of the opportunities of the 1920s.

Born in Chicago in 1877, Schultze graduated from the City College of New York.[7] As was typical of the late nineteenth century, his architectural training was strongly marked by beaux-arts academicism, in which historical—especially classical or Renaissance—forms were appropriated for contemporary building types. Schultze did not go to Paris to study at the École des Beaux-Arts, as did many of the promising young American architects of the period, but he did train in the private atelier of E. L. Masqueray, himself a graduate of the École. Masqueray had moved to New York from France in 1887 and went on to work for two prestigious American firms, Carrère & Hastings and Richard M. Hunt. His atelier, opened in 1893, was devoted to teaching American architects according to the French model.[8] Schultze also studied at the architecture school of the Metropolitan Museum of Art. [fig. 2]

The beaux-arts tradition was the dominant idiom of American architecture in the late nineteenth and early twentieth centuries, a cultural moment sometimes described as the "American Renaissance."[9] Architects trained in classical principles of harmony and order and expert at re-creating elements of Roman temples and Italian palazzos found themselves in demand for both public and private commissions, both structures that embodied high civic purposes and luxurious pleasure palaces. Hunt, for example, designed a major addition to the Metropolitan Museum of Art and the Breakers mansion for the Vanderbilts in Newport; Carrère & Hastings created the New York Public Library and two of Florida's earliest luxury hotels, the Ponce de Leon and the Alcazar. In Schultze's case, beaux-arts training led strongly in just one of these two directions—toward luxury.

After serving in the U.S. Volunteer Engineers during the Spanish-American War (1898), Schultze began working as an architect in 1900. In 1903, he joined Warren & Wetmore, where he spent almost two decades working on one of the most significant projects in New York City's history—the building of Grand Central Terminal and the redevelopment of the land on either side of the terminal and to its north. From 1903 until 1911, he worked on the design for the terminal, a commission that Warren & Wetmore shared with another firm, Reed & Stem. In the following decade, he served as executive in charge of design for the surrounding zone, known as Terminal City. In this capacity he oversaw not only the larger development plan but also the design of a number of individual structures, including office buildings, apartment houses, and hotels. The Biltmore (1913)[10] and Commodore (1919), both large hotels that were part of John McEntee Bowman's growing chain, flanked Grand Central to the east and west, respectively. The Ambassador (1921), located to the north of the terminal on Park Avenue, was a smaller establishment.

[fig. 3]
S. Fullerton Weaver, ca. 1931

In addition to the Terminal City projects, Schultze also worked on other significant commissions during his years at Warren & Wetmore. These included Detroit's Michigan Central Railroad Terminal (1911), a number of suburban railroad stations outside of New York, and the Providence Biltmore Hotel (1922).

When Schultze broke away from Warren & Wetmore, the beaux-arts designer brought to his new partnership the valuable contacts and experience he had gained designing large, complex buildings. He also brought Schultze & Weaver three young colleagues from Warren & Wetmore: Eugene Meroni, William Sunderland, and John Bacon, each of whom would become an associate partner in the firm by the end of its first decade.[11]

It is likely that Schultze's association with S. Fullerton Weaver grew out of the Terminal City project. Among the buildings that Schultze designed was an eighteen-story building on land leased by Weaver at 420 Park Avenue. Born in Philadelphia, Weaver attended a military academy before earning a degree in civil engineering from the University of Pennsylvania in 1902. He formed the Fullerton Weaver Realty Company in New York and went on to serve as an infantry major in France during World War I. He remained active in veterans' affairs after the war, serving as a governor of the Military Order of Naval and Army Officers and working to find employment for returning servicemen.[12] [fig. 3]

It is not clear exactly what role Weaver played once he and Schultze joined forces. Contemporary accounts of the firm's work in newspapers and architectural journals, as well as a small batch of documentary records, make little mention of Weaver and give the impression that it was Schultze who was the primary designer of buildings. Weaver may well have been involved in matters having to do with engineering. Certainly, the connections, knowledge, and resources that Weaver gained in his years as a real estate developer would have been assets for the firm in its early years. Schultze & Weaver's first New York commission, in fact, was for a hotel (the Park Lane) on land that a syndicate headed by the two men leased from the New York Central Railroad.[13]

Weaver was probably an asset in another important way as well. The great-great-grandnephew of President James Buchanan, he had ties to wealth and high society. Parties thrown by Weaver during his bachelor years and, after his 1929 marriage to Lillian Leacock Howell, by the "S. F. Weavers" at their residences in the Park Lane Hotel and East Hampton were often featured in society columns of *The New York Times*. A costume ball hosted by Weaver in the Park Lane's dining room, known as the Tapestry Room, in November 1924 (shortly after the hotel opened) lasted until a 5 a.m. breakfast; awards for the best costumes were handed out by a committee of three judges dressed as "lord high executioners." Guests at these events included such luminaries as New York Senator Royal Copeland; the artist Howard Chandler Christy; General Motors President Alfred P. Sloan; hotel operator Lucius Boomer; Reginald C. Vanderbilt, youngest son of Cornelius Vanderbilt; Merrill Lynch partner Edmund C. Lynch; and New York stockbroker John Vernou Bouvier. Weaver also was active in sporting circles. He served at one time as president of the West Side Tennis Club in Forest Hills, and he was a member of two golf clubs and the Turf and Field Club at Belmont Park, as well as several social clubs.[14]

Although hailing from a less illustrious family, Schultze was often a guest at Weaver's parties; he also hosted his own, on occasion.[15] As Schultze & Weaver grew in reputation, Schultze joined a growing number of exclusive clubs and societies.

The 1929 *Who's Who in New York* listed memberships in the Society of Mayflower Descendants, the Everglades Club in Palm Beach, the Jonathan Club in Los Angeles (designed by Schultze & Weaver), the Scarsdale Golf and Country Club, the Uptown Club, and the Westchester Biltmore Country Club (designed by Warren & Wetmore during Schultze's time there).[16]

Both Schultze and Weaver were insiders, members in good standing of social circles that included the wealthy and the powerful. This status positioned them well to design luxury hotels. Through such circles, they made contacts with developers, executives, and investors who could bring them large commissions. Just as importantly, they possessed first-hand knowledge of the customs and tastes of the people who would form a critical clientele for such establishments. In designing luxury hotels, Schultze & Weaver were designing for people whom they knew—perhaps even for themselves.

Schultze & Weaver's creative capacity was greatly enhanced in 1926, when Lloyd Morgan joined the firm as chief designer.[17] Morgan, a native New Yorker, graduated from the Pratt Institute Architectural School and had additional training at the Massachusetts Institute of Technology, the University of Pennsylvania, and Columbia University. He worked for several architectural firms from 1911 to 1917, starting as an office boy for Dennison & Hirons, and then served in France as a sergeant in World War I. Upon leaving the army in 1919, Morgan remained in France and took exams to study at the École des Beaux-Arts, only to be denied admission due to his weak command of the French language. In 1921, however, back in New York, he won the Paris Prize, sponsored by the Society of Beaux-Arts Architects, which enabled him to return to Paris for three years of study at the École.[18] He remained in Paris for several years after completing his studies, working for several architects, including Victor Laloux, a professor at the École (and designer of, among other buildings, the Gare d'Orsay in Paris). During his time with Laloux, Morgan served as chief designer of the Credit Lyonnais building in Lyons. In France, Morgan also became involved in coordinating the redevelopment of areas damaged during the war.

By the time he joined Schultze & Weaver, Morgan was a seasoned architect who—like Schultze—was deeply immersed in the beaux-arts tradition but was even more extensively trained. A gifted draftsman and designer, he worked on all the major projects undertaken by the firm from 1926 on. The son of an engraver, Morgan probably did not keep the same upper-crust company as his senior partners. There is no record that Morgan belonged to private clubs, though he was a member of the Metropolitan Museum of Art, The American Museum of Natural History, and several professional associations.[19] Morgan also devoted his free time to teaching. For six years he ran an evening atelier for students who could not afford architectural school, and he also served as a professor at Yale University (1928–29) and New York University (1930–35). Among those he taught were four Paris Prize winners.[20]

With Schultze, Weaver, and—from 1926 on—Morgan as key contributors, the young firm was poised to take advantage of the rising demand for luxury by the American public in the 1920s. For a decade after the firm's establishment in 1921, Schultze & Weaver enjoyed prosperity and recognition, culminating in the commission for the enormous and much-publicized Waldorf-Astoria Hotel. During these years, Schultze & Weaver worked all over the country, designing many kinds of buildings, large and small, extravagant and ordinary. But the firm made its biggest mark on two kinds of luxury environments—the resorts of South Florida and the skyscraper hotels of New York City.

The Luxury of Escape: Schultze & Weaver's Florida Resorts

Florida's sunny coastal communities became playgrounds for wealthy northerners beginning in the late nineteenth century. It was during this time that two entrepreneurs, Henry M. Flagler and Henry Plant, built railroads that joined the Atlantic and Gulf coasts of the state to the national rail network and put up resorts along their lines. The resorts Flagler and Plant built in places like St. Augustine, Palm Beach, and Tampa made an extended winter stay in a balmy, beachside destination an annual ritual for the Gilded Age elite. [fig. 4]

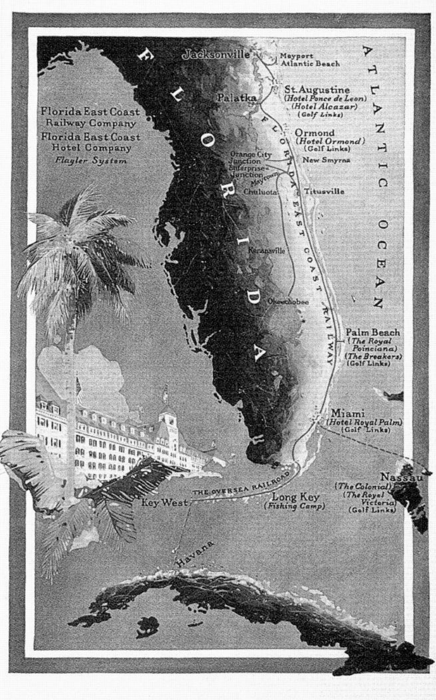

[fig. 4]
Map of the Florida East Coast Railway and Hotel Company, from *Florida East Coast* (ca. 1917)

These early Florida resorts, though by no means identical, shared some important characteristics, which have been detailed in Susan Braden's book *The Architecture of Leisure*. The hotels relied on historical architectural styles—Spanish Renaissance, Islamic revival, and Colonial revival—to produce a sense of fantasy and escape from the cares of ordinary life. Grand entrances leading to ornate interiors signaled to guests their own exalted social standing and privileged separation from the surrounding world. The resort's nature as a self-contained world, able to offer all of the services and entertainment that a guest might want, reinforced this sense of exclusivity. These were big, complex buildings with large numbers of guest rooms (Flagler's Royal Poinciana, for example, had over one thousand) and extensive public spaces, including lobbies, ladies' parlors, grill rooms, dining rooms, and ballrooms. They also had large staffs and a sophisticated technological infrastructure, including elevators, refrigeration, and electrical generators, which were necessary in order to produce luxury in remote places.[21]

The Florida resort hotel was an established building type by the time Schultze & Weaver began designing hotels in the early 1920s. What was new in that decade was that the area around Miami, near the southern tip of the peninsula, had become the most dynamic part of Florida. The extension of Henry Flagler's Florida East Coast Railway south from Palm Beach to Miami in 1896, and the building of his Royal Palm Hotel there, triggered rapid growth in the region. By 1910 Miami had nine hotels and accommodated more than one hundred thousand winter guests. Within a few years, a number of real estate developers, led by the industrialist Carl Fisher, began the expensive, laborious task of turning the mostly uninhabited, swampy barrier island that separated Miami from the ocean into the tamed tropical landscape of Miami Beach. In the early 1920s this investment began to pay off with an enormous jump in land values and the beginnings of extensive building on the island. The 1920s witnessed rapid development in other parts of greater Miami as well. Most notable was Coral Gables, just to the south of downtown Miami, where the real estate developer George Merrick set out to build an ideal American garden suburb. Through a combination of visionary schemes, huge investments, tremendous labor, and brilliant promotion, Fisher, Merrick, and others like them generated a startling boom in 1920s Miami.[22]

Both Schultze and Weaver had connections to key players in the South Florida real estate world. The firm's first project in the region was a hotel commissioned by

[fig. 5]
Nautilus Hotel, Miami Beach, Florida (Schultze & Weaver, 1924), postcard, ca. 1924

Fisher. The owner of a large part of Miami Beach, Fisher saw himself as a real estate developer, not a "hotel man." But by the early 1920s he had invested heavily in dredging, landscaping, and infrastructure on Miami Beach, all for the purpose of increasing land values, and he was severely strapped for cash. The best way to get wealthy prospective buyers to visit the island, he calculated, would be to build luxury hotels.[23]

In 1920 Fisher opened the Flamingo, the first large hotel on Miami Beach. Among the guests during the Flamingo's first winter was S. Fullerton Weaver. A local newspaper article from 1923 recalled that Weaver was one "of the leading hosts" that season, and also a regular spectator at the polo grounds that Fisher built nearby. By March 1923, Fisher was already planning his next hotel on the western shore of Miami Beach on a plot of land facing Biscayne Bay; Schultze & Weaver got the job.[24] The new hotel, the Nautilus, began operating in January 1924 with six stories and two hundred guest rooms. [fig. 5]

Shortly after the Nautilus opened, Schultze & Weaver began working on another Miami-area hotel. This time, the critical connection came through Leonard Schultze. His association with John McEntee Bowman went back to 1914, when Bowman was named president of the Biltmore Hotel in New York, designed by Schultze while he was at Warren & Wetmore. Over the next several years, Bowman took over several more New York hotels (the Ansonia, Belmont, and Murray Hill), as well as the Griswold, in New London, Connecticut, and the Belleview, in Belleair, Florida. By the time he opened the Commodore (also designed by Schultze at Warren & Wetmore) in 1919, his New York properties totaled nearly eight thousand guest rooms and—according to a headline in the *The New York Times*—"encircled" Grand Central Terminal.[25]

Bowman continued to build hotels in the 1920s and looked to Schultze's new firm to design them. The biggest project Schultze & Weaver undertook during its first several years was Bowman's Los Angeles Biltmore, which opened in October 1923. Facing Pershing Square, in the city's downtown, the new Biltmore was the largest hotel west of the Mississippi, with over nine hundred guest rooms. By this time, Bowman had consolidated all his holdings, creating the Bowman-Biltmore Hotels Corporation, which controlled properties worth over $100 million in New York City

alone. During the same year, Schultze & Weaver worked on two other projects for the company—an addition to the Sevilla Hotel (renamed the Sevilla Biltmore) in Havana, and a new 560-room Biltmore in Atlanta; both hotels opened in 1924.

It is not surprising that Bowman began looking to expand into Miami. His opportunity came in 1924, when George Merrick started planning a hotel for his brand-new community of Coral Gables. Merrick, who had accumulated three thousand acres of agricultural and undeveloped land south of the city of Miami, sold his first lot in 1921. In a short time, his team of artists, architects, and landscapers built from scratch a "City Beautiful," with hundreds of new homes in a setting of broad winding boulevards, canals, fountains, flowering plants, and stately trees. Integral features of Merrick's plan were a country club and grand hotel that would serve as focal points for community life and also attract potential property buyers from the north. To realize this expensive project, he enlisted Bowman as a partner, and the two men formed the Miami-Biltmore Hotel Corporation.[26] [fig. 6]

By the time Bowman came on board, Merrick was already working with an architect, Martin Hampton, who had prepared preliminary sketches for both the hotel and country club buildings. Once the hotel became a Biltmore, however, Schultze & Weaver were invited to design the structures. Construction on the hotel began in January 1925 and concluded a year later; the country club opened in March 1925. [fig. 7]

While work on the Biltmore was under way, Schultze & Weaver began a third hotel in the region. This one was for Newton Baker Taylor (N. B. T.) Roney, a New Jersey businessman who had moved to Miami Beach in 1918 and quickly bought enough land to become one of the major developers of the city. Among his properties was an oceanfront plot to the north of a budding zone of urban development. The Roney Plaza, the largest and grandest of the oceanfront hotels built in Miami Beach during the decade, opened in February 1926. [fig. 8]

The 1920s boom was particularly intense in Miami, but it extended to other parts of South Florida as well. Schultze & Weaver happened to have a contact in another major Florida resort community—Palm Beach. William R. Kenan, Jr., the brother-in-law of Henry Flagler and president of the Florida East Coast Hotel Company after Flagler's death, resided in New York at the Park Lane Hotel—the

above:
[fig. 6]
John McEntee Bowman (left) and George Merrick, 1926

top:
[fig. 7]
Miami Biltmore Hotel, Coral Gables, Florida (Schultze & Weaver, 1926), photographic reproduction of rendering, 1924

[fig. 8]
Roney Plaza Hotel, Miami Beach, Florida (Schultze & Weaver, 1926), ca. 1926

Schultze & Weaver–designed apartment hotel that was also the home of S. Fullerton Weaver.[27] In March 1925, one of two large Florida East Coast resorts in Palm Beach, the Breakers, burned to the ground. Kenan hired Schultze & Weaver, who had been designing hotels for his competitors in Miami, to build the new Breakers. By October 1925, the architects had completed their first set of plans for a palatial oceanfront refuge. The 435–room hotel opened at the end of December 1926, just in time for the winter season. [fig. 9]

The Florida boom was over by the time the Breakers opened. Property values had begun to collapse and real estate fortunes had already vanished. Congestion on the rail lines and the blocking of Miami's harbor by a shipwreck in December 1925 delayed deliveries of building materials and cost developers millions of dollars. A powerful hurricane that struck South Florida in September 1926, wrecking buildings and killing hundreds of people, finished off the boom. Florida's "Roaring Twenties" came to an end three years before the stock market crash and the start of the Great Depression across the country.

The end of South Florida's economic boom marked the end of Schultze & Weaver's intense productivity in the region. From 1923 through the end of 1926, the architects designed not only the four hotels, but also two of downtown Miami's largest office buildings: the thirteen-story Ingraham Building (1927), and the seventeen-story Miami Daily News and Metropolis Building (1925). In the years following the boom, the firm had just one significant commission in Florida—a large addition to a private club in Boca Raton—which they completed in 1929.

The Schultze & Weaver hotels were among the most prominent in the region; they became emblematic of their communities, and of the world of leisure and escape that Florida had come to promise. They catered to their guests with the tangible luxuries of good food, comfortable quarters, and facilities for rest and play. Like Florida's earlier Gilded Age resorts, they came replete with extensive lobbies, lounges, dining rooms, patios, terraces, and gardens in which guests could mix with others of their class. They also offered a broad range of services on their ground and main floors. The Breakers, for example, had a number of luxury shops, a hairdressers' parlor (with massage tables), and a men's barbershop; the Biltmore,

[fig. 9]
Breakers Hotel, Palm Beach, Florida (Schultze & Weaver, 1926), presentation drawing, rendered by Chester Price, 1925

a Turkish bath. Outside the hotel buildings, guests could enjoy vast grounds, including golf courses (the Biltmore, the Breakers, and the Nautilus), polo fields (the Nautilus and the Breakers), tennis courts, swimming pools, and beaches.

Schultze & Weaver's South Florida resorts also offered an architecture of luxury, one that created environments designed to produce a sense of pleasure, privilege, and prestige. In both their overall form and their details, the hotels were meant to evoke distant places and times. The firm's Miami hotels, in particular, monumentalized the Mediterranean revival architecture that became one of the region's hallmarks during the boom years. This style was one manifestation of a broader vogue for Spanish architecture that went back to the late nineteenth century, when the Mission style caught on in California and Henry Flagler built his Spanish-style hotels in St. Augustine. Miami, unlike California or St. Augustine, had no history of Spanish settlement, but this did not stop its early developers and architects from appropriating Spanish architecture in order to create an identity—based on an imagined history—for the region.

The Mediterranean revival style, as architectural historian Beth Dunlop has described it, was anything but a systematic, academic recreation of Spain's historical architecture. It was meant to "look Spanish, but it wasn't Spanish; it was a composite of Spanish Renaissance, Andalusian Moorish, Tuscan, Venetian, and Roman architectural elements, with allusions to classical Greece, Baroque France, and virtually any other place or era that seemed to fit."[28] It was a picturesque, highly sellable style that could be adapted for George Merrick's garden suburb in Coral Gables, Addison Mizner's mansions in Boca Raton and Palm Beach, and the resorts of Schultze & Weaver.

The Mediterranean revival was already familiar territory for Schultze & Weaver by the time they began their first projects in Florida in the early 1920s. The firm's first commission, the Los Angeles Biltmore, featured a mix of Spanish and Italian Renaissance elements, from its brick and stone facade to its lounge that reproduced the royal hall of King Ferdinand and Queen Isabella. The focal point of the hotel's spectacular three-story main lobby was a divided staircase with ornate cast-iron railings reminiscent of the famous sixteenth-century Escalera Dorada (golden staircase) in Spain's Burgos Cathedral.[29] [fig. 10]

[fig. 10]
Lobby and stair, Los Angeles Biltmore Hotel (Schultze & Weaver, 1923), from *Architectural Forum* XXXIX, no. 5 (November 1923)

[fig. 11]
Detail of the entrance porch, Nautilus Hotel, 1923

The facades of all three of the firm's Miami hotels invited guests to imagine themselves leaving their everyday world for Spain, frozen at some point in its glorious past. Picturesque towers, ceramic-tile roofs, and ornamental details in cast iron, cast cement, or terra cotta along the roof lines, balconies, and entrances were the chief means of achieving this effect. The Nautilus, for example, was topped by two short towers, each sporting a red copper cupola beneath a flagpole. Occasional balconies, decorated with cast-cement details such as knights and mythological figures, broke the regularity of the guest-room floors. The two entrance porches—one facing the automobile driveway on the east facade of the hotel, the other facing west toward Biscayne Bay—also featured elaborate cast-cement ornamentation, including twisted columns characteristic of Spanish Baroque architecture. [fig. 11] Another typically Spanish touch were the small windows covered by iron grilles that were placed on the ground floor.

The Biltmore and Roney Plaza used similar exterior elements to suggest a Spanish antiquity. But the dominant feature of each of these hotels was a single tower, much taller than the two short towers on top of the Nautilus, which suggested the Giralda bell tower of the Seville Cathedral, one of the most recognizable structures in Spain's architectural heritage. Martin Hampton's proposal for the Biltmore from early 1924, before Schultze & Weaver took over the project, already included a stepped central tower modeled on the Giralda. Schultze & Weaver not only kept a modified version of this tower, rising 315 feet, in their own plan for the Biltmore but also incorporated similar towers in the Roney Plaza and the Miami Daily News and Metropolis Building.[30] [fig. 12]

"Gazing at the beautiful Giralda," gushed a 1926 brochure for the Biltmore, "one's outstanding impression is that one has been suddenly transported to Spain of two centuries ago."[31] The Biltmore's interiors, like those of the other hotels, were designed to keep that impression alive inside the hotel. In the dining room, guests sat on faux-antique Spanish chairs and ate off of china decorated with galleons and tropical flowers and birds. Overhead was a barrel-vaulted ceiling with painted wooden beams, from which were hung wrought-iron chandeliers with colored Venetian glass pendants. [figs. 13, 14] Other public rooms, such as the lounge and main lobby, were furnished with genuine antique chests, chairs, and torchères from Spain and Italy. Wrought-iron rails, columns with ornamental plaster capitals, rugs and draperies with Spanish and Italian designs, and a host of other features all contributed to an atmosphere that combined opulence, antiquity, and exoticism.[32]

Also echoing Mediterranean traditions was the Biltmore's layout, which integrated open-air spaces into the overall plan. The most important feature—one that neither the Nautilus nor the Roney had—was a large central patio, lined by a two-level arcaded loggia, adjacent to each of the public rooms (the lobby, dining room, and lounge) on the main floor. [fig. 15]

The last hotel Schultze & Weaver designed in Florida, the Breakers, offered a different take on Mediterranean architecture. An article announcing the hotel's opening in the *Palm Beach Daily News* called its architecture "modified Spanish, enriched by Italian Renaissance motifs."[33] As in the Miami Biltmore, the main public rooms were arrayed around a large, lushly planted central patio. The most obvious influence on the decoration of these rooms came from Italian Renaissance palazzos.

[fig. 12]
Tower, Miami Biltmore Hotel, from *The Miami Biltmore* (1926)

[fig. 13]
Dining room, Miami Biltmore Hotel, from *The Miami Biltmore* (1926)

[fig. 14]
Plate from the Miami Biltmore Hotel, ca. 1926

[fig. 15]
Patio, Miami Biltmore Hotel, 1926

Guests approached the Breakers from the west, through a long formal garden planted with flowers and palm trees, past a fountain modeled on one from Florence's Boboli Gardens. The hotel's west facade, with its two short, square towers atop a symmetrical base, recalled on a huge scale Rome's Villa Medici. An "Architects [sic] Guide," published in the *Palm Beach Daily News* on the occasion of the hotel's opening, compared Schultze & Weaver's work in designing the interiors with the Medici family's patronage of artists who furnished the interiors of their palace. Thanks to the architects' "wanderings" in search of the finest art and decorations, the interior rooms of the Breakers expressed the "charm and atmosphere of Genoa, Venice, Florence, Bologna and the ever interesting hill top cities of central Italy."[34]

According to the "Guide," the hotel's main lobby, "with its many frescoes, and painted pictures upon the long barrel-vaulted ceiling interrupted by its numerous penetrations," emulated the Palazzo Carrega-Cataldi in Genoa. The South Lounge, which overlooked the Atlantic, was inspired by the Doge's Palace in Venice. A green and gold fresco adorned the ceiling, while portraits of explorers of the New World decorated the walls. The dining lounge suggested the gallery of Rome's Palazzo LeFerno. Its wall hangings and furniture were replicas of Roman and Florentine pieces, while the ceiling was painted with nymphs, mermaids, and other figures. The main dining room, the Grand Loggia, and the patio—the "Guide" claimed—were likewise echoes of Italian originals.[35] [figs. 16, 17]

The luxury that the Breakers provided, as the "Guide" described it, went beyond comfort or even aesthetic pleasure. On offer, thanks to the vast scale of the public rooms and the great care taken by the architects in assembling items from all over the world, was an extraordinary experience of discovery: "It is strange to find this rare collection . . . in this secluded hotel with its shady gardens, patios and porches and it takes a long visit to exhaust its many wonders."[36]

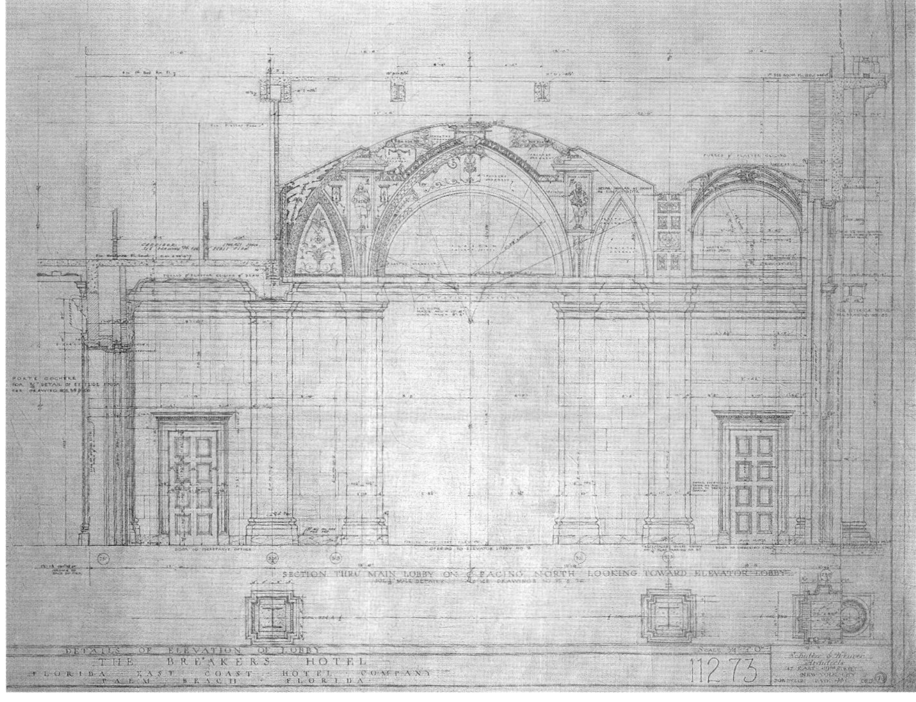

[fig. 16]
Grand Loggia, Breakers Hotel, ca. 1926

[fig. 17]
Main lobby, Breakers Hotel, section drawing (detail), 1925

The Luxury of Continuity: Schultze & Weaver's New York Hotels

Although both Leonard Schultze and S. Fullerton Weaver were New Yorkers and their firm was based in the city, the architects did most of their work outside of the city until the late 1920s. In addition to their commissions in Florida, the firm was especially busy in Los Angeles, where—along with the Biltmore Hotel—it designed a theater, a bank, a private club, a refectory, and a subway terminal building. Other projects completed in the mid-1920s included new hotels in Montauk, on Long Island (the Montauk Manor), and Savannah, Georgia (the General Oglethorpe), as well as one hotel renovation, in San Francisco (the Clift); office buildings in San Francisco and Canton, Ohio; and several buildings in the New York suburb of Scarsdale. Their only New York City jobs during the early years of their partnership were a mixed-use commercial building on Broadway, a J. C. Penney warehouse, and a hotel, the Park Lane.[37]

The Park Lane was one of the first buildings the new firm designed anywhere. In the fall of 1922, Weaver, Schultze, and a third investor, J. Baird, formed a syndicate that assumed a long-term lease on property owned by the New York Central Railroad (and located over its tracks), stretching the length of a Park Avenue block between Forty-eighth and Forty-ninth streets. The thirteen-story hotel opened in the fall of 1923.[38] [fig. 18]

[fig. 18]
Detail of the Park Avenue facade, Park Lane Hotel, New York (Schultze & Weaver, 1923), from *Architectural Forum* LI, no. 6 (November 1924)

The Park Lane, named after a famous establishment in London, was an apartment hotel. Rather than serving short-term visitors, it leased suites of up to six rooms to guests who planned to stay for months at a time or even longer. Within a few weeks of its opening, an article in *The New York Times* noted that the Park Lane, with its elegant and spacious public rooms, had already become a nexus for New York's social elite. Weaver, in the same article, boasted not only that space in the hotel would soon become "practically unobtainable" but that the management had filled it with "eligible acceptable families." Among the charter tenants of the hotel, besides Weaver himself, were C. H. Duell, a former chairman of the New York Republican Party; Clarence M. Wooley, president of the American Radiator Corporation; and D. Rait Richardson, president of Richardson & Boynton, a heating and air conditioning equipment manufacturer.[39]

During the last years of the 1920s, after building a reputation as luxury designers outside New York, Schultze & Weaver won a series of commissions for high-rise luxury hotels in their home city. Two of these, the Sherry-Netherland (1927) and the Pierre (1930), were elegant towers located in the area of Manhattan's Grand Army Plaza. A third, the Waldorf-Astoria (1931), was an enormous 2000-room hotel occupying a full block of land leased from the New York Central Railroad between Park and Lexington avenues and Forty-ninth and Fiftieth streets. All three of these hotels were designed for the upper echelons of the market and rented apartments to long-term guests (the Waldorf-Astoria also had many rooms for transient guests). The firm designed a fourth hotel—the Lexington (1929)—during this period. Unlike the others, the Lexington catered primarily to out-of-town guests who could stay there for as little as four dollars a night, though it also advertised the availability of permanent apartments.[40]

Luxury apartment hotels were the product of dramatic changes to the economic and social fabric of Manhattan over the late nineteenth and early twentieth centuries. During these decades, surging land values—themselves the result of rising population and wealth—encouraged developers to tear down "the city of brownstones and church spires" and replace it with a "modern skyscraper metropolis."[41] Among the victims of this great wave of demolition and reconstruction were the many mansions and town houses that lined Fifth Avenue and other fashionable streets of midtown Manhattan. One by one, the city's patrician families sold or leased their land to developers, who leveled the existing structures—often just a few decades old—to make room for high-rise buildings

As the old mansions fell to the wrecking ball, wealthy New Yorkers increasingly made their homes in elegant apartment towers in the city, or else in suburban houses out of town. Luxury apartment hotels offered another kind of housing option (one that some families combined with the purchase of a large house outside of the city). These hotels were hybrids of apartment buildings and transient hotels, combining some of the features of each. Like apartment buildings, they leased suites of rooms to tenants who made the building their home for all or part of the year and might keep the lease for many years. Like transient hotels, they offered residents the personal services of a full staff of employees and the use of extensive public spaces for dining and socializing. And, because these amenities were provided on a commercial basis for hundreds of residents, they were available for much less than the cost of running a private household.[42]

Building apartment hotels was an attractive option for New York City developers. As long as such buildings did not include private kitchens in the living quarters, they were classified (like other hotels) as commercial rather than residential buildings. This classification exempted them from a variety of residential building regulations, such as stringent limits on height and lot coverage. An apartment hotel could be larger than an apartment building on the same lot, giving the developer the chance to reap a larger return on the investment in high-priced Manhattan real estate.[43]

By the early 1930s, there were approximately one hundred and fifty apartment hotels in the city.[44] For some observers, the apartment hotel looked like it might become the standard mode of luxury urban living. Lucius Boomer, one of the city's leading hotel operators, wrote in a textbook on hotel management that such hotels were "a better machinery of city living," one that might "generally supplant the remaining private city homes and, to a considerable degree, the more exclusive apartment homes because of obvious economic advantages—no investment, no fixed long-term financial obligations, no housekeeping problems, and a minimum of domestic cares."[45] The architectural writer R. W. Sexton called the apartment hotel a "purely modern conception," one that appealed "to those who would be relieved of the cares and worries of housekeeping, who rather prefer the service of hotel life, but who enjoy the suggestion of home life which the apartment offers."[46] The liberating nature, especially for women, of apartment-hotel life was captured by one writer who declared that, in such establishments, a "pen and a checkbook are the sole requisites of housekeeping and homemaking."[47]

The appeal of apartment hotels, however, involved something more than the convenience and cachet of an unencumbered, highly modern lifestyle. Even as they belonged to the new skyline of the 1920s, these hotels also offered an updated version of the urbane luxury of Gilded Age city life. Located at prestigious addresses in the heart of Manhattan, they provided venues where guests could carry on the habits of sociable and opulent living that had taken root in the mansions and

[fig. 19]
Central Park at Fifty-ninth Street in New York, showing from the left: Hotel Pierre (Schultze & Weaver, 1930), Sherry-Netherland Hotel (Schultze & Weaver with Buchman and Kahn, 1927), Savoy-Plaza Hotel (McKim, Mead & White, 1927), and Plaza Hotel (Henry J. Hardenbergh, 1907), post-card, 1933

brownstones of Fifth Avenue a generation or two earlier. Schultze & Weaver's designs for these buildings reveal a desire to keep the atmosphere of this not-so-distant past alive in the most modern of buildings. Their apartment hotels were, to varying degrees, mansions stretched into skyscrapers.[48]

This was true, most of all, of the two hotels Schultze & Weaver designed near Grand Army Plaza, at the southeast corner of Central Park. By the late 1920s, Grand Army Plaza was becoming a center of fashionable hotels, with landmarks like the Savoy-Plaza (McKim, Mead & White, 1927) and the Plaza (Henry Hardenbergh, 1907). [fig. 19] But the same neighborhood also had a longer history as the locale of some of the city's most impressive houses, such as the series of Vanderbilt family mansions that lined Fifth Avenue south of Fifty-eighth Street, and the Astor mansion, a few blocks uptown at Sixty-fifth Street. In the Sherry-Netherland and the Pierre, Schultze & Weaver devised environments where wealthy guests could live a modern way of life in the midst of surroundings that affirmed a connection to the vanishing mansions of the area.

The Sherry-Netherland was the first New York hotel project the firm took on after completing the Park Lane in 1923. The hotel was originally supposed to be named the New Netherland, after the hotel of the same name that had opened at Fifth Avenue and Fifty-ninth Street in 1892. The developer, Samuel Keller Jacobs, closed the original hotel and brought in Schultze & Weaver to work with Buchman and Kahn (a firm with more experience planning tall buildings) on a replacement. The original plan, filed in May 1926, called for a hotel of thirty-six stories on the relatively small (100- by 125-foot) lot across Grand Army Plaza from Central Park.[49]

The project had an eventful path from conception to completion. Just a month after the plans were filed, they were revised to change the establishment from a transient hotel, with rooms for over fifteen hundred guests, to an exclusive apartment hotel with just over one hundred suites of rooms. While the hotel was under construction, Jacobs sold it to the Boomer-DuPont Properties Corporation, a growing hotel chain, that also owned Louis Sherry, Inc., a restaurant company founded by a renowned luxury confectioner, caterer, and restaurant owner. The hotel was renamed the Sherry-Netherland, an advertisement for the quality of the

Up here one lives with the birds. To the north, on a clear day, one can see as far as Spuyten Duyvil; to the west, one overlooks the Palisades and the first of the Jersey towns; to the south, there is the broad panorama of Manhattan, the Metropolitan tower dim in the distance; to the east, there lie Hell Gate, Long Island Sound, and the mellow reds and browns of the roofs of Astoria.

[fig. 20]
Lobby, Sherry-Netherland Hotel, ca. 1927

[fig. 21]
Balcony, Sherry-Netherland Hotel, from *The Sherry-Netherland Fifth Avenue at Fifty-ninth St., New York* (ca. 1927)

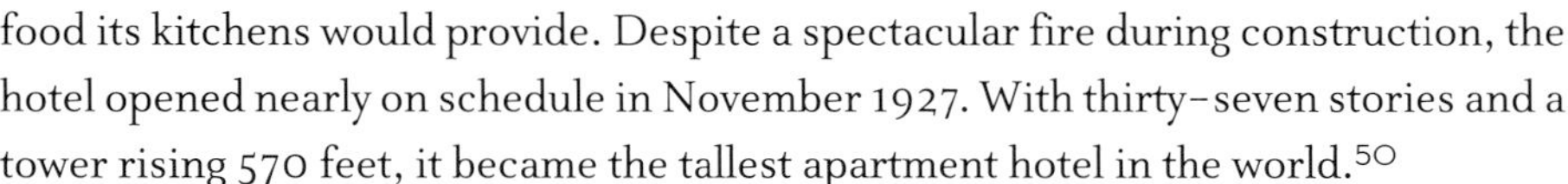

food its kitchens would provide. Despite a spectacular fire during construction, the hotel opened nearly on schedule in November 1927. With thirty-seven stories and a tower rising 570 feet, it became the tallest apartment hotel in the world.[50]

The Sherry-Netherland announced its status as a legitimate successor to the mansions of Fifth Avenue in its entrance vestibule, where two limestone reliefs by the Austrian-born sculptor Karl Bitter were mounted. Bitter's worked graced a number of Gilded Age landmarks, such as the Astor home on Fifth Avenue and Vanderbilt family estates in Newport, Rhode Island (the Breakers) and Asheville, North Carolina (the Biltmore). The panels in the Sherry-Netherland—each depicting a group of girls—were originally made for George B. Post's enlargement (1892–94) of the Cornelius Vanderbilt mansion, at Fifth Avenue and Fifty-seventh Street, where they adorned the carriage porch. When the mansion was demolished in 1927, the new hotel, rising just a block to the north, salvaged the two reliefs.[51]

Visitors to the Sherry-Netherland found a second reminder of the Vanderbilt legacy in the hotel's main lobby, which was decorated with painted panels taken from the same house. The lobby, with its multi-colored marble walls and floors (the plans called for seven varieties) and highly ornate ceiling, and the sky-lit restaurant were the only large public rooms on the ground floor, which was largely occupied by shops. [fig. 20] In the basement was a grill room, decorated with murals illustrating Aesop's fables.

The luxury of the Sherry-Netherland's Renaissance-inspired public interiors was matched by the spacious tenants' living quarters. The lower guest floors—through the sixteenth floor—each had four to six suites of two or more rooms, as well as some single-room apartments for bachelors. Starting on the seventeenth floor, each of the suites possessed a terrace, balcony, or solarium, created by a series of setbacks and notches in the building's facade. [fig. 21] One suite on the twenty-third floor boasted a 50-foot-long terrace overlooking the park. Above that, in the slender tower, each floor consisted of a single suite, culminating in a duplex apartment on the thirty-sixth and thirty-seventh floors. Every suite in the hotel had a small serving pantry, with a refrigerator and "a warming closet," from which a hotel butler could serve meals prepared in the restaurant's kitchen. Along with opulent and comfortable surroundings, sweeping views, a fashionable address, and fine dining, this personal service, by a staff of butlers, maids, valets, and others was one of the hotel's chief selling points. "The Sherry tradition of perfection is drilled into every member of the personnel," boasted a hotel brochure.[52]

The Hotel Pierre, the firm's second apartment hotel in the Grand Army Plaza area, had its own direct links to the past glory of Fifth Avenue. The hotel was the idea of Charles Pierre Casalasco, a Corsican immigrant to the United States and one of New York's best-known restaurateurs. His establishment, located first on Forty-fifth Street and later on Park Avenue, had a loyal following within elite Manhattan society. From these ranks came the financial backers, such as E. F. Hutton and Walter P. Chrysler, for his plan to build a luxury apartment hotel.[53]

Schultze & Weaver had already begun work on the job when the developers announced, in February 1929, that the hotel would go up on Sixty-first Street, just across Fifth Avenue from Central Park. The lot was occupied at the time by several homes, the most prominent of which was a château-style mansion designed by Richard M. Hunt for the prominent lawyer and philanthropist (and descendant of one of America's founding fathers) Elbridge T. Gerry. The Gerry mansion (1894) was known as both a place of learned reflection—it housed a thirty thousand-volume private library—and a hub of elite social life. While Gerry's wife was alive, the family hosted one of New York's most exclusive and anticipated annual balls. But after Elbridge Gerry died in 1927, the mansion stood empty, until his heirs leased the land to the Pierre's developers in early 1929.[54]

Construction on the hotel began in 1929, and it opened in October 1930. The Pierre's broad base ran 270 feet along Sixty-first Street and one-half block south on Fifth Avenue. Like other architects combining the function of a hotel with the form of a skyscraper, Schultze & Weaver used the roofline as the chief expression of the domestic, rather than purely commercial, purpose of the building.[55] From a limestone base, the building rose forty-two stories through a series of setbacks to a tower capped by a copper-sheathed mansard roof—a feature suggestive of some of New York's grand houses from the nineteenth century (such as Hunt's Astor mansion). Otherwise, the exterior decoration on the gray and white building was quite restrained: wrought-iron grilles in a quatrefoil pattern at street level, urns mounted on the terraces and on the upper tower, ornate dormer windows on the roof, etc. [fig. 22]

The hotel offered three entrances (one for the dining room, one leading upstairs to the main ballroom, and one opening onto the lobby) along Sixty-first Street as well as one on Fifth Avenue leading directly to the elevators. The Sixty-first Street entrance halls—with their marble floors, stone walls, and Belgian black marble steps—prepared visitors for the formal luxury they would find in the hotel's many public rooms.

Most of the Pierre's interior spaces were unified by a consistent reference to the Georgian architecture and decoration of eighteenth-century England and Colonial America. On the eastern part of the ground floor was the hotel lobby, with its floor of black Belgian and Alabama cream marble and its pilastered gray and ivory walls, and, adjacent to it, a lounge and writing room for the use of hotel guests. [fig. 23] This room, with white oak walls and shelves, had a marble hearth, over which was hung a large formal portrait in a gilded frame topped by a pediment. The overall effect of the room, according to *The New York Times* critic Walter Rendell Storey, was to suggest the "quiet richness of a great mansion."[56]

[fig. 22]
Hotel Pierre, presentation drawing, rendered by Lloyd Morgan, 1929

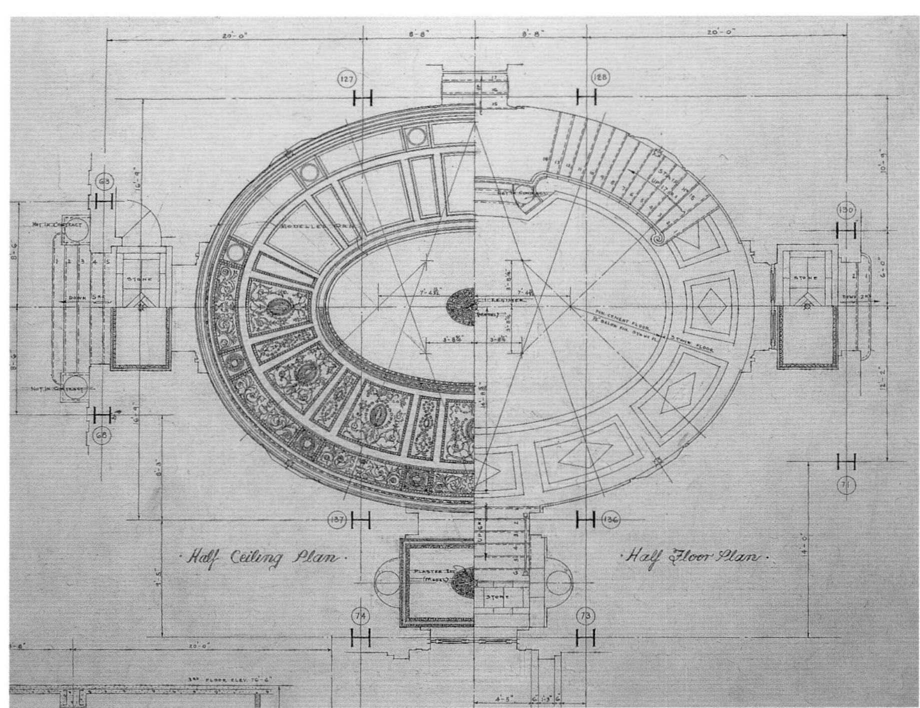

above:
[fig. 23]
Lobby, Hotel Pierre, ca. 1930

top right:
[fig. 24]
Dining room foyer, Hotel Pierre, half-floor and half-ceiling plans (detail), 1929

bottom right:
[fig. 26]
Forty-eighth Street elevation, Hotel Lexington, New York (Schultze & Weaver, 1929), 1928

In the western part of the floor, the oval dining room foyer had stone walls, a ceiling decorated with classical figures in modeled plaster, and marble steps rising to the main dining room. [fig. 24] Called the "Georgian Room," the dining room looked out over Central Park from its central floor, as well as from two raised wings. It was paneled in walnut, with matching pilasters and columns; gold-colored drapes hung in the windows. The main ballroom, on the second floor, was appointed with a maple floor with oak border, plaster walls with inset mirrors and imitation red Verona marble pilasters, and a richly detailed ceiling painted with beasts, vines, and human figures. These and other public rooms—such as the ballroom foyer and smaller function rooms on the second floor, and the roof garden and supper club (originally intended as a breakfast room) on the fortieth floor—featured a similar combination of classical- or Renaissance-inspired decoration filtered through the Georgian style, and materials that were, or appeared to be, both expensive and traditional. Only the basement grill room, with its painted aquatic panels on the walls (the plans initially called for a fish tank), departed markedly from the dominant Georgian theme of the hotel.[57]

The tower rising above these lower stories contained 701 guest rooms, arranged into suites of as many as ten rooms (including parlors, dining rooms, libraries, boudoirs, and dressing rooms), in addition to some single-room units. Some of these rooms were quite generous, such as the parlor for suite no. 407, which measured more than 31 by 18 feet. As in the Sherry-Netherland, each suite had its own serving pantry. White plaster paneled walls with ornamented cornices and pilasters and reproduction period furniture maintained the feeling established in the public floors. In these rooms, noted Storey, could be found "the subtle combination of the lightness, grace and sturdy warmth that we associate with English Georgian furnishings."[58] [fig. 25]

[fig. 25]
Dining room of a typical apartment, Hotel Pierre, ca. 1930

The Georgian revival was an aspect of beaux-arts tradition that did much to shape American architecture from the end of the nineteenth century on. The formal symmetry of Georgian design, in particular, became a favored feature in the homes of the wealthy beginning in the 1890s. Georgian revival architecture served such families, according to the historian Alan Gowans, as a mark of social prestige and of connection to America's historical Anglo-Saxon ruling class.[59] At the Pierre, the application of this style carried an additional layer of meaning: it signaled continuity with the private homes built in this style on Fifth Avenue and other midtown streets, homes that were disappearing to make way for tall buildings like the Pierre itself.

As soon as the hotel opened, the Pierre's public rooms became a center for fashionable social life. On October 26, 1930, Macy's placed an advertisement for its shoe shop in *The New York Times*, claiming that its "devastatingly chic" ladies' alligator or suede step-ins were "just the type of shoe that distinguished women are wearing with woolen frocks to luncheon at the Hotel Pierre." The hotel's roof garden, grill room, and second-floor banquet rooms offered places for private dinner parties and luncheons, while the grand ballroom was booked for debutante and charity balls. Even Elbridge Gerry's descendants, who allowed his mansion to be torn down so the new hotel could be built, used the Pierre's rooms to host parties, such as the bachelor dinner given by Robert L. Gerry, Jr., (Elbridge's grandson) in one of the small ballrooms in April 1934. For families like the Gerrys, the Pierre helped to prolong the tradition of lavish entertaining in the middle of the city.[60]

[fig. 27]
Tower, Waldorf-Astoria Hotel, presentation drawing, rendered by Lloyd Morgan, ca. 1929

In between their work on the Sherry-Netherland and the Pierre, Schultze & Weaver designed the Hotel Lexington, commissioned by the American Hotels Corporation.[61] The Lexington, an eight hundred–room hotel serving mostly transient customers, was located at Lexington Avenue and Forty-eighth Street. Its tower, atop the twenty-four-story building, has been described as "Gothic France . . . sifted through a North Italian sieve."[62] [fig. 26] The same eclectic historicism was on display in the main public rooms: the two-story main lobby, with its oak beamed ceiling, bare stone walls, and arched passageways; the carved oak window seats and "painted antique plaster" ceiling of the Florentine lounge; the American Colonial revival furniture of the Lexington lounge; and the dining room, decorated with mythological figures on the walls and ceiling. The decoration of certain parts of the hotel, however, struck a different note, according to an advertisement announcing the hotel's opening. The Colonial-style furniture in the guest rooms, apparently, had a "suggestion of the moderne," while the jade and silver color scheme of the grill room showed a "conservative modernistic character."[63] The Lexington, which opened in October 1929, hinted at a different kind of luxury, one that Schultze & Weaver would develop with more abandon in its design for the Waldorf-Astoria.

Schultze & Weaver's last hotel, the Waldorf-Astoria, was unlike any other building the firm had designed. It was easily the most prestigious, most publicized, most expensive, and largest project that Schultze & Weaver had undertaken to date, and it remains their most famous building. It was commissioned by Boomer-DuPont Properties as a replacement for the original Waldorf-Astoria (Henry Hardenbergh, 1893 and 1897), once the most renowned hotel in the city, which was torn down in 1929 to make room for the Empire State Building (Shreve, Lamb and Harmon, 1931). In March 1929, the company announced that it planned to build a new Waldorf-Astoria, on an entire block leased from the New York Central Railroad between Park and Lexington avenues and Forty-ninth and Fiftieth streets. Following the announcement, a steady stream of newspaper articles reported on the financing of the project, the progress of construction, and the hotel's innovative and expensive features, such as its private railroad siding and its radio reception system, which would be the largest in the world. In a nationwide radio address broadcast on the evening of the hotel's opening dinner—September 30, 1931—President Hoover saluted the courage of the hotel's management in building "this great structure."[64]

From its 80,000-square-foot base, the hotel rose 625 feet above its Park Avenue entrance, making it the largest and tallest hotel in the world. It contained more than two thousand guest rooms: those for transient customers were located in two slabs facing Park and Lexington avenues, whereas suites for permanent residents were placed in the tower that stood in between. Most impressive of all was the size and variety of the dozens of lounges, lobbies, dining rooms, and ballrooms on the lower floors. These public spaces accommodated "more varied activity," in the words of architectural critic Paul Goldberger, "than any single skyscraper had ever contained."[65]

Just one glance at the building was enough to see that the difference between the Waldorf-Astoria and previous hotels designed by Schultze & Weaver was qualitative as well as quantitative. The earliest sketches of the building, done by Lloyd Morgan, show vertical "spear points" (as they were called by one critic)[66] thrusting from the gray limestone and brick walls, giving the facade a neo-Gothic

[fig. 28]
Park Avenue foyer, Waldorf-Astoria Hotel, presentation drawing, ca. 1930

look similar to that of the Woolworth building downtown. [fig. 27] Revisions to the design, however, stripped these details away, leaving the emphasis on the building's dramatic sculptural form. As Schultze wrote in an article appearing shortly after the hotel opened, "Ornament was eliminated as largely as possible and projections that serve no useful purpose, such as cornices, columns, etc., were avoided."[67] What ornament remained on the exterior—the fins and geometric patterns that adorned the two turrets on top of the tower, and the metal screens that covered the windows on the lower stories—evoked contemporary art moderne fashion rather than historical styles. Unlike any of the firm's previous hotels, the Waldorf-Astoria made no dramatic gesture to the luxurious residences of the past.

Most of the hotel's public rooms harmonized with the building's street presence. A "simple modernistic type of architecture" and "a very restrained modern note" were the expressions that Schultze used to characterize such rooms as the Park Avenue entrance foyer, the main lobby, the main ballroom, and the many adjoining rooms and passages.[68] These spaces were hardly devoid of historical, especially classical, references, such as marble columns and pilasters, but these elements were combined with materials, color schemes, and ornamentation that created a contemporary feel inside the hotel. [fig. 28]

What Schultze referred to as the "modern note" in the hotel's interiors resulted from a number of design choices. The architect himself pointed to two things: the broad wood veneer paneling of many rooms, with minimal use of moldings; and the incorporation of metals to provide variety, together with marble, in the color schemes of rooms. While wrought and cast iron appeared frequently in the public rooms of earlier Schultze & Weaver hotels, reflective metal surfaces were much more in evidence inside the Waldorf-Astoria. Nickeled bronze was the metal of choice, found on pilaster capitals, storefront vitrines, gates, lamps, and mirror frames in rooms throughout the lower floors of the hotel. [fig. 29] Drapes and painted walls complemented the metal work, lending metallic tones—grays, silvers, and golds—to several rooms, such as the main ballroom and its lobby.[69]

The art found in many of the Waldorf-Astoria's public rooms also departed from the historicism that characterized earlier hotel interiors by Schultze & Weaver. Prominently featured was the work of French artist Louis Rigal. He used

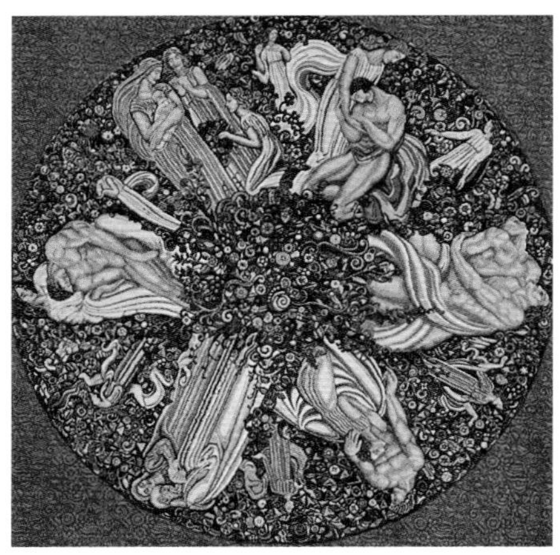

top right:
[fig. 29]
Gates leading to the beauty parlor from Peacock Alley, Waldorf-Astoria Hotel, ca. 1931

top left:
[fig. 30]
Elevator panel, Waldorf-Astoria Hotel, ca. 1931

bottom:
[fig. 31]
"The Wheel of Life" carpet, main foyer, Waldorf-Astoria Hotel, designed by Louis Rigal, from Frank Crowninshield, ed., *The Unofficial Palace of New York* (New York: Hotel Waldorf-Astoria Corp., 1939)

simplified, stylized figures in his design for the "Wheel of Life," which was made into both a mosaic and a rug for the Park Avenue foyer, as well as for bronze panels affixed to elevator doors. [figs. 30, 31] One of the dining rooms off this foyer featured a series of fourteen-foot–high murals by the Spanish artist José Maria Sert, done in dark reds, browns, and black and depicting raucous marriage scenes from *Don Quixote*. (It was Sert who, several years later, painted the mural that replaced Diego Rivera's never completed mural in the RCA Building in Rockefeller Center.) For the Starlight Roof, a restaurant (with a retractable ceiling) on the eighteenth floor of the Park Avenue slab, the American artist Victor White designed wall mosaics of tropical plants and flowers and painted similar scenes in pale green on mirrors.[70]

It is likely that the stylistic shift represented by the Waldorf-Astoria was connected to the leading role in the design process played by Lloyd Morgan, who made the preliminary sketches requested by Lucius Boomer at the end of 1928 and who was responsible for the many renderings of the hotel. Morgan, alone among the firm's partners, had considerable experience overseas, having traveled and worked in Paris during the early and mid 1920s, a time when the art moderne style flourished. As a result of this exposure, the Waldorf-Astoria flaunted a new kind of luxury, one that bowed less deeply to the past and engaged, even if somewhat superficially, with the look of the machine age.

The Waldorf-Astoria's break from historical styles, however, was far from complete. Once guests left the lower floors, they entered a different world, one in which the architects, Schultze wrote, eschewed "anything approaching modernism." The firm hired a host of decorators[71] and instructed them to finish all living quarters primarily in eighteenth-century French and English styles. These rooms had imported antique fireplace mantels, antique and reproduction furniture, and period-style upholstery and drapery fabric. [fig. 32] Even the public rooms on the lower floors were not uniformly contemporary in style. Most notable was the Basildon Room, used for banquets and balls, which was modeled after a room in Basildon Park, a 1776 manor house in Berkshire, England. Included in this function room were a mantelpiece and painted ceiling panels brought over from the original room, as well as reproductions of the original furniture and a rug made from a design by the eighteenth-century architect Robert Adam. [fig. 33] The Empire

Room—which stood across the Park Avenue foyer from the Sert Room—was decorated in the Empire style to provide a link to the room of the same name in the old Waldorf-Astoria. Period styles also guided the design and decoration of a number of smaller function rooms and suites on the fourth floor, as well as private clubs located on the upper stories.[72]

The vast Waldorf-Astoria contained more than one kind of luxury environment. Those parts of the building most likely to be seen by a casual visitor—the facades, the sequence of spaces between the Park Avenue foyer and the main lobby, the enormous main ballroom—offered a vision of elegant "moderne" living infused with the excitement and freedom of the Jazz Age. Less obvious, but no less significant, were the private quarters of residents, as well as the smaller banquet rooms and ballrooms where they might host a dinner party or a wedding reception. In these rooms, much as in the Sherry-Netherland or the Pierre, wealthy guests could live and entertain in an environment that offered the reassurance of continuity with the past.

This mixture of styles bothered Lewis Mumford, who wrote a tepid review of the hotel for *The New Yorker* magazine. "Modernism, revivalism, eclecticism, and plain gimcrackery have all had their hand in producing the Waldorf. Nothing is decisive and clear; that is the capital defect." As a result, Mumford wrote, the Waldorf-Astoria's "sense of luxury is not very convincing."[73]

The qualities that Mumford detected and criticized in the Waldorf-Astoria may have resulted from something more than indecisiveness on the part of the designers. Schultze & Weaver conceived of the Waldorf-Astoria at a time when the meaning of luxury in America was shifting. What people valued as opulent, pleasurable environments was no longer defined by a relatively narrow range of revivalist styles but now also reflected self-consciously modernist trends in the decorative arts and architecture. In the Waldorf-Astoria, Schultze & Weaver designed a building that could not only accommodate an unprecedented number of people and variety of activities but that also encompassed some of the varied conceptions of luxury—both traditionalist and emergent—current in American culture.

[fig. 32]
Eighteenth-century French room, Waldorf-Astoria Hotel, ca. 1931

The Waldorf-Astoria was conceived and planned at the end of a time of great prosperity. Its design reflected the promise of endless growth in the consumption of luxury by the American public. But when the hotel finally opened for business, the Great Depression was already almost two years old, and the hotel struggled from the beginning. Although six thousand people reportedly jammed the ballroom for the opening night dinner, just five hundred guests booked rooms in the hotel, and business did not pick up after that. The Waldorf-Astoria lost money throughout the 1930s and would have done much worse had it not been for steady patronage by the federal government. Only in 1944 did the hotel begin to turn a profit.[74]

Other Schultze & Weaver hotels had even more trouble during the 1930s. The Pierre filed for bankruptcy in 1932 and again in 1939, and the Lexington went into receivership in 1932. The Miami Biltmore Hotel declared bankruptcy and closed temporarily in March 1929, and was sold later in the year for a fraction of the building's original cost. It was not just the Schultze & Weaver hotels that struggled—most American hotels ran into financial trouble during the Depression.[75]

The Waldorf-Astoria was the last hotel that Schultze & Weaver designed. During their ten-year heyday as luxury hotel architects, Schultze & Weaver left a significant mark on two places going through particularly intense building booms.

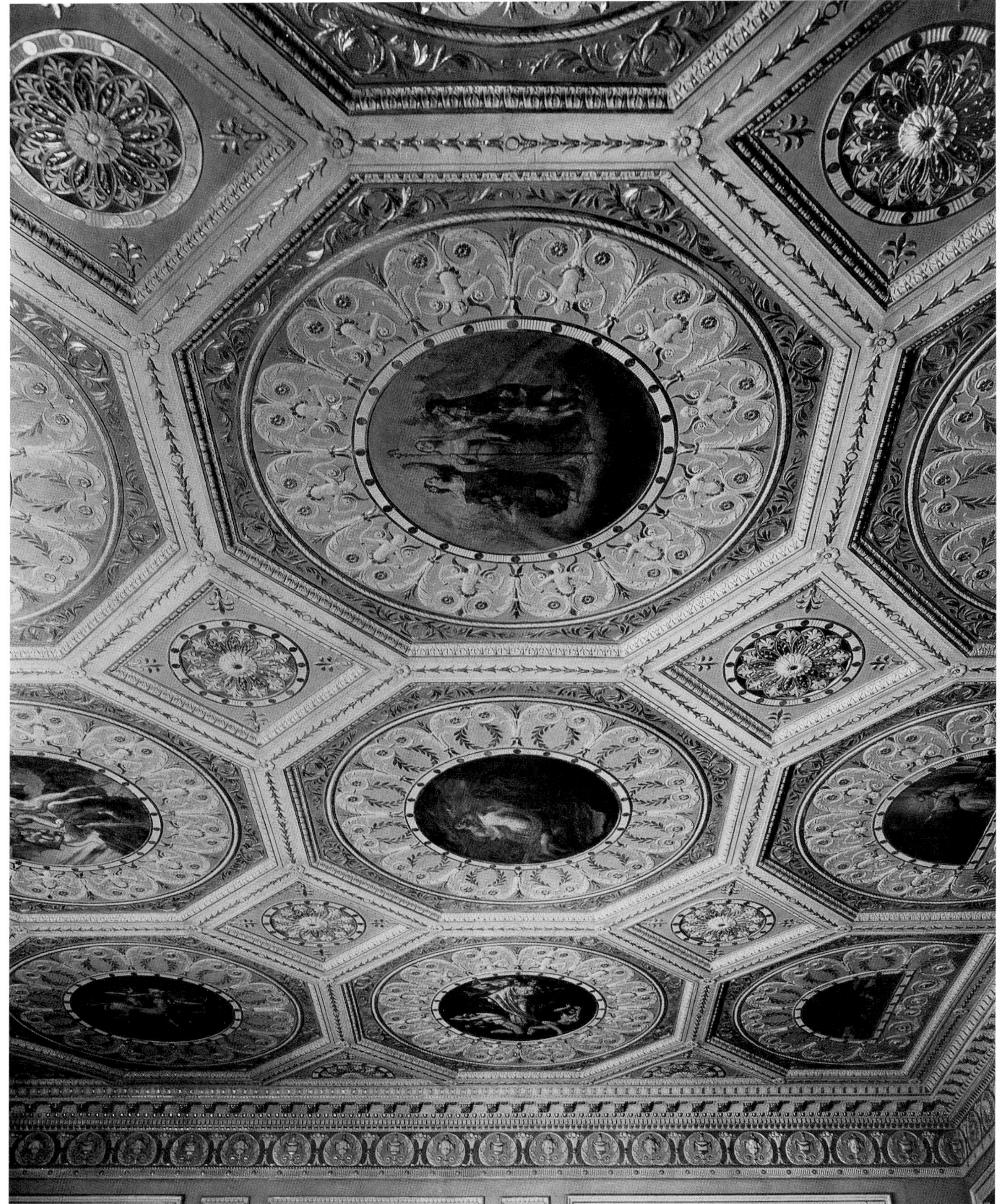

[fig. 33]
Basildon Room ceiling, Waldorf-Astoria Hotel, ca. 1931

In South Florida, especially around Miami, Schultze & Weaver designed resorts that contributed to a surge in development, turning property that had only recently been citrus groves or mangrove swamps into modern suburbs and glamorous vacation destinations. In midtown Manhattan Schultze & Weaver designed several of the world's tallest hotels, helping to complete the transformation of what had been low-rise neighborhoods into a vertical city.

Within these rapidly changing physical and social landscapes, Schultze & Weaver created environments that expressed the self-definitions and aspirations of the American upper class. They did so, in most of their hotels, by loosely applying architecture and ornament associated with the privileged and cultivated classes of former times, whether borrowed from Renaissance palazzos or Georgian country homes. By invoking the past so strongly, the buildings expressed an aloofness from the present, with its dislocations and uncertainties. Schultze & Weaver created atmospheres, in other words, that shielded guests from the very processes of transformation of which their hotels were a part. With the Waldorf-Astoria, however, the architects began to find a language of luxury that was more at home in the modern 'skyscraper metropolis.'

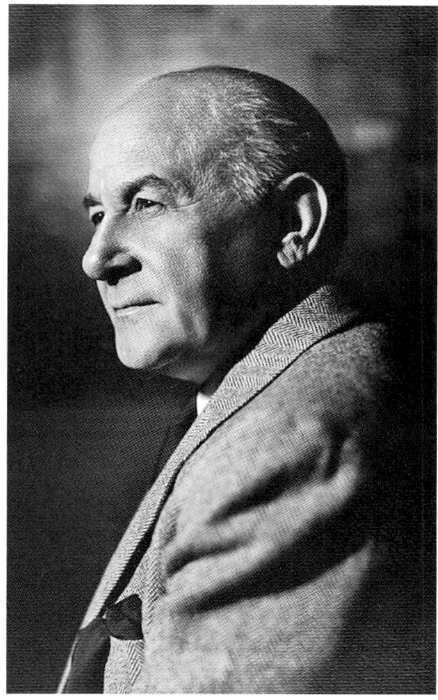

[fig. 34]
Lloyd Morgan, ca. 1950

Ultimately, however, the Waldorf-Astoria was also a dead end for the firm. Not surprisingly, new commissions for hotels dried up after 1931. Schultze & Weaver kept fairly busy over the subsequent years carrying out alterations to existing hotels, especially once the repeal of Prohibition created a demand for hotel bars. But these jobs, like their other projects during this time—a bank, a pumping station, the Food Exhibit building at the New York World's Fair, etc.—were modest compared to the multimillion-dollar hotels and office buildings Schultze & Weaver designed in the 1920s. Only in the last years prior to the start of World War II did larger projects, such as a hospital in White Plains and a Board of Education building in Brooklyn, come their way.[76]

S. Fullerton Weaver died in 1939, and the firm was reorganized as Leonard Schultze & Associates, with Morgan, Meroni, and Sunderland becoming partners. In the early 1940s, business took off again, beginning with large housing developments for the Metropolitan Life Insurance Company in San Francisco, Los Angeles, and Alexandria, Virginia. In 1951, Leonard Schultze died (in Schultze & Weaver's White Plains Hospital). The firm was renamed Lloyd Morgan and Eugene Meroni, and—after Meroni's death in 1955—Lloyd Morgan, Architect. The postwar years brought more big corporate and public commissions, including schools, hospitals, housing developments, and office buildings, and the firm stayed busy into the 1960s. Morgan died in 1970. [fig. 34] While both Leonard Schultze and Lloyd Morgan had long and productive careers after they completed the Waldorf-Astoria, they never reclaimed their preeminence as luxury architects. When a new period of prosperity began after World War II, it was other architects who took up the project of developing a modern idiom of luxury for American hotels.

FROM THE CITY TO THE SEASIDE
Luxury Hotels in New York, Atlantic City, and Miami Beach

Robin F. Bachin

Anthony Trollope, the noted British novelist and travel writer, remarked in 1862 that one of the striking features of American life in the mid-nineteenth century was that "everybody travels in the States." He observed that "the first sign of an incipient settlement [was] an hotel five stories high, with an office, a bar, a cloak room, three gentlemen's parlors, two ladies' parlors, and ladies' entrance and two hundred bedrooms." For an American hotel, he claimed, "size and imposing scale [were] the first requisites."[1] Hotel building signaled a city's place in the emerging commercial economy of the United States during the second half of the nineteenth century. Material prosperity had become a sign of the strength of the nation, and hotel building, a symbol of prosperity. American writer Henry James went so far as to wonder if "the hotel-spirit may not just *be* the American spirit most seeking and most finding itself."[2]

Hotels stood at the nexus of travel and commerce. As the flow of goods, capital, and people, both nationally and globally, accelerated throughout the nineteenth century, central business districts emerged as the locus of commercial activity within cities across the country. Just as the workplace moved outside the home and into urban centers, the hotel emerged as a venue for reuniting the domestic and commercial realms. Like the inns, taverns, and exchanges that preceeded them, hotels served the needs of commercial travelers yet also provided features of domestic life, such as communal parlors and drawing rooms, meals served family style, and (by the early twentieth century) private bedrooms and bathrooms. They also became centerpieces of social life in American cities, offering luxurious settings for entertaining that catered to America's new commercial and industrial elite.[3]

The commerce that prompted the rise of hotels in major cities, facilitated by the development of transportation networks throughout the United States, resulted in the development of travel and tourism as quintessential features of modern American culture. The promotion and expansion of leisure at the end of the nineteenth century offered many Americans the opportunity to transform their sense of personal identity through travel. E. L. Potter, the president of the Clarendon Hotel in Seabreeze, Florida, noted the increasingly close connection between commercial growth, leisure, and travel by the end of the nineteenth century.

[fig. 1]
Tremont House, Boston (Isaiah Rogers, 1829), from William Havard Eliot, *A Description of Tremont House* (Boston: Gray and Bowden, 1830)

"As the country became more prosperous," he explained, "the leisure class increased in numbers and now even the busiest man realizes that he must take time for recreation at different seasons of the year."[4] According to promoters of vacation resorts, travel provided the possibility not only for rest and relaxation but also for an escape from one's everyday life and for an encounter with the exotic.

This confluence of travel, tourism, and modern urban life gave rise to two of the most popular and dynamic vacation destinations of the early twentieth century—Atlantic City, New Jersey, and Miami Beach, Florida. Both places developed as a result of the sun, sand, and surf they offered, but they also incorporated many of the physical features of the modern urban landscape into their design. Although they clearly lacked the industrial and commercial bases that characterized other American cities, they nonetheless offered the excitement and amusement of metropolitan nightlife and an atmosphere that excited the senses. Their whimsical and dazzling architecture, preeminently displayed in the new seaside hotels, showcased building innovations that grew out of hotel and skyscraper designs in cities across the country. And while both Atlantic City and Miami Beach began as vacation spots, their promoters utilized the latest trends in advertising and salesmanship to spark land sales and fuel rising real estate prices, further enhancing their connections to urban commerce. Seaside vacation sites, then, became firmly enmeshed in the culture of consumption and urban growth that shaped America in the early twentieth century.

The Rise of Luxury Hotels in America

The emergence of Atlantic City and Miami Beach as resort destinations represented the convergence of the therapeutic seaside vacation spot with the increasingly luxurious urban hotel. The history of the luxury hotel in America is closely linked to changes in transportation systems, from the rise of the railroad to automobile and air travel. The completion of the transcontinental railroad in the early decades of the nineteenth century made travel throughout the nation easier and more essential, both for business travelers propelling the market economy and for leisure travelers taking advantage of their new-found wealth. Hotels typically touted their convenience to rail lines as a means of attracting customers. Both a symbol and generator of commercial prosperity, the presence of a hotel marked a city as a worthy destination.

The opening of the Tremont House in Boston in 1829 was a signal moment in the history of American hotels. [fig. 1] According to hotel historian Arthur White, "There is little doubt that the opening of the *Tremont* was the start of what we now know as the American Way of Life."[5] The Tremont combined the classical elegance of Greek revival architecture with numerous "modern" amenities (such as indoor plumbing and steam heat), setting the stage for hotels to become leaders in offering technological innovation amidst luxurious surroundings.[6] The stained-glass rotunda at the Tremont was the first hotel lobby presided over by a clerk; previously, guests entered directly into the barroom or exchange. The design of the hotel included three separate entrances, a luggage room of great "formality and dignity as well as optical grandeur," numerous piazzas and porticoes, and "first-class French decorating."[7] The elegance of the Tremont reflected the hotel's role as a centerpiece of both commerce and civic life in Boston.

Following the success of the Tremont, a flurry of hotel construction took place in the 1850s, with luxury emerging as the order of the day. Social commentator Russell Lynes explained in *The Taste-Makers* that hotel architects were trying to please the "national palate that hungered for comfort dipped in a sauce of glitter and gold." New York's St. Nicholas Hotel (1853) was the first to cost over one million dollars.[8] Not to be outdone by Boston and New York, other cities embarked on hotel-building projects. The Hotel Continental opened in Philadelphia in 1860, on the corner of Ninth and Chestnut streets in the heart of the emerging downtown. The main corridor featured a travel office, telegraph office, news stand, smoking saloon, billiard room, gentlemen's café, and business offices.[9] In Chicago, Potter Palmer opened his Palmer House in 1870, only to see it burned in the great Chicago fire of 1871. Vowing to build an even better and more luxurious (as well as fireproof) Palmer House, he quickly set to work rebuilding his hotel on the same block on State Street. The completed hotel, which officially opened on New Year's Day, 1874, included plate-glass windows, an ornate entrance, and the first barber shop in an American hotel, featuring 225 silver dollars set within the tiled floor. The now-requisite rotunda of the lobby created a transitional space between the city street and the hotel interior, where local merchants as well as guests gathered to drink, smoke, lounge, and converse.[10] [fig. 2]

The creation of the Palace Hotel in San Francisco marked the apex of the palatial, masonry-constructed hotel in America; it also signaled the transcontinental scope of travel, leisure, and luxury in the nation. When the Palace, which cost $5 million to build, opened in 1875, it was the most expensive hotel ever constructed. According to an article published in *Frank Leslie's Illustrated Newspaper* in 1878, "The immense court, with its circular carriage sweep, broad promenade, banana trees, and palms, lending a tropical note, impressed itself on the memory of countless visitors."[11] The Palace also included some of the most elegantly appointed spaces reserved for women. That consideration for female guests played such an important role in hotel design suggests the extent to which the function of hotels had shifted, from being primarily about housing business travelers to becoming increasingly about creating elegant spaces that could serve as social centers in the midst of America's downtowns.

[fig. 2]
Grand Rotunda, Palmer House, Chicago (John M. Van Osdel, 1873), from *Palmer House Illustrated* (Chicago: J. M. Wing & Co., 1876)

[fig. 3]
Waldorf-Astoria Hotel, New York (Henry J. Hardenbergh, 1893, 1897), postcard, ca. 1915

Ladies' parlors and drawing rooms typically were located on the second floor of the hotel, with the ground floor reserved for (male) commercial activity. The parlors often included floor-to-ceiling mirrors, richly appointed furnishings, gilt wood, and rich drapes and carpets. According to an 1849 description of a ladies' parlor of the Astor House, the floor-to-ceiling mirrors allowed the female guest to see herself "reflected at full length whichever way she turns, and her likeness is set in very ornamental surroundings."[12] The design of the ladies' parlors positioned women, both literally and figuratively, at the nexus of domesticity, commerce, and the emerging consumer culture shaped by travel, fashion, and display.[13]

That the hotel should be more things to more people was captured in a statement made by architect Henry Hardenbergh, the designer of the original Waldorf-Astoria (1893, 1897) in New York. In defining the functions of a hotel, he stated, "The modern hotel should not only afford ample means of furnishing lodging and food to those seeking those necessities, but such privacy, comfort, luxury, or means of entertainment as may be secured in a private domicile, and in addition every means of carrying out the domestic, public, or social functions of life."[14] Business, leisure, and domesticity should all be features of the modern hotel, and Hardenbergh's Waldorf included them all.[15] [fig. 3] According to one contemporary account, the hotel offered "every pleasure and convenience of metropolitan life . . . a grand ballroom, a theater, a banqueting hall, a full suite of rooms for wedding celebrations, lecture rooms, club rooms, and even a hall furnished specially for meetings of secret societies." The hotel also boasted broker's offices, a photographic gallery, hairdressing salons for men and women, Turkish and Russian baths, and a roof garden that was "painted in Pompeian red . . . with trellised vines, palms, evergreens and flowers."[16]

[fig. 4]
The Plaza Hotel, New York (Henry J. Hardenbergh, 1907), ca. 1910

One of the most significant innovations at the Waldorf-Astoria was the elimination of the separate ladies' entrance and ladies' parlors. Architect Hardenbergh explained that "the setting apart of rooms for . . . women is being abandoned."[17] Instead, women utilized the public spaces of the hotel previously off limits to them, further signaling the emergence of hotels as centers of urban social life and leisure. As a result, the lounges in hotels like the Waldorf became even more elaborate, with domed ceilings, elegant murals and frescoes, velvet and damask draperies, and exquisite chandeliers. The design of the Palm Garden Dining Room, with large plate-glass windows that looked out onto Fifth Avenue, introduced another opportunity for female guests to be seen in public. The Palm Garden faced the Waldorf's main entrance and was, according to some, the most fashionable restaurant in the country. Now observers outside the restaurant, walking along Fifth Avenue, could view the privileged diners—the elite of society—inside. Indeed, the "Palm Room," as it was called, played such a central role in the success of the Waldorf that it became a fixture of luxury hotels thereafter.[18]

The Waldorf ushered in the era of the hotel as the centerpiece of the social world for the nation's emerging leisure class. Other hotels quickly followed suit. The new Plaza Hotel opened in New York in 1907 at Central Park South and Fifth Avenue, one of the most fashionable districts in the city.[19] [fig. 4] Like the Waldorf, the Plaza catered to those who wished to use hotels as the sites of fashionable entertainment and elegant living. The first visitors to sign the guest registry at the opening of the Plaza included the leading business people of the day, such as the Vanderbilts, the Goulds, the Wanamakers, and the Dukes.[20] Likewise, the guest list at the Bellevue-Stratford, which opened in Philadelphia in 1904, featured the names of some of the foremost entertainers of the day, including motion picture stars Ethel Barrymore, Rudolph Valentino, Douglas Fairbanks, and Mary Pickford.[21] In addition to offering the finest and most elegant surroundings, hotels now occupied a central place in the emerging world of leisure, fashion, and entertainment. They had become places to see and be seen. Rather than simply housing travelers who came to a city to experience the urban attractions outside of their elaborate front doors, hotels had themselves become part of the attraction.

The Lure of Atlantic City

The notion that hotels were destinations in and of themselves had been a feature of spa resorts since the nineteenth century. These resorts catered to the wealthy who were seeking the therapeutic benefits of mineral springs and fresh air as sources of physical rejuvenation. The supposedly curative elements of mineral spas and ocean air inspired the emergence of domestic tourism. Colonial Americans traveled to Stafford Springs near Hartford, Connecticut, and White Sulphur Springs in (what is now) West Virginia. By the middle of the nineteenth century, some Americans, critical of what they perceived as the growing materialism of American life in the so-called Gilded Age, sought retreat and spiritual regeneration through closer contact with nature. Many saw in the seashore a place of religious renewal and revival and established seaside communities devoted to temperance, prayer, and communalism.

The early history of the New Jersey shore reflects efforts by some Americans to seek refuge from the commercialism of American urban life. The shore began attracting summer visitors as early as the 1790s. Travelers took coaches from Philadelphia or New York on trails through the Pine Barrens or sailed from either city to reach the seashore. There they sought rest, relaxation, and the therapeutic effect of ocean breezes.[23] The first resort area to emerge at the shore was Cape May, which by 1840 had become a leading American vacation spot, rivaling Saratoga Springs in western New York. The first "luxury" hotel in Cape May, the Mansion, was built in 1832, and was followed by the more expansive Stockton House, modeled on the historic Tremont House of Boston. Because Cape May was a vacation destination with little development surrounding it, the resort hotels included bowling alleys, archery and pistol ranges, ice cream salons, bands and orchestras, and large porches for socializing, playing cards, and promenading. The recreational options at Cape May signaled the integral nature of spaces for entertainment in resort hotels.[24]

Other parts of the Jersey shore began to develop once rail service linked both Philadelphia and New York with the seaside in the 1850s. Religious communities increasingly dotted the shore and helped make the area one of the first middle-class resorts in America. Methodists founded Asbury Park and its neighboring community Ocean Grove, and by the end of the nineteenth century, both were attracting crowds numbering in the tens of thousands. Although they had lost some of the religious zeal that characterized their founding, they nonetheless provided a counterpoint to the increasingly risqué amusements featured at New York's Coney Island and the Jersey shore's Atlantic City.[25]

First Annual Excursion of Phila. Lodge, No. 1, B. O. of Buffaloes,
TO ATLANTIC CITY.
Wednesday, Aug. 17, '81.
Adults' Tickets, $1.00,
BY THE
CAMDEN & ATLANTIC R. R
[The Old Reliable.]
REGULAR EXCURSION TRAIN LEAVES
VINE AND SHACKAMAXON STS. FERRIES
AT 6-30 A. M.
SOUTH ST AT 6-20 A. M
SPECIAL TRAIN FROM
VINE ST AT 7-30 A. M
RETURNING LEAVE
AND 10-30 P. M.

[fig. 5]
Advertising card for Camden & Atlantic Railroad, 1881

During the last decades of the nineteenth century, Atlantic City was becoming the most popular seaside resort in America. Atlantic City began its growth after rail service was established from Philadelphia in 1854, but it took a couple of decades for the city to grow in earnest. [fig. 5] The introduction of a boardwalk and, later, amusements helped catapult the seaside town into one of the hottest in the country, sending land values soaring. The same technology that brought the electric railroad also contributed to the advent of more sophisticated amusements, in turn attracting more and more vacationers from various backgrounds to the beach. Middle-class whites began taking extended vacations at the hotels and small cottages available for rent, and working-class groups took day-long excursions to the beach, often as part of workplace-sponsored programs.[26]

Atlantic City's Boardwalk (designated a street in 1896) constituted the physical symbol of the dual nature of the city's offerings, for it literally divided the natural space of the shoreline on one side from the emerging commercial center of mass amusement on the other. [fig. 6] The idea for a boardwalk came from Alexander Boardman, a railway conductor, and Jacob Keim, the proprietor of the Chester Country Hotel, one of the early wood-frame hotels at the beach. Together they petitioned the city in 1870 to build a footpath along part of the beachfront so that travelers would not track sand into the railcars or hotels. The Council approved the project, and on June 16, 1870, Atlantic City dedicated its first boardwalk, which stretched one mile and was built at a cost of $5,000.[27] The initial resolution stipulated that there could be no buildings on the ocean side of the boardwalk, but the land side soon became populated with stalls and shops that offered a plethora of goods and services, including photographers, sun parlors, book sellers, Japanese flower painters, fortune tellers, and vaudeville theaters. To traverse the boardwalk visitors first used wheeled chairs, which were later replaced by the ubiquitous rolling cars.[28]

The commercialization of the Boardwalk helped define the texture of the seaside resort Atlantic City was becoming. The area took on an urban feel as a result of the wide variety of goods sold there and the density of buildings adjacent to the ocean. Stores catering to tourists sprang up and helped meld the experience of seaside vacationing with urban commerce.

[fig. 6]
The Boardwalk, Atlantic City, postcard, ca. 1900

The creation of piers jutting out from the Boardwalk and into the ocean [illegible]r bridged the "natural" and urban elements of Atlantic City. [fig. 7] By the late [illegible]enth century, wood and even iron piers were constructed for recreation and relaxation. The first successful amusement pier, opened in 1884, was a multi-decked, 625-foot-long extension into the ocean. It offered picnic areas, sunbathing pavilions, an area for baby strollers, and an ice-water fountain. The 1898 Steel Pier, designed by James H. Windrim, would be the most ambitious of its time. It stretched 1,780 feet into the sea and became known as the "Showplace of the Nation" for the vaudeville and minstrel shows it featured as well as its famous "High Diving Horses."[29] [fig. 8] George C. Tilyou's 1904 Steeplechase Pier offered more daring amusements, including the Whirlpool and the Whip, which shook and twirled riders with new mechanical contrivances.

The hotels of Atlantic City complemented this dynamic and whimsical urban fabric. While early hotels were modest in size and built in the Queen Anne or stick styles common to resort architecture, those built in the early twentieth century added flamboyance and grandeur to the seaside streetscape. The history of the Marlborough-Blenheim Hotel highlights the changes taking place in hotel construction in Atlantic City at the turn of the century and the important role urban hotel design played in transforming seaside resort architecture. Owner Josiah White was a significant figure in the development of Atlantic City hotels, as he became the first hotel operator in Atlantic City to remain open year-round. The creation of new kinds of mass amusement, from roller coasters and carousels to halls of mirrors and oddity shops, meant that the resort no longer had to rely on the lure of the seaside in summertime to attract travelers. In 1902, when White made plans to enlarge his Marlborough Hotel by creating an annex, he sought a daring design that would reflect the modern character of the city by the sea.[30]

White chose Philadelphia architects William L. Price and M. Hawley McLanahan for the annex, which would be called the Blenheim Hotel. One of the leading concerns of builders at that time was fireproof construction. Several resort towns, including Atlantic City, had been devastated by fires, spread as a result of the pervasive use of wood-frame construction for hotels and piers. The Blenheim would be the world's first fireproof hotel built of a revolutionary material—reinforced concrete.

top:
[fig. 7]
The ocean and piers, Atlantic City, postcard, 1921

bottom:
[fig. 8]
Diving horse attraction, Atlantic City, postcard, 1929

top:
[fig. 9]
Marlborough-Blenheim Hotel, Atlantic City (Price and McLanahan, 1906), postcard, 1925

bottom:
[fig. 10]
Traymore Hotel, Atlantic City (Price and McLanahan, 1915), postcard, 1915

Price and McLanahan pioneered the use of concrete in building, recognizing its advantages not only in technological terms but also in the area of innovative design.[31]

According to Price, the use of new kinds of building materials forced a reconsideration of design. Explaining the use of concrete, he said, "It is evident that this would and should make a wide departure from Classic forms and accepted styles—that it means, in fact, a new architecture, although it will not be necessary to abandon all precedent. . . . But in a material so plastic the forms of openings and mouldings may be expected to vary much from those necessary to an architecture dependent on arches and lintels."[32] Price advocated a "modern" architecture to fit a modern age and saw no better place to unveil it than the quintessential modern resort town of Atlantic City.

The fifteen-story Blenheim, built in 1906, was connected to the Marlborough via a long passageway across Ohio Avenue. Its Moorish design featured domes, minarets, curves, and spires evoking elements of exotic lands alongside the sandy shores of New Jersey. [fig. 9] The facade reflected its seashore setting by incorporating cast tile and terra-cotta ornamentation of shells, crabs, mermaids, and sea horses. The exterior painting of the hotel had touches of beige and turquoise, thereby blending the colors of sea and sand. While some architects ridiculed the design for its flamboyance, Price explained, "[I]t is an expression of the purpose for which it was built and of the place where it was built: that it is an expression of the gay and sumptuous life, as it was meant to be, of the people that go to Atlantic City."[33] In the Blenheim, Price and McLanahan had used the latest building technologies, combined with playful visual references to the seashore, to create a model for the modern resort.

Price and McLanahan continued their experimentation with form when they received the commission to expand the Traymore Hotel at Illinois Avenue and the Boardwalk. The hotel, across Park Place from the Marlborough-Blenheim, was owned by Josiah White's cousin Daniel White. For the Traymore, Price and McLanahan's design was more austere but no less experimental. [fig. 10] They created a raised central block with domed towers rising 234 feet above the ocean. The height and scale of the new six-hundred-room hotel clad in sand-colored bricks created the image of a giant sandcastle rising up from the Boardwalk when it opened in 1915. According to architectural historian George E. Thomas, the Traymore "established the sinewy and structurally expressive forms that became the model for both the tapering skyscrapers and muscular mid-rise buildings that became standards of eastern cities."[34] Indeed, a contemporary critic said of the Traymore, "[It] is really the old picturesque seaside hotel, purged of its gambrel and filigree translated into the terms of stern modernism, with its picturesqueness preserved."[35]

Price and McLanahan, as well as other Atlantic City hotel designers like William Macy Stanton, created an architecture of entertainment that turned the streetscape of the Boardwalk into a pleasure paradise. Juxtaposed with the amusement piers, taffy shops, and fortune tellers, the hotels became essential features of an urban fantasyland. While they reflected the latest building techniques and design innovations, they also promoted a playfulness that belied their importance in the larger history of modern skyscraper construction. By combining building innovation with fanciful design, the architects of Atlantic City hotels showcased the confluence of resort architecture and urban skyscraper design.[36]

[fig. 11]
Lucy the Elephant, Margate, New Jersey (James V. Lafferty, 1881), after 1881

The splendor of Atlantic City hotels not only drew vacationers but also helped promote increasing real estate values as a result of land speculation. First, owners of rail lines and hotel proprietors and then others invested in stretches of land behind the Boardwalk to sell or rent to seasonal tourists and even those who chose to stay year-round. Both the hotels, with their towering observation decks, and the amusements like the Ferris Wheel that whisked revelers high into the sky, served the interests of advertisers promoting real estate development. The entire iconography of the Boardwalk, with its billboards, electric lights, and souvenir shops, catered to the process of commodifying the seashore.

Nothing represented the practice of using the fantastical design innovations of the hotel in the service of sales better than the creation of Lucy the Elephant. [fig. 11] Lucy, a small hotel built in the shape of an elephant, was constructed in order to lure potential land buyers to an area just south of Atlantic City. The hotel quickly became a destination not just (or even) for potential property owners but for tourists who saw her as one more curiosity in the pantheon of oddities offered in Atlantic City. Entertainment, amusement, sales, and spectacle all merged together in the "city by the sea," making the pursuit of pleasure one of the central features of this urban resort.

The Florida Resorts

For those who wished to pursue fantasy farther afield, destination resorts in Florida furnished a perfect balance of civilization and the exotic. Through the development of rail transportation, locales such as Miami Beach emerged as a vacationer's paradise, replete with balmy winters, subtropical beaches, and all the amenities the wealthy had come to expect. [fig. 12] Florida was built on promotionalism, on selling the image of paradise through new forms of advertising and media emerging at the turn of the century. Owners of railroads used new advertising and sales techniques to entice travelers to these tropical destinations, or as one promoter put it, "Where Summer Spends the Winter."[37]

[fig. 12]
Brochure for the Illinois Central Railroad (1930)

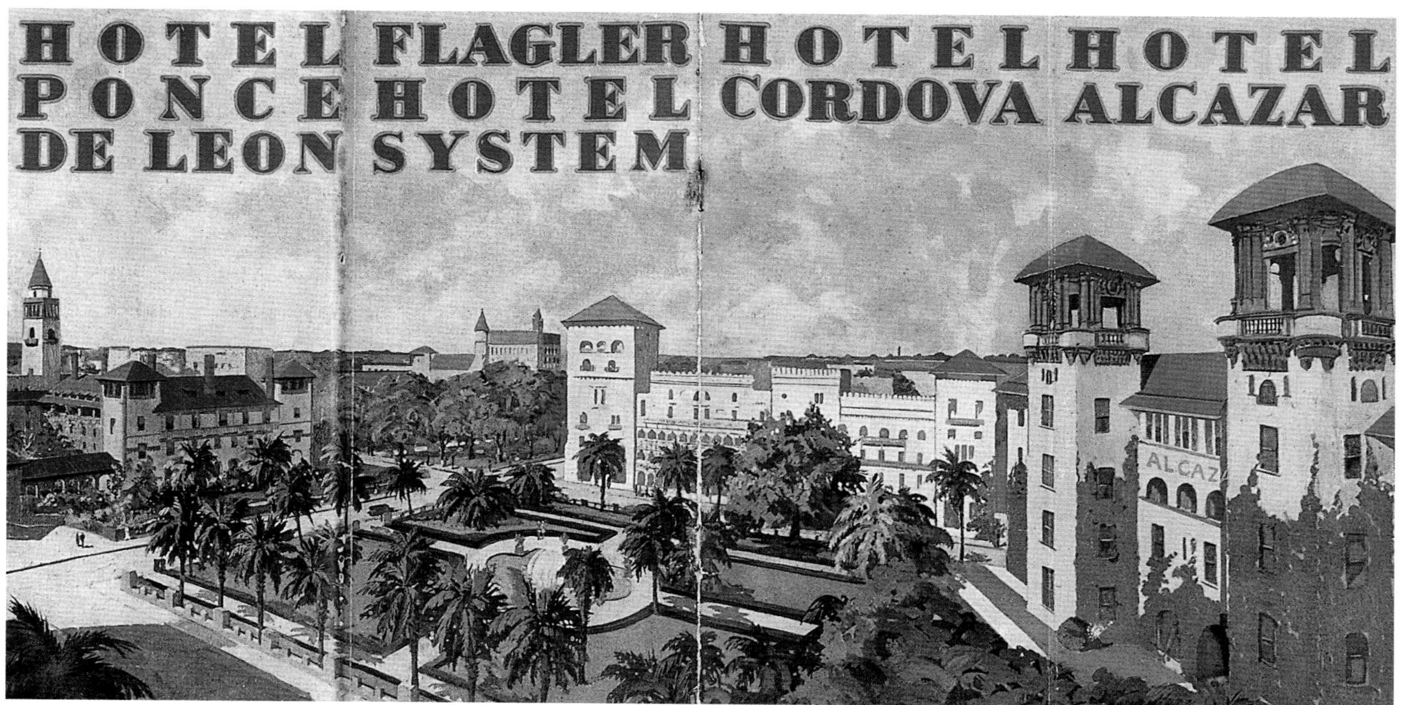

[fig. 13]
View of St. Augustine hotels, from *Flagler Hotel System* (ca. 1930)

Like other seaside resorts, the growth of rail lines throughout Florida prompted the boom of resort hotels there. Henry M. Flagler, a colleague of John D. Rockefeller at Standard Oil, started a railway company that eventually would reach all the way to Key West. Along with developing the Florida East Coast Railway, Flagler also created his Model Land Company to sell tracts of land along the rail line. As historian Charles Funnell has explained, "[I]t was a happy arrangement: the railroad would increase the value of the Land Company's holdings, and the sale of land would bring customers for the railroad."[38] As a means of enticing travelers to use his railroad and perhaps buy land from his holding company, Flagler created some of the most elaborate resort hotels to date. He and other promoters of vacation destinations who came later developed fantastic sketches and drawings of Florida's fantasylands whose themed designs promised exoticism and escape.

The first of what would eventually include six hotels in Flagler's Florida East Coast Hotel system was the Ponce de Leon in St. Augustine, Florida. St. Augustine was unique in that it already was an established city (indeed, the first continuously inhabited city in the United States). Unlike some of the other resorts Flagler would develop, St. Augustine already had an advanced urban infrastructure, housing stock, and amenities for tourists. Still, Flagler saw the potential in making St. Augustine into an elite vacation destination that would attract tourists from across the nation. [fig. 13] To design the hotel, he selected architects John M. Carrère and Thomas Hastings, recent graduates of the Écoles des Beaux-Arts in Paris. Construction on the hotel began in the summer of 1885, and the building opened in January of 1888. The building material consisted of a blend of cement, sand, and coquina-shell gravel, a ubiquitous material found along the shores of the Atlantic that had been used by Africans in the construction of slave quarters at many northern Florida plantations prior to the Civil War.[39]

The four-story Spanish Renaissance revival structure cost $2 million and included 450 guest rooms along with private parlors, reading and game rooms, and lounges. [fig. 14] Like his counterparts in Atlantic City, interior designer Bernard Maybeck used fanciful seaside embellishments for the interior, including dolphin motifs and doorknobs modeled after seashells. Inside the front gate was a 10,000-square-foot garden court surrounded by vine-covered verandas and filled with bubbling fountains and exotic plants. Beyond the garden court stood an archway

[fig. 14]
Front entrance, Ponce de Leon Hotel, St. Augustine, Florida (Carrère & Hastings, 1889), from *Florida the American Riviera. St. Augustine the Winter Newport* (1887)

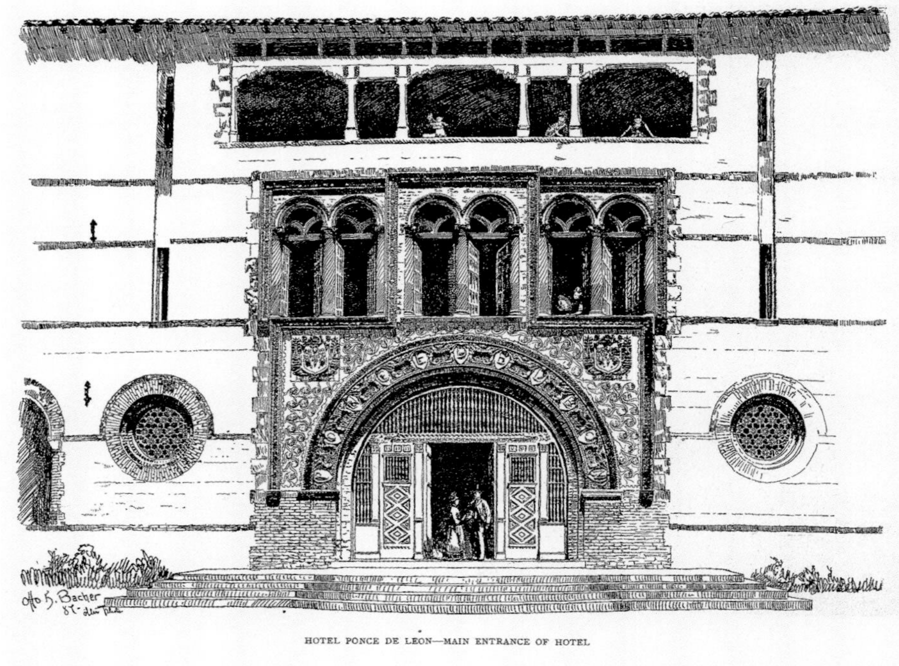

that led to a rotunda eighty feet tall. The ballroom off the rotunda was capped by Tiffany chandeliers, while the dining room featured Tiffany stained-glass windows and a ceiling decorated with artist George Maynard's depiction of the four seasons as well as a pictographic history of Florida.[40]

The construction of the Royal Poinciana in Palm Beach epitomized the intimate connection between rail construction and resort hotels. In 1893, Flagler bought a tract of land in Palm Beach to begin a new hotel, building even though his rail line had not yet reached the location. Construction of the Royal Poinciana started on May 1, 1893, with materials brought in by steamer. The E-shaped, six-story structure was the largest wooden building ever erected. Its corridors were lined with exclusive shops on the order of those on Fifth Avenue, making it the Floridian equivalent of the Plaza or the Waldorf-Astoria in New York. One contemporary journalist described Palm Beach as a place "where people who have more money than they need spend their time industriously as society climbers, fashion plates, scandal mongers, whiskey guzzlers and gamblers."[41] [fig. 15]

In 1907 Henry James described the scene at the Royal Poinciana itself as "Vanity Fair in full blast—and Vanity Fair not scattered, not discriminated and parceled out, as among the comparative privacies and ancestries of Newport, but compressed under one vast cover."[42] In fact, it was largely the same clientele that hosted teas and galas and took up permanent residence at the Waldorf-Astoria and the Plaza that made their way to Palm Beach for the winter. The register of hotel guests included names such as William Vanderbilt, John Jacob Astor, George Jay Gould, and John Wanamaker, virtually replicating the guest list at the Plaza on its opening day.[43]

The opening of the Breakers Hotel further established Palm Beach as the winter destination of the rich and famous. By 1895, the Royal Poinciana had become so successful that Flagler decided to build another, less grand, hotel on the ocean side of Palm Beach to absorb the overflow crowds. Flagler soon made additions to the Palm Beach Inn and renamed it "The Breakers," but the wooden structure was consumed by several fires. In 1925, Flagler's company decided to build a more modern, fireproof, and grandiose structure and hired the architectural firm of Schultze & Weaver to design it.[44]

[fig. 15]
Brochure for Palm Beach (1914)

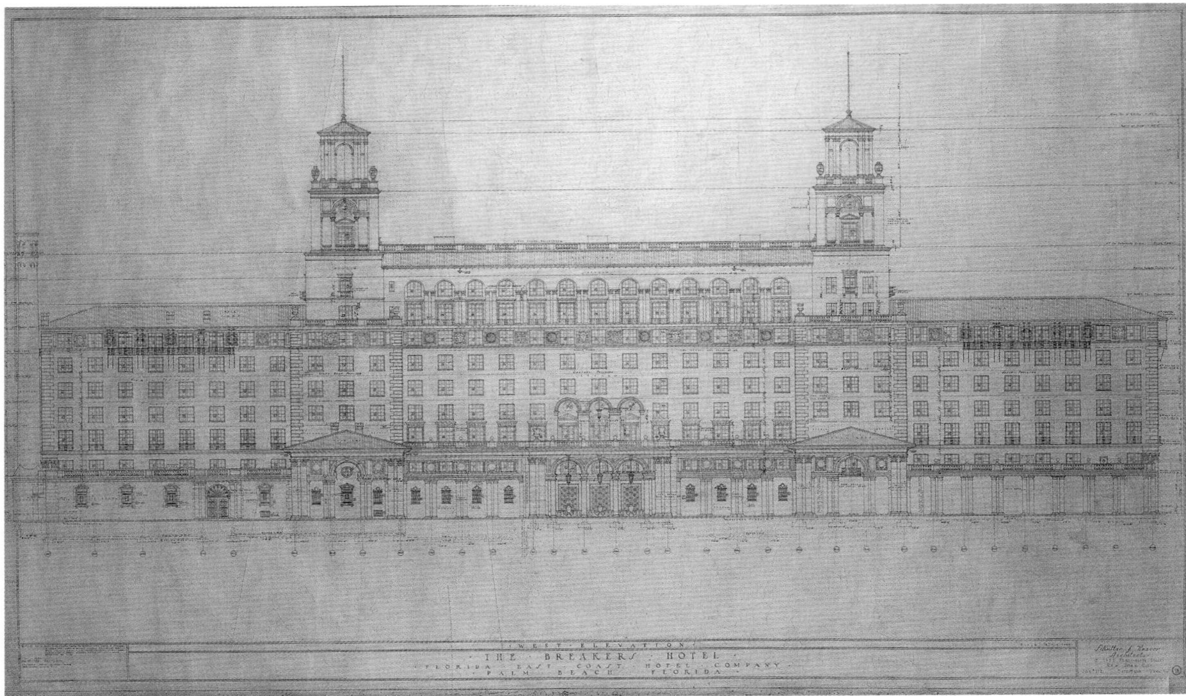

[fig. 16]
Breakers Hotel, Palm Beach (Schultze & Weaver, 1926), 1926

Leonard Schultze and S. Fullerton Weaver had already earned reputations as two of the most talented creators of resort hotels that combined modern building techniques with historic architectural design. The firm designed the 1923 Los Angeles Biltmore in the Spanish Baroque revival style—a style that increasingly and with slight variations would shape resort hotel design throughout Florida. For Schultze & Weaver, buildings were designed in their totality. Scenes of Arabian nights, Oriental landscapes, and Egyptian hieroglyphs combined to create a sense of fantasy for those who visited. The Breakers, an Italian Renaissance-inspired hotel, evoked the Villa Medici in Rome; the towers of the building, as well as its H-shaped plan featuring plazas, loggias, and columns, recalled the sixteenth-century palace. [fig. 16] Like Price and McLanahan, Schultze & Weaver used the latest building technologies to create the illusion of Old World grandeur. Yet the structural steel and reinforced concrete frame and stucco exterior made the building thoroughly modern. All the hotel's attractions were incorporated into one complex, so guests could enjoy the casino, swimming pool, and golf course without leaving the grounds of the Breakers. The success of the Breakers prompted further land speculation in Palm Beach, fulfilling Flagler's plan of linking luxury travel with property promotion.[45]

While resorts in northern and central Florida attracted well-heeled crowds both as vacationers and land buyers, the success of tying hotel development with real estate promotion reached its apex in South Florida. Numerous promotional brochures linked the tropical climate, lifestyle of leisure, and opportunity for effortless wealth supposedly offered in South Florida at the turn of the twentieth century. [fig. 17] One brochure touting the allure of Coconut Grove, the oldest settlement in Miami, claimed, "The winter days are filled with sunshine flecked by fleecy clouds, while stars and moon glow at night with a brilliancy unknown at the North."[46] The author of this description, a physician from Cornell University, then stated: "Such, in brief, are the conditions that make for health and comfort—no grippe, no pneumonia, no malaria, but dry air, perfect drainage and equable temperature."[47] Like the early promoters of Atlantic City, developers in South Florida highlighted the healthful benefits of its sun and sand while linking these features to the promise of pleasure and fantasy. Real estate offices multiplied in

MIAMI BEACH
Florida
is
Calling you

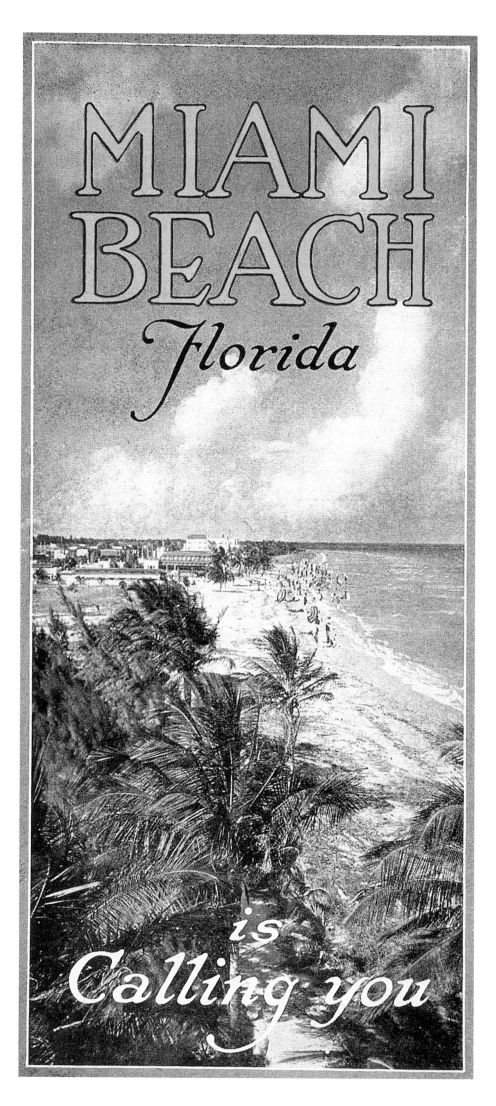

[fig. 17]
Brochure for Miami Beach (ca. 1922)

[fig. 18]
Babe Ruth (left) and Al Smith playing golf at the Miami Biltmore Country Club, 1930

South Florida as Miami became known as "America's playground," not only because of its year-round sunshine but also as a result of its generous offerings for elite recreation, from yacht racing to polo playing.

Land speculators and builders seeking to promote economic growth in South Florida abounded. Developers created exotic, fantasy-inspired subdivisions to entice tourists to remain in South Florida and make the vacation resort their permanent home. George Merrick created perhaps the most successful and enduring planned community in South Florida: Coral Gables. With elaborate Spanish revival architecture, grandiose public spaces, and monumental civic buildings, Coral Gables embodied the urban planning ideals of the City Beautiful movement, which came to maturity in the years prior to World War I. It combined a focus on aesthetic beauty with economic growth, seeing the two as integrally related. The construction of the Miami Biltmore Hotel, the centerpiece of Merrick's community, highlighted the seminal role that hotels would play in this urban planning strategy as icons of the lifestyle of leisure.[48]

Merrick hired Schultze & Weaver right before the firm received the commission for the Breakers in Palm Beach. The Biltmore incorporated the Spanish revival style that permeated all of the buildings in Coral Gables. It was modeled on the Giralda tower in Seville, Spain (an element that would reappear in other Schultze & Weaver projects in South Florida, including the Miami Daily News and Metropolis Building). While the Biltmore incorporated many of the same design elements of the Breakers, including open courtyards, vaulted ceilings, elegant terraces, and grandiose ballrooms, the hotel became famous for its million-gallon swimming pool, reportedly the largest in the world. The pool, around which the outdoor patios were arranged, highlighted Merrick's intention of making the Biltmore "the center of sports and fashion."[49] The hotel would host not only wealthy travelers like those who vacationed at the Breakers but also prominent figures from the emerging professional sports and entertainment crowd of the 1920s. Gene Sarazen, Ginger Rogers, Bing Crosby, and Babe Ruth were popular guests [fig. 18], as was Olympian swimmer Johnny Weissmuller; Weissmuller actually served as the swimming instructor at the Biltmore before landing the film role of Tarzan. A promotional booklet promised, "This Hotel and Country Club will attract the right kind of people to the land"; by luring the

MIAMI BEACH
CITY OF HEALTH
A CONSTANT TEMPERATURE—WINTER and SUMMER
MIAMI BEACH
winter home of champions
PERFECT PLAY IN PERFECT CLIME
MIAMI BEACH
IS CALLING YOU
SPACIOUS ACCOMMODATIONS REASONABLE RATES
MIAMI BEACH
on the ocean front
PARKER
MIDWINTER TEMPERATURE—AIR—70° WATER—70°

[fig. 19]
Brochure for Miami Beach (ca. 1926)

wealthy, the Biltmore would "draw the South to the attention of the moneyed men of the country."[50]

Like Merrick, Miami Beach developer Carl Fisher was a master at using luxury to sell land. Fisher made his initial fortune with Prest-O-Lite, the company he developed to manufacture headlights for automobiles. Fisher was interested in more than just the practical elements of the automobile, however. He used much of his profit from Prest-O-Lite to construct the Indianapolis Motor Speedway, the grandest racetrack in the world.[51] According to his biographer, Mark S. Foster, the energetic Fisher helped to popularize such elite and glamorous sports as race car driving, boat racing, and polo playing.[52]

Fisher brought his passion for the fast-paced sporting life and his flair for publicity to his efforts to develop Miami Beach. By 1919, the resort had a polo field, golf course, tennis courts, and piers for boat races. Fisher also lured high-profile celebrities and athletes to his newly built Roman Pools, including Bill Tilden, Gertrude Ederle, Jack Dempsey, and Gene Tunney. According to one historian, "For those whose idea of sport was to wear resort clothes and sit, drink in hand, watching other people play, Miami Beach provided champions to look at."[53] [fig. 19]

From the start it was clear that Fisher was interested in developing the area for the purpose of making money through land sales. According to an account in the *Miami Metropolis*, "Mr. Fisher acquired the land purely for speculation, and he has given it out as his intention to make of the place as near a tropical garden as money can produce; one that will be a fit setting for the beautiful homes to follow."[54] Fisher encouraged some of his business associates from the automobile industry to buy property on Miami Beach, including Prest-O-Lite partner Jim Allison, by then head of Union Carbide; Arthur C. Newby, president of National Automobile Company; Frank Seiberling, head of Goodyear Tire; Harvey Firestone, president of Firestone Tires; Jim and George Snowden, both oil men; and Henry McSweeney, attorney for Standard Oil. Together several of them organized the Miami Ocean View Company in 1916 and built Star Island.

The centerpiece of any destination resort, of course, was a luxury hotel. Here, the hotel was used as a vehicle not only for attracting visitors to Miami Beach

[fig. 20]
Flamingo Hotel, Miami Beach (Price and McLanahan, 1920), from *Souvenir of Miami Beach, Florida* (ca. 1926)

to enjoy the sun and surf, but also as a site for selling the idea of permanent settlement to the wealthy guests. In 1919, Fisher and Jim Allison hired Price and McLanahan, the firm that revolutionized seaside architecture in Atlantic City, to draw up plans for a hotel on Miami Beach. On January 6, 1920, the *Miami Metropolis* reported that the staking off of the grounds had been completed and construction would begin just a few days later.[55]

Fisher chose to name his new hotel the Flamingo. [fig. 20] The name, with its "flavor of something rare and brilliantly tropical," was well-suited to the new hotel; it highlighted the element of exoticism that a tropical vacation on Miami Beach promised.[56] The Mediterranean revival style of the hotel set the standard for the grandeur and elegance of Miami Beach development. The style reflected Old World aesthetics and suggested a sense of timeless beauty in the service of newly generated wealth. America's industrial elite could experience the elegance of Europe within the framework of the fast-paced life of leisure that Americans celebrated in the Jazz Age. Indeed, an advertising brochure for one hotel boasted that the newly built hotels of Miami Beach were even more appealing than those of Europe: "Their breath-taking beauty not only rivals—but because of Florida's glamorous setting—by far outdoes all Europe has to offer."[57] Conflating the appeal of Europe and Miami, a brochure for another hotel, called the Montmartre, claimed, "If you dream of Paris . . . and you like the sun, fun, and frolic . . . you'll love the Montmartre!"[58]

The interior of the Flamingo incorporated elements of the exotic and the exclusive. Tropical colors dominated the decor, with blue and tan carpets and draperies, and mahogany for beds, chairs, and dressing tables. The walls all were ivory, though the great lounge was done in light yellow with large black and yellow tiles on the floor. The sunroom featured soft green draperies along with "flamingo pink" and blue furnishings.[59] Fisher ordered $218,709 worth of furnishings from friend and fellow Miami Beach property owner John Wanamaker's Department Store in Philadelphia to complement the interior design.[60]

The Flamingo featured lush landscape design as well to enhance the aesthetics of the building. Grapefruit, orange, and mandarin trees were planted on the grounds, as were flowering shrubs. Fisher hired two Japanese landscape gardeners, Tashiro and Kataro Suto, to introduce exotic plant species that would enhance the

[fig. 21]
Corner of the lobby, Flamingo Hotel, ca. 1925

sense of extravagance and romance of the hotel. They incorporated "Arabian jasmine, Brazilian pepper, Chinese holly, Canary Island date palms, Hong Kong orchids, Mexican flame vine, Rangoon creeper, [and] Surinam cherry." According to one account, "the new greenery was as artificial as the soil in which it was planted."[61]

Fisher also attempted to introduce exotic animals to the hotel. In 1920 he embarked on an expedition to hunt flamingoes in the tidal marshes of the Bahamas, hoping to bring back several specimens that would stroll the grounds of the hotel. *National Geographic* advertising director John Oliver (Jack) La Gorce and noted naturalist artist Louis Agassiz Fuertes, among others, accompanied Fisher on his trip. The gamesmen captured hundreds of flamingoes, all of which died on the boat trip back to Florida. Undeterred, Fisher introduced pheasants and peacocks to the grounds, which fared much better. Still, the hotel was named the Flamingo, so in place of living flamingoes, Fisher had Fuertes decorate the lobby with paintings and plaster reliefs of the birds.[62] [fig. 21] The use of tropical flourishes in the décor of the Flamingo became a staple of Miami Beach interior design, as did the introduction of Oriental elements. The whimsical features that Price and McLanahan introduced on the Jersey shore and then imported to Miami Beach set the stage for further experimentation there.

In addition to exoticism, the Flamingo promised exclusivity. Rates started at $15 per day, thereby excluding all but the wealthy. Its one hundred and fifty rooms each featured private baths as well as views of either the ocean or the bay. Private docks and bathhouses, men's clubs, piers for viewing yacht races, and a resident elephant all contributed to the extravagance of the Flamingo.[63] Fisher went so far as to import forty Guernsey cows from Wisconsin so that his guests could "drink the most expensive milk in America" (the cost of transporting the cows to Florida topped $7,000).[64] The hotel's amenities also ensured a well-heeled clientele. The shops and services at the hotel included Black, Starr & Frost, a leading Fifth Avenue jeweler; the Bonwit Teller and Company department store; Don Ferris, a men's haberdasher; Max Littwitz, purveyor of lace and linens; and Thomas and McKinnon, a broker's office and member of the New York and Chicago stock exchanges.[65] Like the Royal Poinciana, then, the Flamingo catered to travelers seeking urban amenities amidst a tropical backdrop.

Promotional materials for the Flamingo and later, the Roney Plaza—a 1926 Schultze & Weaver hotel on Miami Beach—highlighted the importance of exclusivity in attracting visitors to the hotels. A *Vanity Fair* advertisement for the Roney Plaza showcased a fit young woman sitting at a pool, and stated, "Socially comfortable, if you know what I mean . . . a lot of our crowd."[66] Like the Palm Room at the Waldorf-Astoria, the promenade at the Roney Plaza provided society ladies the chance to showcase their latest fashions. [fig. 22] Local newspapers featured the activities of Miami Beach socialites staying at the new hotels. The *Miami Herald* printed the guest lists of hotels, the attire of the guests, and the color themes, decorations, and refreshment choices of popular hostesses. Under a section published daily called "Miami Beach Personals," the newspaper reported the arrival and departure of prominent guests. Popular activities for socialites included such upscale entertainments as gala dinners, tea parties, garden dances, and yachting races, further contributing to the feeling of exclusivity at the beach.[67]

Exoticism and exclusivity came together in these social activities as well. At the Nautilus Hotel—designed by Schultze & Weaver for Fisher in 1924—tea dances

[fig. 22]
Outdoor café, Roney Plaza Hotel, Miami Beach (Schultze & Weaver, 1926), postcard, ca. 1945

were all the rage, especially after Prohibition took liquor, at least officially, out of the ballrooms and restaurants of resort hotels. According to one advertisement, "Every afternoon on the grounds of several of the larger hotels in the Miami district, under cocoanut palms and multi-colored umbrellas and canopies of an oriental atmosphere, society enjoys the smiling out-of-doors of this sub-tropical section."[68] Here the hint of the exotic, with the air of Orientalism, also implied exclusivity; only the well-heeled, suggested the ad, would be expected to partake in the tropical pleasures and social graces of outdoor Japanese tea gardens.

Exclusion took a more blatant form through restrictive policies and covenants. Hotels prohibited the letting of rooms to African Americans. A deed from one of Fisher's transactions with his Alton Beach Realty Company was typical of restrictions placed on property ownership. The deed stated that the owner "is not and shall not be permitted to sell, lease, or rent the said real estate in any form, manner . . . to any person or persons other than the Caucasian Race."[69] Despite the fact that black workers, both from the South and from the Bahamas, made up the bulk of the work force on Miami Beach, they were even prevented from using the beach itself. The *Miami Metropolis* reported, "The arrival of Negroes at south beach Sunday caused a little stir among the owners of places of amusement."[70]

While there were no formal restrictions on Jews, there were visible signs that much of Miami Beach—at least in Fisher's section north of Fifteenth Street—was off limits. Hotel promotional brochures boasted that their clientele was "Gentile Only" or "Restricted"; some hotels even featured signs on their facades stating, "No Jews or Dogs."[71] Yet Jews were a vital presence in the area, and many were close friends and associates of Fisher. Ironically, Julius Fleischmann, of Fleischmann's Yeast, was Fisher's polo partner but could not go to Fisher's clubhouse or rent a room at the Flamingo.[72] Fisher claimed that these restrictions further showcased the exclusive character of Miami Beach and helped drive up its desirability as a destination, as well as the prices of its real estate. Indeed, real estate values rose 1,000 percent between 1914 and 1924. In 1924, the *Miami Herald* reported that Fisher's Alton Beach Realty Company sold over $1 million in nineteen days.[73] Many attributed this boom, at least in part, to the policies of exclusion that made Miami Beach a tropical playground for the rich.

[fig. 23]
Colony Hotel, Miami Beach (Henry Hohauser, 1935), reproduction of rendering by Henry Hohauser, ca. 1935

The presence of blacks and Jews, however, fed into the exoticism and fantasy that area promoters were selling. Nothing illustrated this better than Fisher's plan to introduce gondolas at the Flamingo Hotel. In a letter to La Gorce, Fisher explained his idea of having Edward D. Purdy, president of Purdy Boat Company on Biscayne Bay, import the boats from Italy for the purpose of escorting hotel guests around the bay. "I had Purdy come down on a rush order and we are going to build six [of the boats] in twenty days. I have some of the most wonderful Bahama Negroes you ever saw to push these gondolas around. They are all going to be stripped to the waist and wear big brass ear rings. And possibly necklaces of live crabs or crawfish. Too bad you can't say anything about this in the front pages of the *Saturday Evening Post*."[74]

Other hotels and vacation resorts also used African Americans as features of exoticism and spectacle. One of the leading entertainments for visitors to Atlantic City was the minstrel show. In addition, African Americans helped to create the experience of an urban fantasyland for the white, middle-class visitors to Atlantic City by pushing them down the Boardwalk in rolling chairs. At Flagler's Royal Poinciana, which featured three miles of connecting corridors, black workers pedaled guests through the hotel in "Afromobiles," single-seat wicker chairs that were the Florida equivalent of the rolling chair.[75]

The visibility of blacks as entertainers and participants in exotic displays was paralleled by their invisibility as real-life workers whose labor was essential to the functioning of the hotel. Of course, all hotels did what they could to hide the realities of hotel labor from guests. But resort hotels faced unique problems with maintaining this separation between labor and leisure, black and white, since they were not situated in fully developed urban environments. Atlantic City differed from other seaside resort destinations in that, given its close proximity to New York and Philadelphia and in light of the amusements and diversions it offered year-round, it had developed as a place of permanent settlement for vacationers and workers alike. Blacks lived in boarding houses and small rental cottages that, while segregated, still allowed them easy access to their jobs on the Boardwalk and in hotels.[76]

By contrast, at Florida resorts there was little in close proximity to the hotel other than the railroad depot that deposited guests there. Many Florida hotels employed workers who came for the season and then returned to jobs in northern hotels during the summer months. These seasonal workers had to be housed, and often that housing was racially segregated. The Ponce de Leon in St. Augustine, for example, included a wing over the kitchen that housed migrant hotel chefs, waiters, musicians, guards, and maintenance workers. The hotel's black employees, including laundresses and porters, were housed in "colored barracks" several blocks away, thereby maintaining the exclusivity of the hotel, even in its staff quarters. At the Royal Poinciana, Flagler created a worker's community in nearby Lake Worth to preserve the exclusivity of the hotel surroundings.[77]

Clearly, fantasy, exoticism, and exclusivity were bound together in the creation of destination resorts like Miami Beach. Ironically, it was largely groups that had been excluded from the luxury hotels of Miami Beach in the 1920s that would help sustain the resort town through the economic devastation of the Great Depression. By the late 1920s the southern tip of the beach was being transformed into a community that, within two decades, would become largely Jewish and would cater to a mixed-class clientele, in part, as a result of the much less restrictive practices of property owners to the south of Fisher's development.[78]

[fig. 24]
Traymore Hotel, Miami Beach (Albert Anis, 1939), postcard, ca. 1939

The architects who designed the new buildings for Miami Beach, including Henry Wright, Roy France, Henry Hohouser, and L. Murray Dixon, employed the symmetrical, streamlined styles of modernist Art Deco design and adapted them to the tropical landscape. [fig. 23] They drew on the architectural innovations of Price and McLanahan and Schultze & Weaver, but they utilized these to create high-density, modestly priced hotels that reflected a machine-age aesthetic and a Depression-era sensibility. Their hotels featured tropical murals and etched glass flamingoes like those of their predecessors while introducing modern materials like Vitrolite (a type of colored glass) to interior fixtures.[79] Many of these designers also embraced the communal ideals articulated by proponents of modernism, including Le Corbusier and Walter Gropius. As a result, they saw in Art Deco not just a style uniquely symbolic of a modern aesthetic but also one that could introduce greater efficiency and egalitarianism to urban design. Miami Beach, then, emerged as an ironic counterpoint to the flamboyant luxury hotels developed decades earlier.[80] By affixing names of grand northern hotels such as the New Yorker, or even Atlantic City's Traymore, on much more modest buildings, promoters of these new Art Deco hotels celebrated their connection to architectural innovation even as they advertised their status as imitations. [fig. 24] In doing so, however, they opened up travel, tourism, and even exoticism to a larger segment of the population, thereby helping to democratize leisure in America.

The central place of travel in American society by the early decades of the twentieth century made both the urban luxury hotel and the seaside resort popular destinations for the new leisure class. That many of the elites who entertained at the Waldorf-Astoria also vacationed in Miami Beach was no accident; the increasing reliability, efficiency, and comfort of railcars, and later, automobiles, made leisure more accessible in destinations far from the centers of business activity. Indeed, many of these elites made their fortunes in the transportation industry and used these funds to promote real estate development and acquire land in the emerging seaside resorts. Miami Beach was tied to New York not just by the railroad but also by the patterns of travel, leisure, and land acquisition that made both places hubs for the fashionable set. The physical development of Atlantic City and Miami Beach further attests to the symbiotic relationship between urban hotel life and seaside resorts. In their designs for urban hotels, architects introduced tropical flourishes and exotic decor to suggest the possibility of escape as part of the hotel experience. Similarly, seaside resort developers looked to urban hotel design for guidance in architecture, interior appointments, and elegant furnishings. While both Atlantic City and Miami Beach offered the therapeutic and restorative benefits of sun and surf, they also promised the allure of modern luxury. They represent a unique contribution to the history of vacation resorts, melding the tranquility of the seaside with the glitz and glamour of modern urban culture.

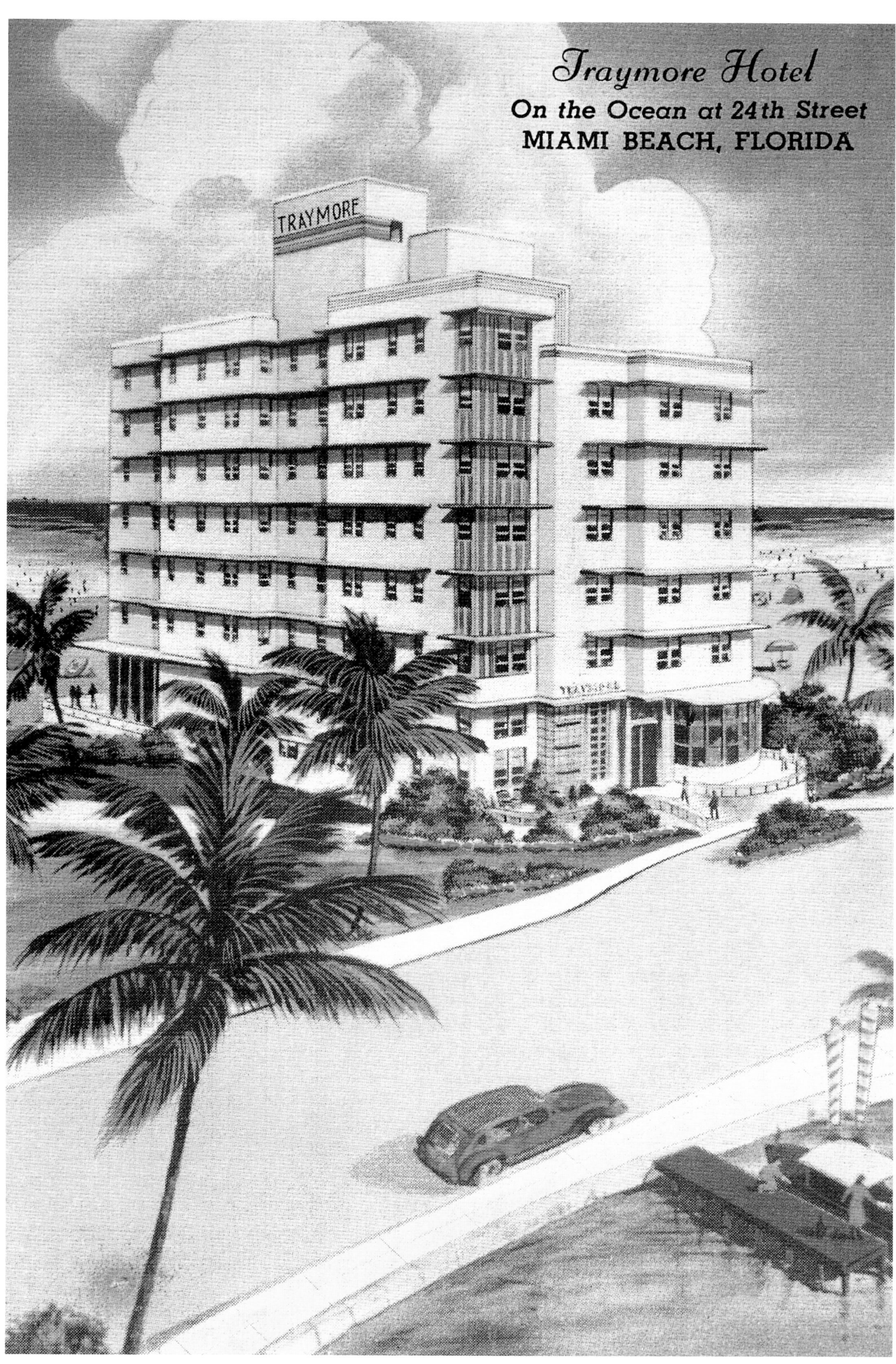
Traymore Hotel
On the Ocean at 24th Street
MIAMI BEACH, FLORIDA
TRAYMORE

THE SKYSCRAPER AND THE CITY

Schultze & Weaver's New York Hotels

Keith D. Revell

"Leonard Schultze has the reputation of knowing more about hotels than almost anyone else," declared architect and critic Kenneth Murchison in May of 1929. "He has certainly done lots of them, here in New York and all over the country."[1] Schultze & Weaver's success at solving the "hotel problem"—creating buildings that responded effectively to the financial demands of their owners, the operational concerns of their managers, the personal preferences of their guests, and the critical scrutiny of commentators and other architects—rested on their ability to deal creatively with the often conflicting pressures generated by the multiple contexts of the hotel trade. While their hotels can, of course, be understood as brilliant artistic achievements, they were also shaped by distinctive economic, social, and legal developments that tested the architectural imagination of the firm.

Like their competitors, Schultze & Weaver worked with a basic hotel plan that had emerged in the late nineteenth century and had been replicated, with minor variations, in cities around the country: sub-basements and basements for kitchens, laundries, and storage; a showplace lobby and dazzling public lounges; the requisite ballrooms and restaurants (usually a fabulous main dining room and a more masculine grill room); commodious guest rooms and residential suites; and working space on the upper stories for ventilation, elevators, and other equipment. But the particular challenges that emerged in the 1920s as a result of urban growth, the increasing difficulties of hiring and managing domestic servants, changes in the economics of the hotel industry, and recently enacted zoning regulations profoundly influenced the firm's adaptations of this basic model—both at the level of floor plan and exterior—and help to explain why Schultze & Weaver's buildings took on the forms they did. The five major hotels they completed in New York City during this period—the Park Lane (September 1924), the Sherry-Netherland (November 1927), the Lexington (October 1929), the Pierre (October 1930), and the Waldorf-Astoria (October 1931)—showed just how responsive Schultze & Weaver became to the peculiar demands of this building type in the nation's largest metropolis while at the same time excelling at resort hotels in locations where the parameters for successful design were quite different.

Schultze & Weaver became experts in designing hotels to serve a decidedly high-end clientele: no small accomplishment considering that building a first-class residential skyscraper in New York City during the 1920s meant entering a crowded market with very high land costs. Two competing trends conspired to push up land values year after year. First, midtown Manhattan was becoming increasingly desirable as a residential location, and those residences were almost exclusively in apartment buildings. Second, residential areas were under constant pressure for redevelopment from commercial interests, in spite of zoning regulations that prevented businesses in those districts. Together, these trends made it much more expensive for even wealthy families to live in the city. Growth squeezed everyone's housing budget, prompting a search for new ways to live well in Manhattan, and Schultze & Weaver were among those architects who responded with a new approach to the urban home that allowed the well-to-do to abandon their brownstones and mansions for skyscraper hotels.

Although the 1920s can certainly be characterized as an era of suburbanization and the growth of single-family home ownership, midtown Manhattan witnessed its own residential boom in apartment living, beginning along Park Avenue. As part of the massive redevelopment project that included Grand Central Terminal (completed in 1913), the New York Central Railroad electrified its rail operations and covered its tracks, creating new cross streets north of Forty-fifth Street. "The effect was magical," reported economist Edwin Spengler. "The New York Central itself built new structures within the newly created blocks, and many hotels and office buildings were quick to follow. Further north, apartments and fine mansions were rapidly constructed."[2] Park Avenue led the way, but Lexington Avenue and eventually Fifth Avenue were swept up in the movement as well. In 1921–22, property on Lexington Avenue in the ten blocks north of Forty-second Street rented for between $16 and $25 per square foot; by 1928, prices topped $100 per square foot, a fourfold increase in an era when property values for the city as a whole increased by a sizable 150 percent. The population of New York City continued to shift from Manhattan to Brooklyn, Queens, and the Bronx, but already crowded Manhattan added apartment dwellers at a rate far exceeding any other place in the country.[3]

Simultaneously, the older residential areas in midtown were becoming business districts, which meant increasing competition for prime locations, especially along the major avenues and on corner lots—precisely where Schultze & Weaver's hotels stood. Improved transportation facilities made it more convenient to live outside of Manhattan while continuing to work and shop there. The rows of brownstones that occupied the streets east of Central Park gave way to businesses, in spite of restrictive covenants designed to maintain the residential character of the area. Even apartment buildings had a hard time competing. "Many of the apartments along Park Avenue command rentals of $15,000 to $20,000, and from a few much greater sums are realized," one observer noted in 1929, "yet real estate operators get larger revenue from office structures, with consequent increases in property values."[4] Zoning restrictions designated a large section of the Upper East Side for homes and apartments, but competition for space was so intense that enterprising developers frequently purchased property in residential zones as a pretext for petitioning city authorities to change the zoning district to allow for business. Schultze & Weaver made their name in this market, where their ability to design sumptuous hotels that could still turn a profit—in spite of legal constraints and in the midst of intense competition for customers' dollars and soaring land prices—brought them some of the most prestigious clients in the city.[5]

Previous waves of development had prompted earlier generations of wealthy residents to move their mansions ever northward on Manhattan Island, and the boom of the 1920s would probably have been no exception to this pattern had it not been for two additional factors driving the well-to-do into residential skyscrapers: the domestic servant problem and the redefinition of luxury living. Both created a demand for full-service, low-maintenance, trouble-free apartments, and Schultze & Weaver responded with specific architectural features designed to make their hotels appealing to developers and potential residents alike.

The problem of finding, managing, and keeping competent, honest domestic labor became acute during the 1920s: a difficulty that shaped the requirements of the clientele Schultze & Weaver served. Between 1910 and 1920, the number of domestic servants in the United States declined by nearly 25 percent, from 1.3 million to just over a million, while the number in New York City fell from 113,409 to 84,615.[6] "The servant in the house is passing," noted one observer in 1922. "If the present tendency keeps up, there will literally be nobody there but the family."[7] The shortage of domestic workers did not abate with the return of prosperity after World War I, and those women who were available asked for higher wages, shorter hours, and more choice over the tasks they did. The "critical servant problem" was soon blamed on the restrictive immigration laws of 1921 and 1924, prompting calls to revise quotas to let in more women for domestic service. So great was the clamor to amend the law that the Bureau of Labor Statistics made a special study of the problem, only to conclude that "economic and social causes having little or no relation to immigration" were responsible, since immigration quotas had mainly restricted the flow of Eastern European women who rarely went into domestic work, and the preferred ethnic groups for household labor—English, Irish, German, and Scandinavian—continued to enter the country in more or less the same numbers as before the war.[8]

THE ADAM STYLE OF ENGLISH ARCHITECTURE IS SUGGESTED IN DESIGN OF DECORATIVE DETAILS

[fig. 1]
Park Lane Hotel, New York (Schultze & Weaver, 1924), from *Architectural Forum* LI, no. 6 (November 1924)

The real sources of the servant problem were the status and drudgery of domestic work combined with the growth of employment options for women. "The fourteen-hour day of the domestic servant has long been defended with the counter-argument of a pleasant home and good food," but it did not take long for household laborers to learn that "a good home" usually meant "low wages" and unceasing demands.[9] Economic growth and changing mores created more choices for women, and it was not just white collar work that outranked domestic service. "The girls prefer to do factory work and have their evenings and Sundays free," reported one expert.[10] Jobs as waitresses or chambermaids, though essentially the same as household labor, paid more and had higher status and more regular hours. Domestic workers, conscious of these options, became more difficult to manage. As a result, "Housewives beg for an old-time maid or servant," commented Mary Patton, assistant secretary for the YMCA's Employment Department.[11] In 1927, a group of "society women" in New York City, led by Mrs. Richard Boardman (who lived on the Upper East Side and moved in the same social circles as those who would take up residence in Schultze & Weaver hotels), even responded by organizing Scientific Housekeeping, Inc., in an effort to train household servants. Staffing a household and managing the traditional retinue of servants necessary to run a large home were thus becoming more expensive and more onerous.[12]

Residential hotels offered a solution to both the rising cost of home ownership in Manhattan and the difficulties of managing a household staff. Schultze & Weaver created a particularly successful model of this response to the problems of

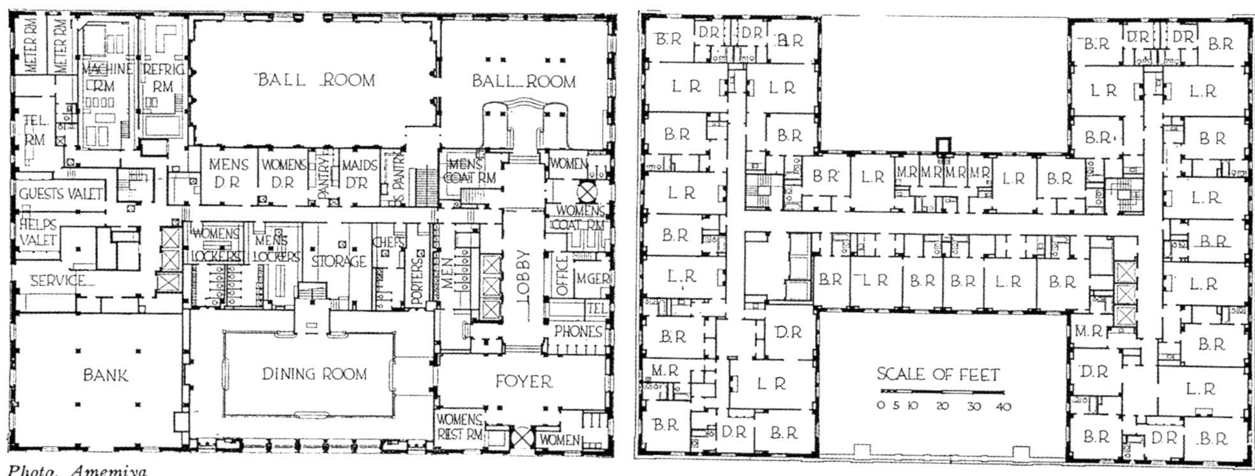

[fig. 2]
Floor plans, Park Lane Hotel, from *Architectural Forum* LI, no. 6 (November 1924)

high-class living, beginning with the Park Lane in 1924. [figs. 1, 2] The Park Lane was located between Forty-eighth and Forty-ninth streets in a cluster of apartments "at the very gateway to Park Avenue" north of Grand Central Terminal. The adjacent buildings at 270, 290, and 300 Park Avenue, home to Marguery's, Pierre's, and Sherry's restaurants, constituted a new social and residential center for elite New Yorkers, and the Park Lane represented a new level of refinement in the "ideal of city living" signaled by this distinguished group of buildings.[13] As Matlack Price noted in 1924,

> For a long time the ideal of those who wished an adequate and impressive dwelling in New York was the great private house, with its full staff of servants and with all the elaborate ceremony of an Italian palazzo of the Renaissance . . . . Today the situation has changed, and these houses, no longer an essential part of a changed social fabric, are burdensome, and constitute a responsibility in maintenance, which has become uncongenial to their owners.[14]

S. Fullerton Weaver had been among the pioneers of this trend along Park Avenue, and he designed the Park Lane to serve "eligible acceptable families to whom social atmosphere and environment are prerequisites."[15]

Key to securing this "most representative tenantry" for the Park Lane was Weaver's use of serving, or butler's, pantries. These alcove spaces leading into the dining rooms of suites in the Park Lane were not large enough for cooking, nor were they equipped for it; instead, they provided the physical link between private dining and entertaining and professional hotel management that became a central feature of upper-class apartment life during the 1920s. As Weaver observed, "This innovation provides for the service of meals in the apartments, but prepared in the hotel kitchens. It relieves the hostess of all responsibility."[16] Squeezed by rising land costs and mounting labor difficulties, the rich turned to architects like Schultze & Weaver for a redefinition of urban living; the architects responded by creating residential hotels that freed their tenants of the responsibilities of maintaining an elaborate household while retaining the very highest levels of personal service expected by the leisure class.

below:
[fig. 3]
Service pantry (detail of an advertisement for Monel Metal), Sherry-Netherland Hotel, New York (Schultze & Weaver with Buchman and Kahn, 1927) from *Architectural Forum* XLVIII, no. 1 (January 1928)

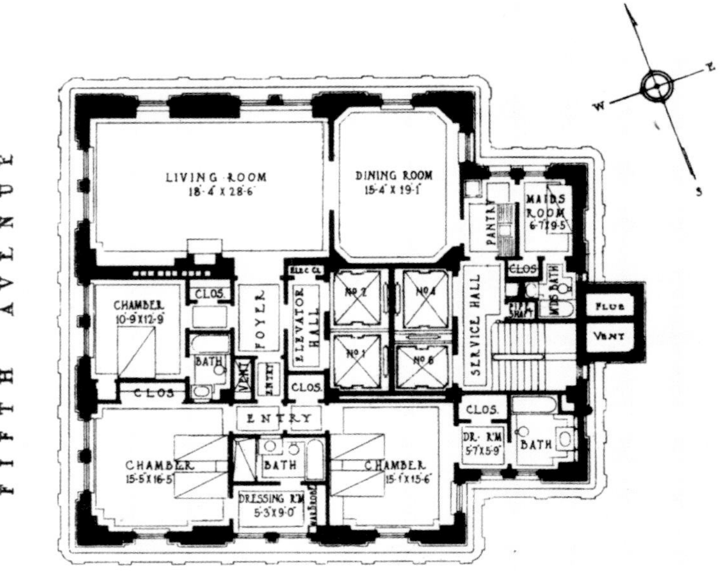

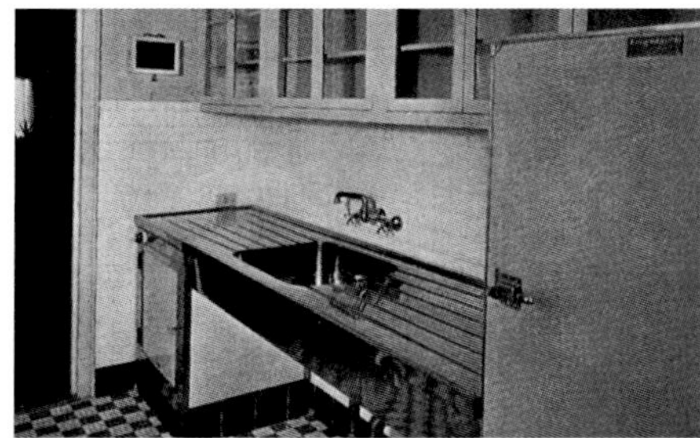

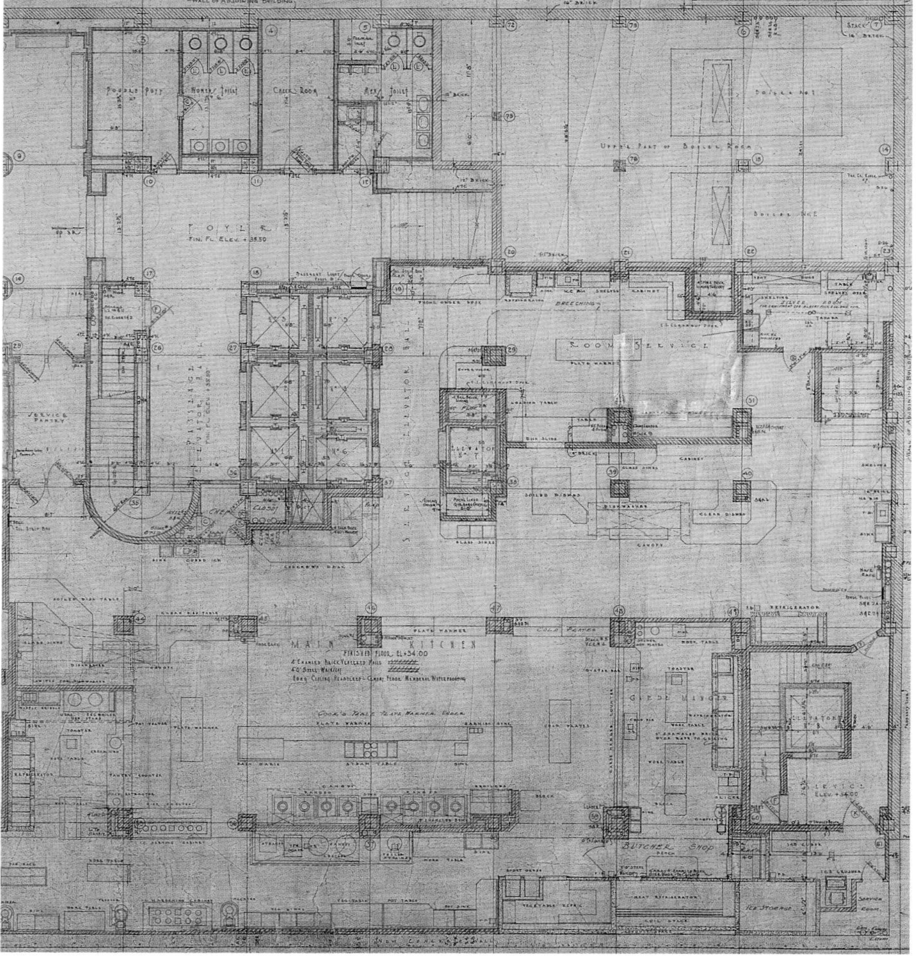

top right:
[fig. 4]
Plan of the thirtieth to thirty-sixth floors, Sherry-Netherland Hotel, after 1927

bottom right:
[fig. 5]
Plan of the basement (detail), Sherry-Netherland Hotel, 1926

The Sherry-Netherland epitomized the use of serving pantries as a solution to the domestic servant problem. These spaces, approximately 70 square feet in area (roughly 7 by 10 feet, depending on the floor), contained a small refrigerator, a metal sink and drain boards, and cabinets for service items. [fig. 3] Residents undoubtedly used them to store cold foods, as a sort of kitchenette, but they were not intended for cooking; their design and placement reveals a more important purpose. A typical pantry in the Sherry-Netherland was connected by a doorway to a capacious dining room (roughly 15 by 20 feet), but it also opened onto either a service hall adjoining a main hallway (as on the third through sixteenth floors) or a service hall completely separate from passageways used by residents and guests (as on the thirtieth through thirty-fifth floors). [fig. 4] This allowed the professional service staff of the hotel to transport food from the basement [fig. 5], up a set of service elevators conveniently located right in the kitchen, into service areas on each floor, through a special entrance to the service pantries, and then into the private dining room of each resident—all unseen and unheard by tenants.

The service pantry was one of the features that made the Sherry-Netherland a model of carefree living for those who could afford it. "Sherry domestics will care for their apartments. Sherry food will be served in their dining-rooms. Sherry butlers will become their butlers, Sherry valets and ladies'-maids their personal attendants . . . . What an ideal scheme of things!" trumpeted one of the hotel's first advertisements. "One is free to stay or flit—Europe, Palm Beach, Long Island. Yet one's perfect household goes on forever."[17] Lucius Boomer, whose company ran the Sherry-Netherland, knew that this new way of living hinged on freeing residents from the burdens of household management. "The personal domestic service will offer not only complete relief from responsibility," he lauded, "but, considering that the residents are put to no direct expense for a permanent staff of skillful servants and also that household expenses will cease when absent [if, for instance, the owner flitted off to Europe], there will be no expenditures for upkeep, and the net cost to tenants will be very reasonable."[18] Thanks to the clever arrangement of space, living well in Manhattan could now be redefined, not in terms of having a mansion and servants, but as complete lack of responsibility for household affairs, which could happily be left to a professional staff of personal servants managed by proprietors who understood what it really meant to be wealthy. To be sure, even a professional staff could get out of hand: there was that time, for example, in 1928 when the employees of the Sherry-Netherland, "all seated on gilt chairs . . . secretly moved from a dining room," gathered in "an ornate suite on the fifteenth floor" to watch a boxing match between Ruddy Ott, captain of the waiters, and his assistant Ernest Sefflin, but it was a "corking good bout," according to doorman and referee George McClune, and service to the tenants continued without interruption.[19]

The Hotel Pierre represented yet another variation of the new approach to full-service apartment hotels. Like the Park Lane and the Sherry-Netherland, the Pierre had service pantries accessible from service elevators connected to the hotel's main kitchen, which suggests just how compulsory this architectural feature had become in this class of building. But the Pierre stands out among the Schultze & Weaver hotels for its extraordinary entertainment spaces. From its very conception, the developers of the Pierre had intended it to continue the social function of the Gerry mansion it replaced; that venerable home, designed by the great Richard M. Hunt, "was the scene of many functions which made social history."[20] The

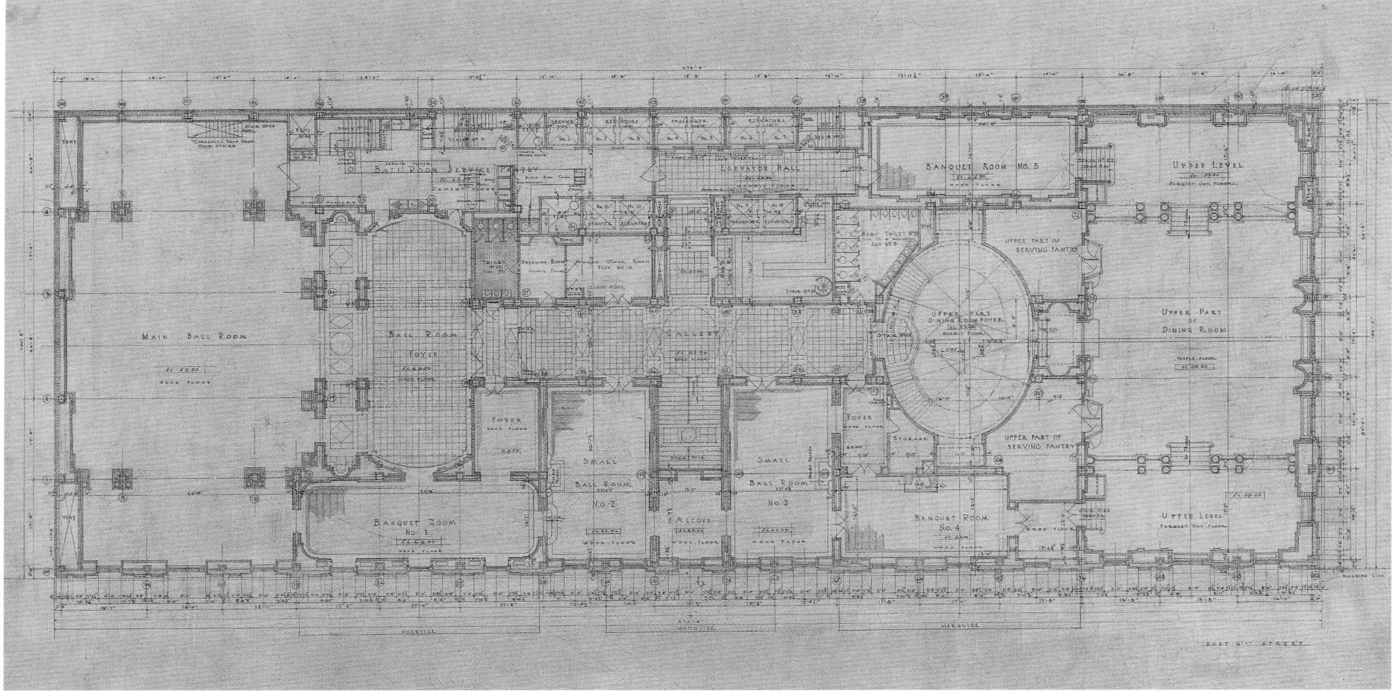

[fig. 6]
Plan of the ballroom floor, Hotel Pierre, New York (Schultze & Weaver, 1930), 1929

[fig. 7]
Grill room, Hotel Pierre, ca. 1930

[fig. 8]
Kitchen, St. Regis Hotel, New York (Trowbridge & Livingston, 1904), from *The St. Regis Hotel* (1905)

"prominent New Yorkers" behind the new Pierre planned "to make it one of the distinctive social centres of New York City" by building it to such proportions that "the largest social events can be staged without cramping its quarters."[21] The Pierre would offer everything from banquet rooms served by the city's premier catering service to a secretariat "where members of the staff will be available to perform for the guests all the duties ordinarily entrusted to a social secretary" and a "committee of chaperones . . . of unimpeachable character and social recognition for the entertainment of younger persons who visit New York alone," allowing the wealthy to economize on staff while entertaining even more lavishly than they could in private homes.[22]

The layout of the Pierre reflects this distinctive set of functions. The site itself was quite large; with 100 feet along Fifth Avenue and a roomy 270 feet along Sixty-first Street, the 27,000-square-foot base of the Pierre was more than double that of the Sherry-Netherland (on a site 100 by 125 feet just two blocks south). This gave Schultze & Weaver space on either side of the tower of the building to create an expansive ballroom—capable of seating more than a thousand guests—and a large main dining room for the principal hotel restaurant. The ballroom boasted a nearly 64-foot-high ceiling, and the dining room had a 56-foot-high ceiling in spite of being set atop the grill room, which had a 38-foot-high ceiling. [figs. 6, 7] The size of the site also allowed the architects to include six other large banquet rooms on the massive ballroom floor, all for use by hotel residents for their private social events. The Pierre thus had the entertainment spaces that we would associate with a modern convention hotel, only for a permanent clientele.

Entertaining on this scale required extensive service facilities. Although large kitchens had long been common for first-class hotels [fig. 8], the Pierre's were particularly impressive, since they performed three distinct functions. They provided regular meals for the tenants, who had no kitchens of their own and relied on the same arrangement between the main kitchen and service pantries as residents of the Sherry-Netherland. They also catered the social events held by the residents and furnished meals for the restaurant that served the main dining room. The hotel's kitchen occupied a large section in the center of the basement next to the grill room. It featured two ample work areas (one 28 feet long and another 21 feet long) with gas ranges and salamanders (or broilers), comparably large areas for

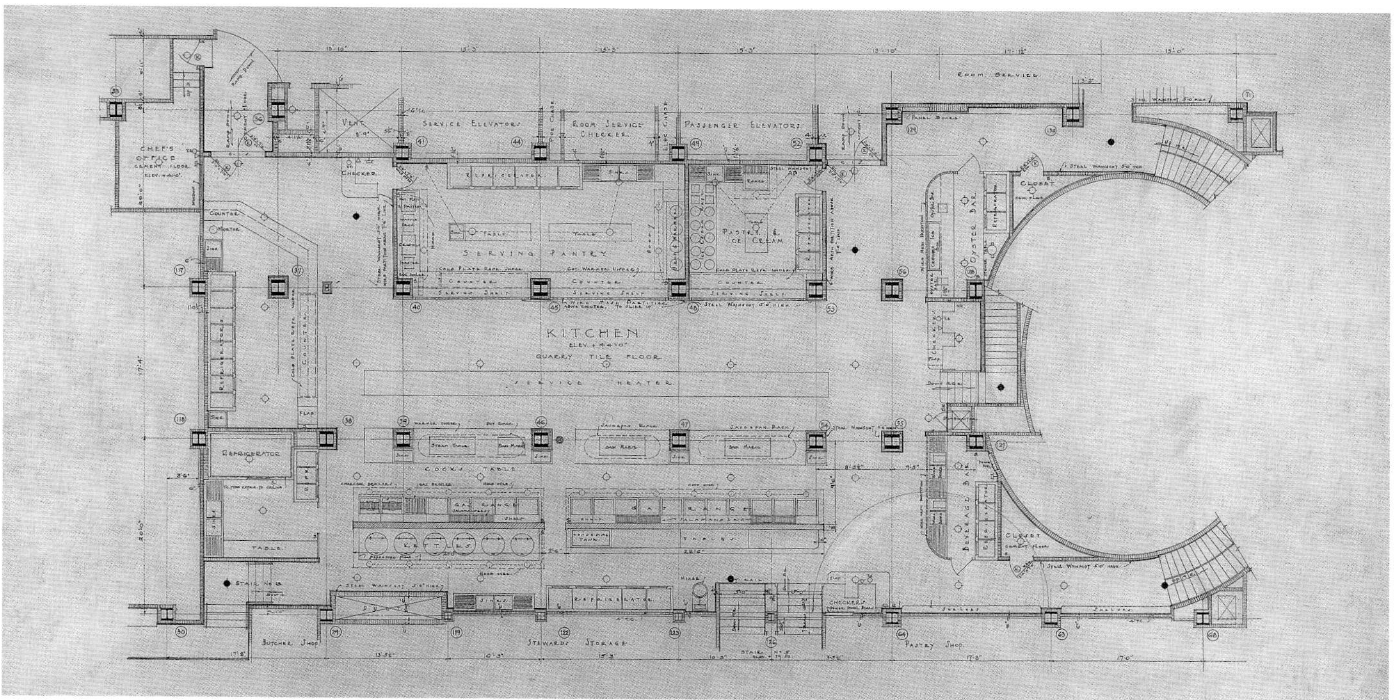

[fig. 9]
Plan of the kitchen (detail), Hotel Pierre, ca. 1929

steam cooking, and a service heater (for keeping food warm before serving) some 50 feet long. [fig. 9] Storage rooms for poultry, meat, smoked meat, vegetables, cheese, and fruit were tucked alongside separate rooms for ice cream and candy making, vegetable preparation, a bakery, and a pastry shop. The laundry was also indicative of the level of entertaining carried out at the Pierre; while many hotels had elaborate laundry rooms for cleaning service linens and tenant clothing, the two 120-inch flat work ironers and four large washing machines were undoubtedly intended for the sizeable tablecloths used in the ballroom. And because the employees of the Pierre served, in effect, as a shared household staff for residents who were accustomed to having servants at their call, the hotel included more than a dozen servant bedrooms, in addition to all the other spaces necessary to house and feed the help—from lounges to dining rooms.

Such facilities represented a very deliberate attempt to connect the Schultze & Weaver hotels with a tradition of style and luxury associated with the great hotels and restaurants patronized by high society during the late nineteenth and early twentieth centuries—a connection made both through the level of service offered to patrons and in the personnel associated with that service. The Pierre was named for Charles Pierre, proprietor of Pierre's restaurant—that "pretentious" establishment that had moved from East Forty-fifth Street to 290 Park Avenue in 1920, when Park became the social center of elite New York, and finally found its proper place in the Hotel Pierre in 1930. Pierre, as he was known in the world of hospitality, was born Pierre Casalasco in Corsica. This son of a hotel proprietor ran away to Monte Carlo at age eighteen and worked his way through the ranks of restaurant and hotel jobs in Paris and London, where in 1903 he met Louis Sherry, ringmaster of Sherry's in New York City, which was second only to Delmonico's among entertainment venues for the social elite.[23] Sherry followed a similar career path, from Vermont to Montreal and thence to New York City, where he distinguished himself as a waiter who studied "the eccentricities of the palate" and the individual tastes of his guests.[24] When he started his own restaurant, he made fine service its hallmark. "From the start," Sherry recalled, "I determined not to let anything go out of my house that was not made in the best possible way out of the best and most expensive materials on the market."[25] To appeal to wealthy clients, Sherry

top:
[fig. 10]
Louis XVI parlor, Hotel Savoy, New York (Ralph S. Townsend, 1892), from *Hotel Savoy Illustrated* (ca. 1893)

bottom:
[fig. 11]
Palm Court, Ritz-Carlton Hotel, New York (Warren & Wetmore, 1910), from *The Ritz-Carlton Hotel of New York* (1919)

THE PALM COURT REFLECTS AN ATMOSPHERE OF CONTENTMENT, WHERE ONE MAY THOROUGHLY ENJOY COMPLETE RELAXATION AND REPOSE

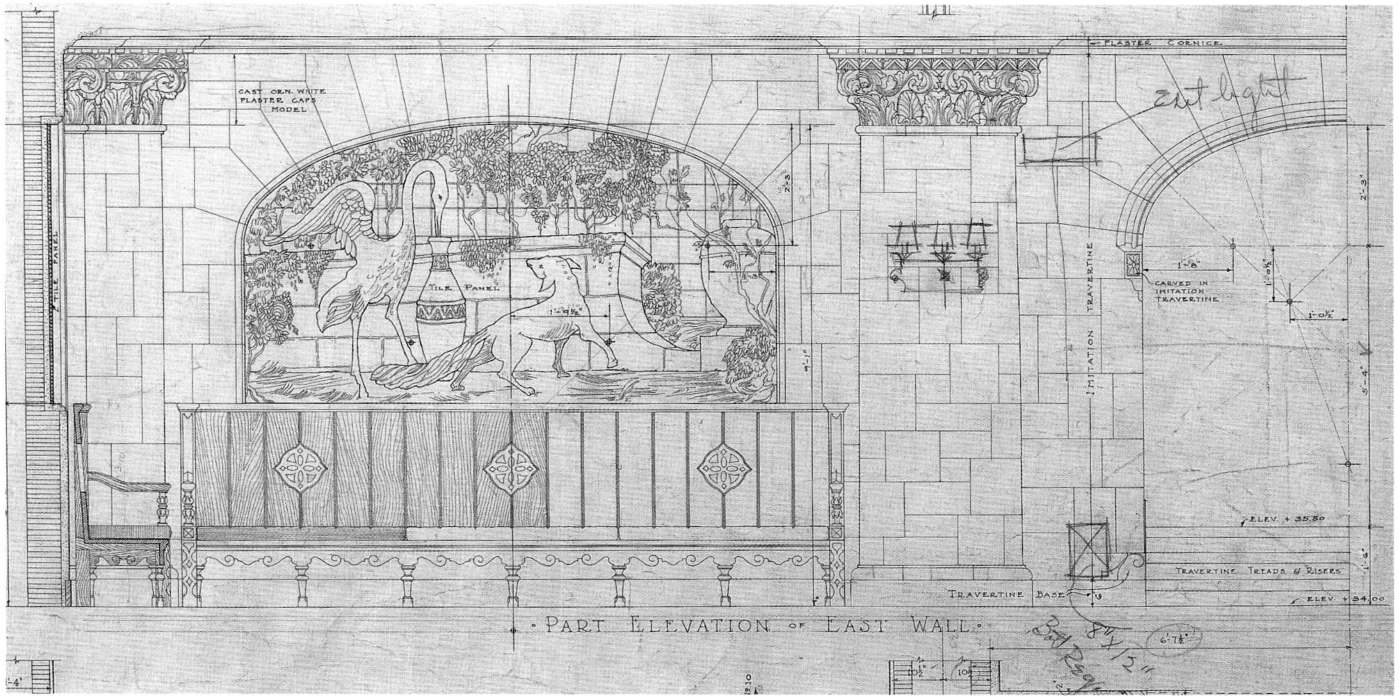

and Pierre knew that they had to dazzle and flatter. "One of the secrets I had learned was that nothing goes further with dainty people than dainty decorations," said Sherry. "Novelties of service," lavish preparations, and intimate knowledge of customer tastes transformed Sherry into a "society caterer" to the "ultra fashionable."[26] The wealthy relied on him to put on their debutante balls and charity dinners. Though he died in 1926, the company that bore his name carried with it a tradition: "Sherry service" meant only the best. Pierre inherited that tradition, and the Hotel Pierre represented the fulfillment of this style of service.

Although Schultze & Weaver continued this tradition of luxury service in their hotels, economic considerations forced them to revise the use of ground floor space in particular. The ground floor of a first-class hotel performed at least two important roles: as a reception area for guests and residents and as a public social venue. Hotels like the old Waldorf-Astoria (1893, 1897), the St. Regis (1904), the Astor (1904), and the Knickerbocker (1906) had ground floors devoted to elaborate public rooms typically decorated in ornate period styles, such as billiard rooms, reception rooms, libraries, and a "palm room" or other unusually decorated space (like the Orangerie in the Astor, which was designed to represent an Italian garden). These spaces served as public meeting areas and often the site for business meetings. [figs. 10, 11] Hotels could afford many such rooms in part because they also had bars and could serve alcoholic beverages in their restaurants. But Prohibition put an end to hotel liquor service in 1920, and the charming rooms that had lured guests and impressed visitors became unproductive space. By the early 1920s, architects felt increased pressure to design revenue-generating hotel spaces. Not surprisingly, the lower floors of the Sherry-Netherland and the Lexington look nothing like those of the Astor or Knickerbocker. Shops replaced period rooms along the street facade, where they might entice potential customers passing by. Using the ground floor for retail was so important that the restaurant of the Sherry-Netherland was tucked into a windowless corner of the building away from both of the street facades, unlike the dining rooms at the Park Lane and Pierre, which featured large windows looking onto the street. And the sumptuous grill room, where Schultze & Weaver lavished attention on murals and marble decoration, was located in the basement.[27] [figs. 12, 13]

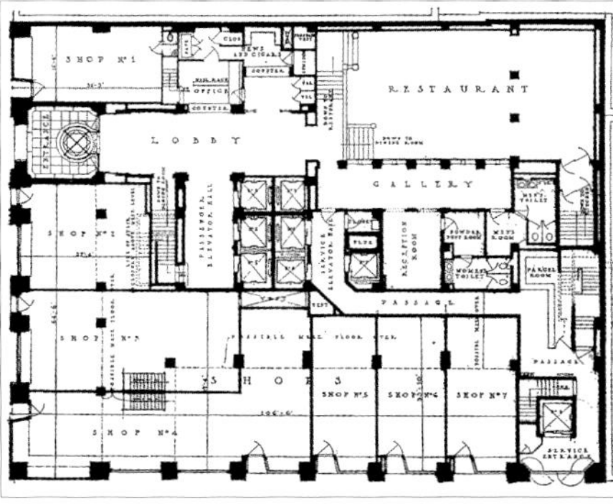

above:
[fig. 12]
Plan of the ground floor, Sherry-Netherland Hotel, from *Architecture* LVI, no. 6 (December 1927)

top:
[fig. 13]
Part elevation of the east wall, dining room (detail), Sherry-Netherland Hotel, 1926
This room, designated as the "dining room" in the plans for the hotel, was renamed the grill by the time the hotel opened.

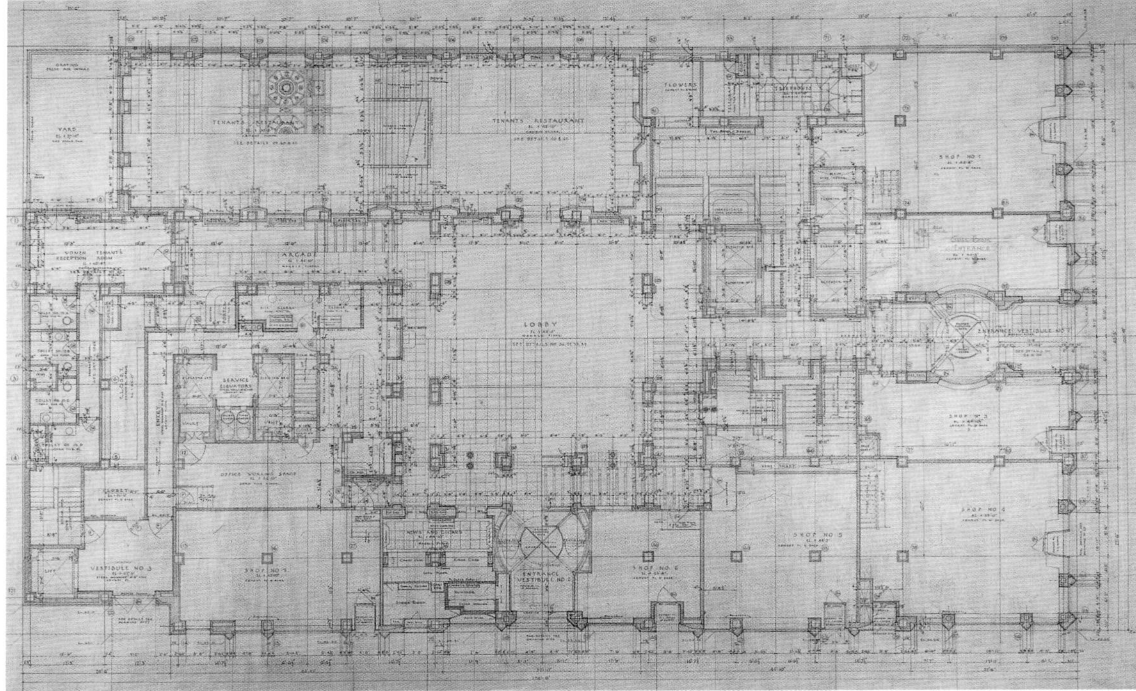

[fig. 14]
Plan of the ground floor (detail), Hotel Lexington, New York (Schultze & Weaver, 1929), ca. 1929

Of all the Schultze & Weaver hotels, the Lexington shows most clearly this emphasis on utility, for it came the closest to serving a transient population. The Lexington had permanent tenants, as revealed by the presence of a tenant's restaurant, but the building had no serving pantries; unlike the Park Lane or the Sherry-Netherland, the Lexington also had no private dining rooms. The kitchen itself was not as impressive as that of the Pierre, or even of the Sherry-Netherland; in spite of the fact that the Lexington was a first-class hotel with eight hundred rooms, it had but one showplace restaurant—the mandatory grill room—headed by a well-known French chef. Beyond the restaurants and a modest lounge, however, the Lexington did not have entertainment facilities. Indeed, the Lexington was "distinctive among the higher class New York hotels by reason of the fact that it offers no banquet or convention facilities."[28] Instead, American Hotels Corporation, which operated the building, emphasized "that the promise of no convention crowds assures greater comfort for the individual guest, transient or permanent."[29] And there would be almost nothing to distinguish the transient from the permanent, since the plans of the building indicate that this was a hotel of single rooms (which were nearly identical on every floor in spite of the diversity of floor plans) and not suites, as in the Park Lane, Sherry-Netherland, and Pierre. Whatever space might have been devoted to banquet facilities was reserved for shops. Both the ground floor and the second floor had retail spaces (nine distinct shops in all), with additional rooms in the basement designated for shop storage. In fact, retail space ringed the lobby of the Lexington, making this the most clearly commercial of all the Schultze & Weaver hotels. [fig. 14] Although the Lexington was located just a block south of the new Waldorf-Astoria, and even though it was designed by the same firm for largely the same class of clientele, its interior spaces reflect a rather different solution to the hotel problem.

This emphasis on retail space in the Lexington makes it all the more surprising that the Pierre had no space for shops at all. The lobby served as an entrance to the residential and entertainment spaces of the building, making it unique among the Schultze & Weaver hotels. Even the Park Lane had space for a bank in one corner of the ground floor. Aside from its restaurants, the Pierre was given over entirely to its residential and social functions. This certainly makes sense, given the purposes for which its sponsors intended it, but there was more at work here than a desire that retail space should not intrude upon banquet rooms for debutante parties. The Pierre had no retail space because it stood in a designated residential zone; retail was forbidden by law anywhere in the building. This was but one of the ways that legal considerations affected the Pierre and all of Schultze & Weaver's New York buildings.

New York City's 1916 zoning ordinance forced Schultze & Weaver to create hotel plans that, in addition to making economic and aesthetic sense, could pass muster with the local officials who interpreted the law and issued building permits. Because zoning regulations varied both from city to city and, in New York, from block to block, legal limitations frustrated efforts to develop a standard hotel design that could be used in multiple cities and on multiple sites, even in an era when rising property values encouraged standardization as a means to cut costs. Thanks to zoning, noted Schultze in 1923,

> It is . . . virtually impossible to determine a universal type of building, either in exterior architecture or in plan, that will fit any two localities. In Boston the limit of height of a building has only recently been raised to 155 feet; in Los Angeles it is limited to 150 feet, while San Francisco places no limit. Chicago allows a maximum height of 260 feet. The zoning law of New York creates a problem entirely different from that in any of the other cities mentioned.[30]

While it is true that hotels (like other skyscrapers) were built from the inside out, with the "typical guest room floor" as the central consideration, they also had to be built from the outside in, with the zoning ordinance determining their massing to a large extent. The zoning ordinance thus had a great deal to do with the diversity demonstrated by Schultze & Weaver's New York hotels, since architects had to make decisions about floor plans and external ornament within the "envelope" created by the law.[31]

That envelope could be very complicated, thanks to the height and setback requirements of the ordinance. Rather than adopting a single fixed height limit for all buildings, New York City created five districts, with building heights based on multiples of street widths, ranging from "one times" to "two and a half times." Above that, buildings had to be set back from the street wall according to a specific formula that also varied from district to district. So, for example, the street wall of a building in a "one and a half times" district on a 100-foot-wide street could not rise above 150 feet; after that, the building had to be set back from the street wall: it could rise another 3 feet if it were set back from the street by another foot proportionally (an additional 60 feet if set back 20 feet, etc.). [fig. 15] The ordinance allowed additional height for cornices, parapet walls, and towers occupying no more than 25 percent of their lots. Because street widths differed all over the city, the height limitations created a bewildering variety of possibilities for architects.

The ordinance carved up midtown into an array of height and use districts. Park and Lexington avenues around Grand Central Terminal were in a "two times" district, but above Fiftieth Street, buildings could be no higher than one and a half times the street width; both avenues were also business districts, which meant that the Park Lane and the Lexington stood on property that could be used

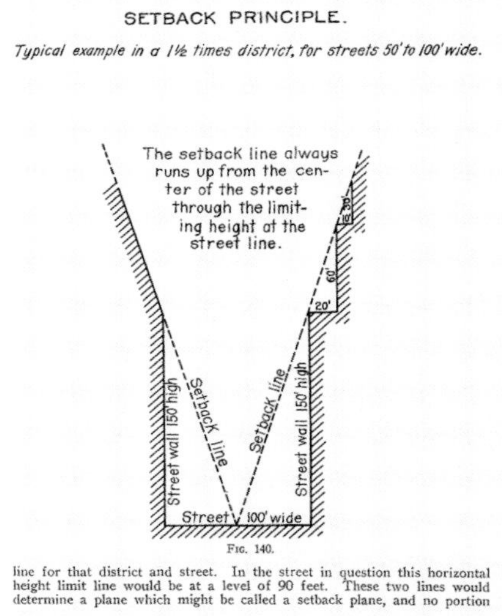

[fig. 15]
Setback principle, from the Commission on Building Districts and Restrictions, Final Report, June 2, 1916 (New York: Board of Estimate and Apportionment, Committee on the City Plan, 1916)

[fig. 16]
Fifth Avenue and Fifty-ninth Street elevations,
Sherry-Netherland Hotel, ca. 1926

for business purposes. The ordinance designated Fifth Avenue from Thirty-first to Fifty-seventh streets as a "one and one-quarter times" height district—the most restrictive designation received by any area in Manhattan. But from Fifty-seventh to Sixtieth streets, Fifth Avenue was a "two times" district, and above that—from Sixty-first Street, all along Central Park, up to the Harlem River—it was a "one and one half times" district. Although most of Fifth Avenue below Central Park had been designated for business, above Sixty-first Street the ordinance mandated residential use only, suggesting that Central Park East would remain the last (and, in fact, the only) purely residential section of the avenue. Of all Schultze & Weaver's hotels, only the Pierre was spared competition from business uses by virtue of its location in a residential zone.

The effect of zoning regulations on Schultze & Weaver's hotels depended on three variables: the width of the widest street the property fronted, the height district designation, and the size of the plot upon which the building stood. Both the Sherry-Netherland and the Pierre fronted Fifth Avenue, which was 100 feet wide, but because they stood on different sized plots and in different height districts, Schultze & Weaver could respond differently to the legal constraints they faced.

The Sherry-Netherland stood in a "two times" district, which meant that the street wall of the building could not extend higher than 200 feet (two times the width of Fifth Avenue). There was no requirement that architects build to the limit of the law, but because the Sherry-Netherland occupied very high-priced land, Schultze & Weaver were compelled to push it right up to the legal maximum. As their elevation drawing shows, the street walls of the Sherry-Netherland rise to precisely 200 feet on both the Fifth Avenue and Fifty-ninth Street frontages before receding from the property line as required by the ordinance. [fig. 16] Schultze & Weaver even noted "1ST SET-BACK" on the drawing, making this linen unique among surviving architectural drawings of period buildings. The zoning ordinance specified further that buildings in "two times" districts could rise further only if they were setback from the street in a ratio of four to one: for every foot the structure was set back from the street wall, it could rise an additional 4 feet.[32] Although the linen identifies three setbacks, these are really the beginning, middle, and end points of two setbacks: one bounded by the seventeenth and twenty-first floors, and the second bounded by the twenty-first and twenty-third floors. At the first setback, the building recedes by 11 feet, 9 inches (or 11.75 feet) and extends upward for 47 feet (four floors, from the seventeenth to the twenty-first): precisely 4 feet up for every 1 foot back. For the second setback, the building recedes an additional 6 feet (5 feet, 11 inches) and rises a further 24 feet (two floors, from the twenty-first to the twenty-third): again, in a four to one ratio. The solariums on the northwest, southeast, and southwest corners at the first setback exceeded the prescribed street wall height, as did the bays on the twenty-first and twenty-second floors, but the ordinance specifically allowed such architectural features to pierce the setback envelope.[33] These projections broke up the mandatory setbacks and demonstrated how architects exercised their aesthetic judgments even when squeezed between legal limits and economic demands. The setbacks on the Sherry-Netherland became selling points, creating terraces with commanding views of Central Park and the city beyond.[34] [fig. 17]

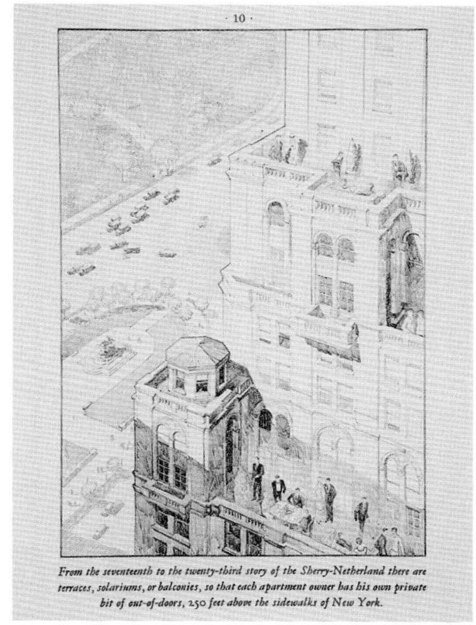

10
From the seventeenth to the twenty-third story of the Sherry-Netherland there are terraces, solariums, or balconies, so that each apartment owner has his own private bit of out-of-doors, 250 feet above the sidewalks of New York.

[fig. 17]
Terraces, solarium, and balcony, Sherry-Netherland Hotel, from *The Sherry-Netherland Fifth Avenue at Fifty-ninth St.*, New York (ca. 1927)

The zoning ordinance placed even greater constraints on Schultze & Weaver's choices for the Pierre. Like the Sherry-Netherland, the Pierre fronted

Fifth Avenue; but because it was in a "one and a half times" district, its street wall could not exceed 150 feet (although according to the elevation drawing the Pierre rises 2 and ¾ inches above that: a difference the city apparently considered too small to protest). In a "one and a half times" district, the setback ratio was one to three. On the Pierre, the setbacks on the east and west only rise 69 feet, although the building receded from Fifth Avenue on its western side by nearly 50 feet, which would have allowed an increase in height of 150 feet (note that the building is slightly asymmetrical; the eastern section of the base of the building is just over 56 feet wide, or about 7 feet wider than the western section, probably to accommodate the ballroom). The architects could not take advantage of that calculation because the lot was too narrow. The Fifth Avenue frontage of the building was only 100 feet, which would have meant that an increase in height of 150 feet required the building be set back from Sixty-first Street by 50 feet, leaving only 50 feet of depth: thus turning the upper stories of the Pierre into a narrow wall-like tower.

Schultze & Weaver solved this problem by giving the Pierre two principal setbacks. The building receded 20 feet from Sixty-first Street at both the fourteenth and the twentieth floors. The middle tier of the building—between the base and the tower—thus had a footprint of approximately 170 feet along Sixty-first Street and 80.5 feet along Fifth Avenue (or 13,671 square feet); though this section of the building is carved by numerous courts, it occupies almost exactly half of the site (13,670 square feet). The second setback created a tower of 112 feet by 60.5 feet: 6,767 feet, or a fraction over one quarter of the site. The ordinance permitted towers of unlimited height, so long as they did not occupy more than 25 percent of the site. Thus, Schultze & Weaver were able to make the maximum allowable use of the tower limitation of the ordinance while remaining within the setback limits and giving the building a clear sense of proportion from base to tower. [fig. 18]

To understand just how influential the zoning ordinance was, it is worth noting that the site where the Pierre was built had actually been in a "three-quarters times" zone from 1921 to 1924. For that brief period, the city had imposed a skyscraper ban along this stretch of Fifth Avenue by creating the most restrictive height district in the entire metropolis. Even on a 100-foot-wide street like Fifth Avenue, a "three-quarters times" district designation would have meant that the street wall of the Pierre could have been only 75 feet; the setback ratio would have been an exceedingly restrictive 1 to 1.5 (in other words, the building could rise only 1.5 feet for every foot that it was set back from the street wall). The base of the hotel would have been confined to something like seven stories (since the floors on the Pierre were roughly 11 feet in height), rather than fourteen, and the tower would have started on the thirteenth or fourteenth floor, rather than the twentieth. Had the 1921 skyscraper ban remained in force, therefore, the Pierre would have been a rather different building than it turned out to be.[35]

Schultze & Weaver showed yet another solution to the difficulties posed by the ordinance in their treatment of the Lexington. [fig. 19] This site was located in a "two times" district, which meant that the architects faced the same setback ratios as they did with the Sherry-Netherland. But the Lexington fronted on Forty-eighth Street, which was a mere 60 feet wide, and on Lexington Avenue, which was only 75 feet wide. This meant that the building could not exceed 150 feet at the street wall. Fortunately, the site stretched for nearly 175 feet along Forty-eighth Street, which allowed Schultze & Weaver to make up for space lost because

[fig. 18]
Hotel Pierre, presentation drawing, ca. 1930

[fig. 19]
Hotel Lexington, presentation drawing, 1929

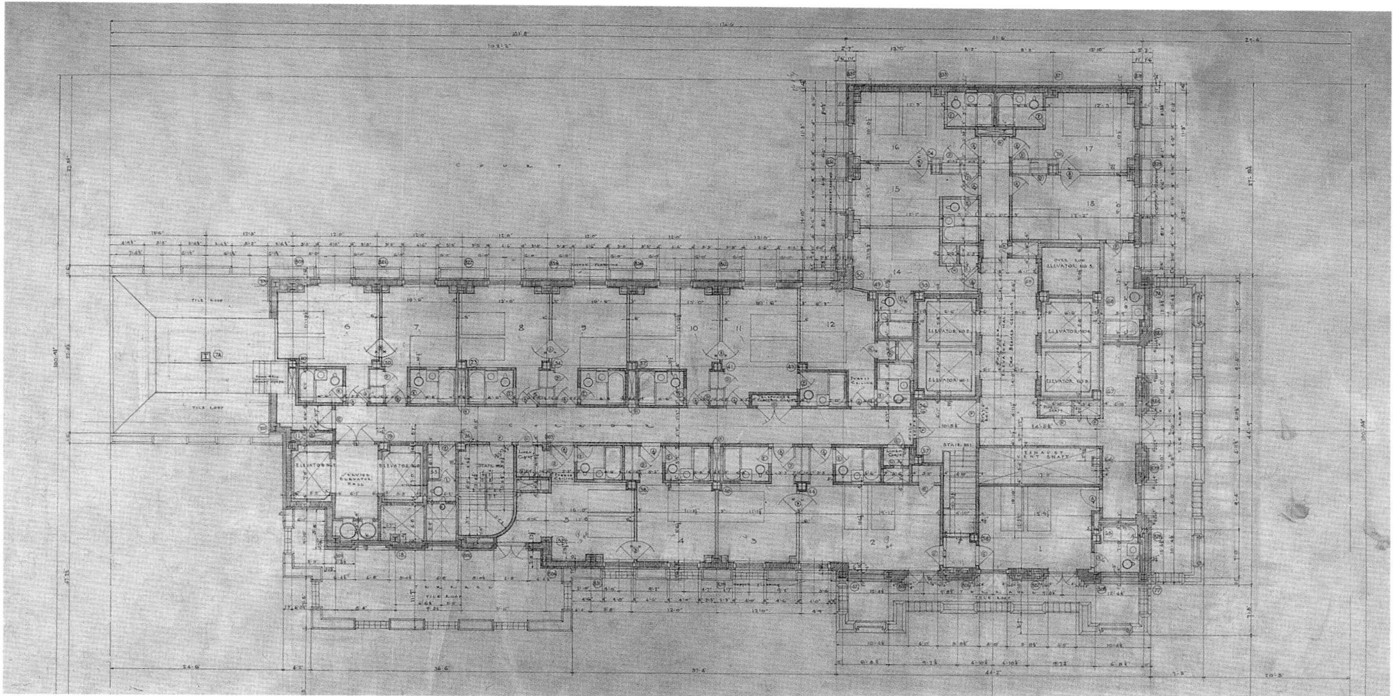

of narrow street widths. Above the mezzanine, the building takes on the shape of a key, with thirty-nine nearly identical rooms arrayed around the perimeter. Thanks to light courts at the corners and rear of the building, each room has a window: an essential feature of a first-class hotel. At the fifteenth floor, however, the setback requirements of the ordinance chiselled into this basic floor plan. Schultze & Weaver trimmed rooms from successive floors, creating six additional floor plans—for the fifteenth and sixteenth floors, the seventeenth and eighteenth, the nineteenth, the twentieth through twenty-second, the twenty-third, and the twenty-fourth—to retain as many rooms as possible within the setback envelope. The twenty-fourth floor has only eighteen rooms—fewer than half as many as at the base of the building—because of the setback requirements, and this effort to maximize space (and minimize the loss of rooms on upper floors) in spite of the legal limitations gives the Lexington its deeply carved facade. [figs. 20, 21]

Important though it was, the influence of the zoning ordinance on Schultze & Weaver's hotels cannot be separated from the economic context confronting the architects and the market that each building served, a point illustrated most clearly by contrasting the Lexington, with its multiple floor plans and Gothic massing, with the staid Park Lane. If zoning had been the determining factor for the Park Lane, the building would have looked very different than it did. Situated on spacious Park Avenue in a "two times" zone and a business district (where it had to compete with commercial properties fetching higher rents), the Park Lane should have pushed up to the maximum height limits as did the Sherry-Netherland, the Pierre, and the Lexington, with setback upper stories and perhaps a tower. But the Park Lane shows no evidence that it was influenced by the zoning ordinance. Instead, it looks like other buildings on Park Avenue: dignified but unimaginative hat boxes with similar, if not identical, cornice lines, designed to give the boulevard a harmonious appearance, reminiscent of the beaux-arts ideal of a wide residential street. That image had been the goal of those developers, like Weaver, who attempted to shift the social center of New York City from Fifth Avenue to Park Avenue in the years after World War I. But the defeat of the skyscraper ban on Fifth Avenue and the feverish pace of real estate development during the mid-1920s overwhelmed the vision that began on Park Avenue. Hotels and apartment buildings followed office buildings as

[fig. 20]
Plan of twenty-fourth floor (detail), Hotel Lexington, ca. 1929

[fig. 21]
View from Lexington Avenue, Hotel Lexington, from *The Architect* 13 (January 1930)

[fig. 22]
Waldorf-Astoria Hotel, New York, (Schultze & Weaver, 1931), presentation drawing, rendered by Lloyd Morgan, ca. 1930

property values compelled architects to work very close to the limits of what the zoning ordinance allowed. The result was a new generation of skyscraper hotels—Schultze & Weaver's chief among them—that created a bridge between the beaux-arts ideal and architectural modernism.

The Waldorf-Astoria, which was constrained by precisely the same set of legal limitations and street widths as the Lexington, shows how far Schultze & Weaver had travelled down this path during the 1920s. [fig. 22] The new Waldorf stood on high-priced land in a densely developed part of the city just north of Grand Central Terminal; indeed, most of the building was directly above the sprawling underground rail yard, which meant that engineers had to design special pilings to isolate the hotel from the vibrations caused by train movements.[36] To amortize the cost of the land, the hotel had to occupy an immense site: a lesson taught by the Pierre and the Lexington, both of which demonstrated just how much rentable space the zoning ordinance could carve from a building. Like the Lexington and the Sherry-Netherland, the new Waldorf would have shops to help pay the rent. Like the Pierre, the new Waldorf included the most spacious of entertaining facilities, but here they would serve both residents and transients, to spread the cost over a larger customer base. Like the Park Lane, the Pierre, and the Sherry-Netherland, the new Waldorf was designed to embody a "new ideal in city living" by retaining "an atmosphere of individual and homelike beauty," even as it housed thousands of guests.[37] Like the Sherry-Netherland and the Pierre, it continued a tradition of service and luxury associated with an earlier era; where Louis Sherry and Pierre Casalasco had connected those hotels with the golden age of fine living in Manhattan, so too did Oscar Tschirky, the renowned maître d'hôtel of the old Waldorf-Astoria, provide the linkage that helped the new Waldorf-Astoria make a place for itself within the already crowded market for first-class hotels by capitalizing on a nostalgia for days gone by.[38]

By the time they designed the new Waldorf-Astoria, therefore, Schultze & Weaver had learned how to work creatively within the limits of the law, in spite of the economic pressures of building in a crowded market with rising property values, to respond to the demands of a clientele who associated luxury with an earlier era and an older style. With the new Waldorf, the architects made their break from the aesthetic trappings of that tradition and sculpted a massive hotel according to the new set of design principles that their buildings had helped establish. In the process, they turned economic and legal necessities into design virtues and married received expectations of luxury—and the working requirements of a first-class hotel that they required—with a new image of skyscraper design.

LLOYD MORGAN
SCHULTZE & WEAVER
ARCHITECTS
15 EAST 48TH ST N.Y.C.

THE HOTEL MACHINE

Management and Technology in the Skyscraper Hotel

Kenneth J. Lipartito

In Steven Millhauser's novel *Martin Dressler,* the title character, an entrepreneur in late nineteenth-century New York, reflects on the hotel as an artifact of technology. It appears to him as "a system of order, a well-planned machine that drew all these people to itself and carried them up and down in iron cages and arranged them in private rooms."[1] As the novel progresses, Dressler builds, tears down, and then rebuilds a series of increasingly grand, elaborate, and fantastic hotels, which become worlds within worlds, dreamscapes that seek to fulfill every desire and fantasy of their patrons and of the entrepreneur himself.

Millhauser's fiction tracks quite precisely changes in the hotel as an artifact and emblem of the modern technological landscape. By the 1920s, astute hotel entrepreneurs were creating, as Martin Dressler had imagined, worlds within worlds that offered patrons a new definition of luxury and urbanity, one that was both exclusive yet widely available in hotels of great size. Like the architects of mass consumption, hotel builders sought to deliver an efficient service. Yet efficiency competed with the sense of luxury and even fantasy that grand hotels advertised. In constructing hotels as systems of technology, hotel entrepreneurs also sought to retain the sense of individuality and personal attention that had made the urban hotel of the nineteenth century attractive to upper-class patrons. This project would combine the talents of engineers, businessmen, university-trained hotel managers, and above all architects, the select few of whom included Leonard Schultze and S. Fullerton Weaver. [fig. 1]

As hotels moved from familiar figures of the vernacular city landscape in the nineteenth century to tools for a modern industrial and urban society in the twentieth, they changed in both form and function. They recreated and "renovated" themselves in each generation, harnessing the forces of steam and electricity, adding grand displays of artificial illumination, and employing technologies of locomotion, heating, and air conditioning to serve guests' needs and pleasures, indeed to define new pleasures. But as ordered environments, responsible to the capitalists who financed them, hotels also ordered their patrons' lives in a technological womb of security and service.[2] The food guests ate, the linens they slept on, and the domestic artifacts and furnishings of their rooms were mass-produced as hotels grew to giant size by the 1920s. Technology was both necessary to functioning on this scale and also a point

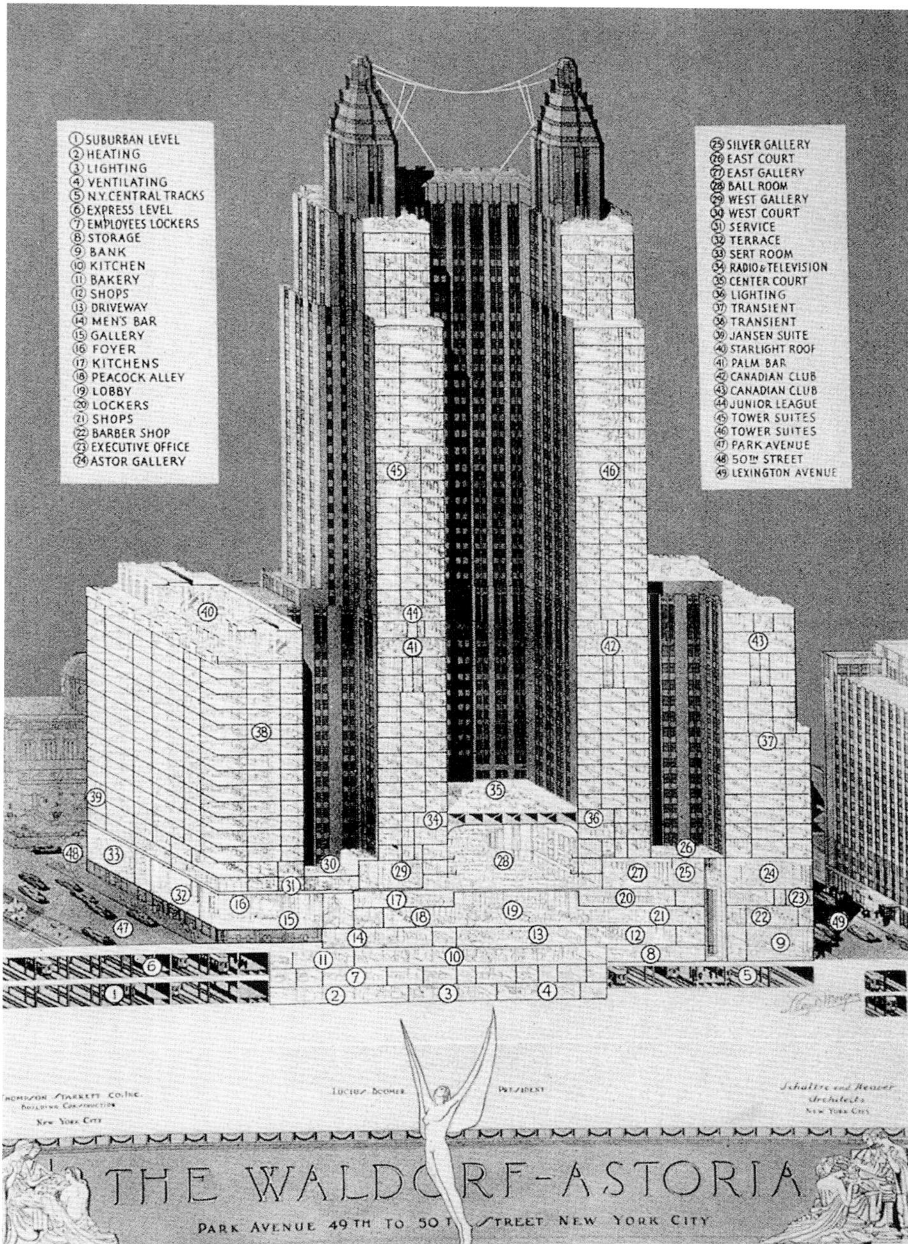

[fig. 1]
Waldorf-Astoria Hotel, New York (Schultze & Weaver, 1931), from Frank Crowninshield, ed., *The Unofficial Palace of New York* (New York: Hotel Waldorf-Astoria Corporation, 1939)
The skyscraper hotel combined an impressive street-level appearance with a complex, specialized division of space to assure profitability.

of consumer advertising; new hotels touted the comforts of cool air, electric lighting, rapid elevators, and other luxurious, mechanically produced amenities that both rich and middle-class customers could enjoy within the confines of a large hotel. At the same time, hotel architecture, which embraced modern design hesitantly in the early twentieth century, couched structural innovations behind a facade of familiar architectural elements. Designed to make use of new technology, hotels also worked to conceal that technology from the sight of guests. [fig. 2]

The evolution of the urban hotel can be followed through a series of building types that appeared in Boston, New York, and other large cities starting in the late eighteenth century. Buildings for housing transient travelers began to appear in major cities during the colonial era. These new edifices contrasted with older boarding houses, which commonly occupied existing structures, as well as humble inns and taverns. In 1794, New York's City Hotel, financed by a company of stockholders, defined the word *hotel* as not merely a public building or elegant private home but a large, impressive, centrally located facility for the comfortable lodging of traveling strangers serving quality food and drink and attracting attention for the dances, balls, and parties it hosted as well as the prominent guests it served.

[fig. 2]
Tower, Sherry-Netherland Hotel, New York (Schultze & Weaver with Buchman and Kahn, 1927), presentation drawing (detail), rendered by Chester Price, 1926
The historical ornamentation of the Sherry-Netherland's roof concealed the elevator machinery at the top of the tower. (See page 196 for full drawing.)

The opening of Boston's Tremont House in 1829, followed quickly in New York by Isaiah Rogers's Astor House in 1834–36, expanded the notion of the hotel as a center of social and commercial life. Hotels became increasingly grand, large-scale buildings of architectural distinction and beauty. No longer simply superior inns for citizens of the new republic, hotels were arbiters of style and stages upon which to display wealth. They employed new technologies, such as steam-powered pumps that fed water to baths on the upper floors. Many of the hotels built in the antebellum era sought to outdo their rivals by adopting the latest in technology, such as gas lights at New York's American Hotel of 1835 and private baths *en suite* at the New Yorker Hotel of 1844. Some technologies were developed specifically to suit the needs of the hotel, such as the "perpendicular railway" that moved guests to upper floors in the Fifth Avenue Hotel of 1859 before the invention of the passenger elevator.

In the late nineteenth-century Gilded Age, distinctiveness, luxury, and cutting-edge technology continued to define the fashionable urban hotel. In 1882, the Hotel Everett located on New York's Park Row became the first to use electric lights. In 1889, the Holland House in New York installed electromagnetic annunicators in each room that allowed guests to dial up as many as 140 different services. With the expansion of urban telephone networks, the Hotel New Netherland installed the first switchboard for room phones in 1894, increasing the hotel's connection to local, and later national, networks of communications.

Still, for all these changes and innovations, the pattern of hotel evolution before the turn of the twentieth century was one of individual and "unsystematic" growth. At least that was how later hotel professionals would see it. Life within the hotel was marked by an abundance of personal servants catering to the whims of the well-to-do. The buildings themselves, though distinctive, were still highly unstandardized and haphazard in their adoption of technologies to permit profitable operation. By the twentieth century, a new generation of hotel professionals set upon a mission to modernize not only the physical attributes of the hotel but its entire method of operation as well.

Hotel architect J. Otis Post noted that until 1910, "the requirements for a hotel were almost as individual as those of a private residence."[3] Designs were made for "laymen owners." Professionalization of management and intervention by profit-seeking capitalists increased the emphasis on efficient service and design.[4] Architects responded to new demands for efficiency by designing even larger hotel structures and paying greater attention to opportunities for systemization and organization of space. The shift in the size and design of space, in turn, required new internal organization and management. Urban hotels from the early twentieth century on began to evolve a new style and approach, the culmination of which was Schultze & Weaver's massive Waldorf-Astoria of 1931. This hotel would represent the fullest expression of the skyscraper hotel model and employ the most advanced behind-the-scenes technologies and methods of operation. [fig. 3]

Changes in the design and conception of urban hotels by the twentieth century were, of course, reflected in the buildings and their internal spaces, but one of the best gauges of the changing nature of hotels is the language used to describe them. When writers addressed the hotels under construction in New York and other major cities around the turn of the century, their words revealed a preoccupation with the size and scale of the buildings and the flow of activities within them. Technological marvels, these new hotels were evaluated in scientific terms.

[fig. 3]
Tower, Waldorf-Astoria Hotel, presentation drawing, ca. 1930
Schultze & Weaver's rendering of the Waldorf-Astoria's tower, with art moderne details and beams of light, suggests a positive engagement with technology.

above:
[fig. 4]
Steam supply system, Waldorf-Astoria Hotel, from *Behind the Scenes at the Waldorf-Astoria* (ca. 1939)
The Waldorf-Astoria used enough steam to heat eight hundred homes; it also used steam to run the compressors of more than sixty refrigerators.

top right:
[fig. 5]
Main salon, St. Regis Hotel, New York (Trowbridge & Livingston, 1904), from *The St. Regis Hotel* (1905)

It was the number of floors, rooms, and guests under one roof that distinguished the best hotels from lesser establishments. The amount of water and electricity consumed or the number of towels and linens washed each day became quite literally the measure of success. Writers offered up impressive lists of the tonnage of food served (and sometimes, thrown away), blocks of ice crushed, glasses of water filled, and banquets held in hotel restaurants—a necessary amenity for any respectable establishment.

The figures quoted were indeed remarkable. A good-sized hotel accommodating three hundred guests would, on an average day, serve 130 pounds of beef loin, 150 pounds of lamb, 75 pounds of ham, 120 pounds of veal, 115 pounds of pork, and some 30 roasting chickens.[5] Schultze & Weaver's Waldorf-Astoria was especially subject to quantitative description. In a year, the massive operation used enough electricity to supply six thousand homes, while its thirty-one elevators traveled the distance from Earth to the Moon.[6] [fig. 4] Even the small details were astounding: its Persian garden rug was reported to be "probably the largest hand-tufted carpet ever woven in a single piece," with over twelve million knots.[7] Its internal telephone switchboard could serve a medium-sized city, and its guests washed themselves each day with 750,000 gallons of water.

Sometimes, in fact, scale took on nauseating proportions. With hotel kitchens turning out meals for three hundred, five hundred, perhaps a thousand guests plus outside patrons, the garbage disposal problem was enormous. Incinerators could handle much of it but, noted one engineer, "Owing to the amount of grease which is always present, the heat from burning garbage is terrific."[8] Incinerators had to have a separate flue leading to the hotel's highest point, where a smokestack would belch out the undigested bits of diners' meals, thoroughly insulated from the rest of the structure.[9]

Such quantitative analysis providing a ranking for achievement has a long and cherished place in American culture. For hotels, however, quantity was something new and, increasingly, problematic. A generation before, the measure of a hotel's success might be in the wealth or social position of its patrons. Hotel owners pointed with pride to the grandeur of the main hall or lobby or the expense of the furnishings. These remained important measures of hotel distinction in the early

[fig. 6]
Park Avenue foyer, Waldorf-Astoria Hotel, presentation drawing, ca. 1929

twentieth century as well. [figs. 5, 6] The new century, however, saw increasing reliance on mass production rather than an emphasis on class distinction as the hotel industry's strategy for success. Even the high-end urban hotels designed by the respected architectural firms Holabird and Root, George B. Post and Son, and Schultze & Weaver were forced to confront the quantity issue. Hotel profits depended to a greater and greater extent on large-scale operations, and yet, at the same time, the move from class to mass threatened to undermine the very qualities of distinction that made hotels enticing spaces within the urban landscape. The best hotels were pressed to fend off competition from low-end establishments while delivering luxury and personal service on a grand scale, using as efficient means as possible.

The business problems confronting hotel managers increased with the boom economy of the 1920s. By 1928, the United States had twenty-six thousand hotels, supplying one-and-a-half million rooms, accounting for $5 billion in invested capital. Unfortunately for the would-be capitalist, the industry kept on expanding until it reached the point of overcapacity—the bane of any large-scale, capital-intensive enterprise. Supply outstripped demand, and hotel occupancy rates fell from a World War I high of 85 percent to below 70 percent by 1928. Revenue per room declined, and failures of hotels shot up after 1925. In the long run, consolidation might cut back excess capacity, but in the mean time, hotels scrambled not to be one of those sacrificed to balance supply and demand.[10]

Lucius Boomer, the most thoughtful student of hotel management of the times, noted the double-edged nature of the capitalist sword. [fig. 7] On the one hand, hotels were big business; as the nation's fifth largest industry, they were significant contributors to the economy, in a league with General Motors and Standard Oil. This status put pressure on operators to show profits. "Now that such large sums are invested, bankers and investors are looking into [the hotel industry's] business phases most carefully," Boomer observed.[11] Hotels tapped the national capital market, their giant mortgages financed by banks and sold to bond companies.[12] There was far less tolerance for the individual quirkiness of the jovial old innkeeper. Management of hotels had to be modern and, at the same time, somehow avoid the repellent aspects of large-scale operation and the soulless conformity of bureaucratic organization.

[fig. 7]
Lucius Boomer, ca. 1931

Boomer argued in his authoritative treatise, *Hotel Management*, that the hotel, though still a home, was home to such vast numbers of people that it had to promote "the scientific use, combination and concentration of resources."[13] Words such as "modern," "system," and "scientific" enjoyed a vogue in the early twentieth century. Although they sounded good, what did these words mean, and, more specifically, what did they mean in the context of the hotel?

Answers to these questions reflect the range of commercial strategies available in business thinking of the time. One strategy, mimicking the chain stores of the retail sector, found moderate acceptance in the hotel industry by the 1920s. Famous hotels of distinction became part of small, exclusive chain operations. Hotel expert Boomer teamed with DuPont heir Coleman DuPont to form the Boomer-DuPont Properties, which operated the Waldorf-Astoria and other establishments. John Bowman's Bowman-Biltmore Company controlled hotels in New York, Los Angeles, Miami, and elsewhere. Perhaps the most extensive of the chain hotels were the Statler properties. E. M. Statler offered reasonable rooms at a reasonable price, though he also operated a number of more expensive hotels as well. He pioneered design concepts that allowed for the efficient operation of his purpose-built properties, such as uniform guest rooms wrapped around a single plumbing shaft and centralized groupings of passenger and service elevators to economize on space and move guests quickly to upper floors.

Rational design, it was hoped, would provide the profits that an increasingly competitive and expensive industry needed to keep growing. Historian Lisa Pfueller Davidson writes of a "melding of early twentieth-century business, architecture, and technology" leading to hotels that were "fundamentally modern in their rationalized response to complex functional requirements."[14] "Eliminating wasteful design through efficiency" was essential to the hotel's profits; this meant a design that was the "epitome of convenience and efficiency."[15]

As design embraced efficiency, architects had to adjust their approach to hotel commissions. Although there was a danger that business and technical imperatives might strip the architect of his traditional role as form-giver, in fact, if handled correctly, a hotel project could increase the power of the architect as the "total designer" of the building, its engineering, and its operations. After all, only good design could ensure the proper arrangement of heating, lighting, and ventilation. Mistakes in these key systems could not be corrected easily once the building was finished. Using a "simple and intelligent style in which to clothe modern construction," hotel architects could produce buildings that would allow "a suitable return on the money invested and maximum comfort and convenience for the hotel guest."[16]

Schultze & Weaver were unusually well prepared to handle this new sort of architectural work.[17] S. Fullerton Weaver, a socially prominent New Yorker, not only had the necessary contacts for securing commissions but he was also an engineer by training. His partner, Leonard Schultze, had prior experiences that included work on Terminal City, a complex of offices, hotels, and apartments above the Park Avenue tracks of the New York Central Railroad.[18] Systematizing hotel design and operations meant dealing with a complicated, interrelated set of technical, architectural, and organizational issues. "As the plan of a modern hotel is of such a complicated nature," explained W. Sydney Wagner of the firm of George B. Post, "it is essential that an architect who has had no previous experience in hotel planning should obtain the services of a hotel consultant and a hotel manager who is capable

[fig. 8]
Kitchen, Hotel Commodore, New York (Warren & Wetmore, 1919), 1919
The kitchen of the Hotel Commodore was designed for efficient preparation and delivery of food. Quantity management, more than quality and originality, defined the cuisine of the large-scale hotel.

of reading plans."[19] If done correctly, though, such complicated design work helped to ensure the success of a hotel project. "No longer," wrote J. Otis Post, "do bankers consider the financing of a hotel a dangerous experiment."[20] Nor did they have to rely on the "personality," or the integrity, of the owner (or other subjective factors) when making loans. System, professionalism, and management were what they looked for, and the architect could aid in furthering these desirable characteristics by offering a rational design.[22]

In the early twentieth century, "efficiency" carried certain specific connotations. With regard to production, it implied standardization of products, the tools to make them, and, indeed, the workers who used the tools. In a factory setting, it meant as well the rationalization of space to permit the fastest flow of work on the assembly line with minimal kinks or bottlenecks impeding worker motion.[24] Advocates of modern hotel management asked architects to provide similar standardization and rationalization in their spaces of production. [fig. 8] Architects reduced the detail, variation, and complexity of rooms and baths. They eliminated the odd corners and columns that hampered the flow of patrons into the lobby and up to the rooms. They collaborated with mechanical and structural engineers to plan and construct space for maximum return on investment and to provide room for the complex technical systems of heat, light, and water needed in a hotel that proposed to be up-to-date in its appeal.[23] [fig. 9]

[fig. 9]
Engine room, Knickerbocker Hotel, New York (Trowbridge & Livingston, 1906), after 1906

To speed production, Henry Ford and other revolutionaries of manufacturing integrated operations, controlling their raw materials and opening or controlling outlets for their goods. This vertical integration ensured that the factory floor never lacked for parts or materials and that output never sat idle waiting for a customer. Hotels could do the same thing by operating their own laundries and china-painting shops and keeping upholsterers, mechanics, plumbers, and carpenters on duty full time. [figs. 10, 11] Or they could secure exclusive deals with manufacturers of various goods who would produce a limited series of standard designs exclusively for the hotel. The modern hotel, noted Boomer, "not only assembles within the building the domestic essentials . . . but frequently goes far into the field of manufacture, with departments for fabricating silverware, furniture, fixtures, uniforms and bedding." A good sized hotel kitchen operated, for all

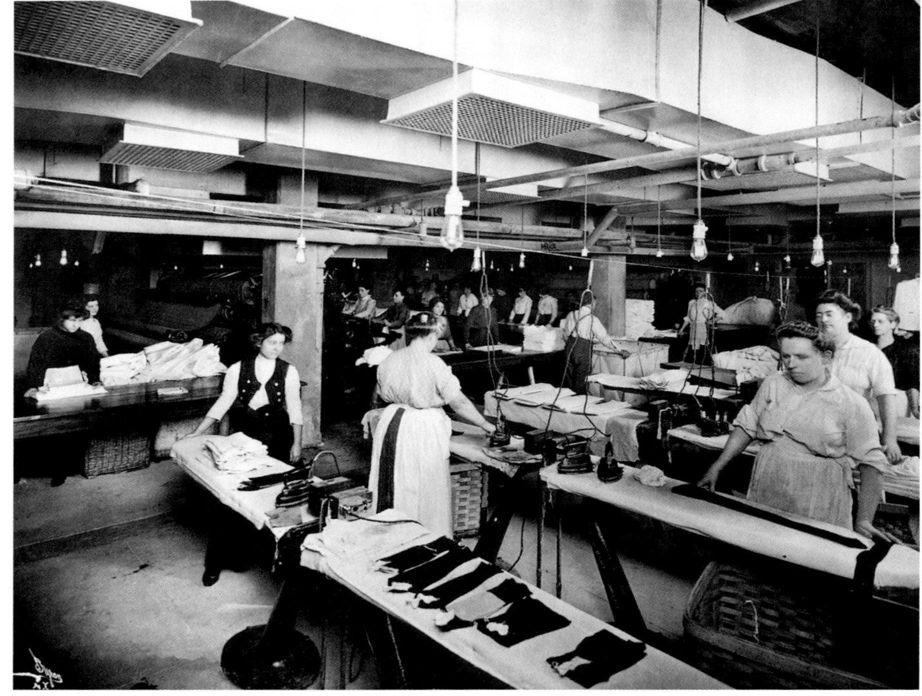

top right:
[fig. 10]
Laundry, Knickerbocker Hotel, after 1906

bottom right:
[fig. 11]
Laundry, Biltmore Hotel, New York (Warren & Wetmore, 1913), ca. 1913
Providing guests and dining rooms with fresh linens on demand required hotel laundries to operate at an industrial scale. Like other industrial establishments, hotels drew their labor force from the city's immigrant populations, including women.

above:
[fig. 12]
Bakers, Waldorf-Astoria Hotel, from Henry B. Lent, *The Waldorf-Astoria* (New York: Hotel Waldorf-Astoria Corporation, 1934)

intents and purposes, its own bakery, ice cream parlor, and candy shop, among other things. It was "hard to set a limit to the services that a hotel should undertake," Boomer reflected.[24] [fig. 12]

Hotels had to bring guest services under direct control to assure quality and consistency of experience. They might franchise out some things, but they were wise to manage important hotel functions themselves. Having "complete control" over laundry, for example, was considered essential in a first-class hotel; otherwise, as one expert put it, "a constant supply of snow-white, clean-smelling linen" could not always be assured.[25] For similar reasons, hotel porters retrieved luggage for guests from train stations and ships. Even tangential operations such as coat checks, candy and cigar shops, and florists, might be brought under the establishment's control—providing an extra source of profit while ensuring patrons received the same level of service throughout the hotel.[26] [figs. 13, 14]

Creating a total hotel experience through vertical integration could only be done in a large-scale operation. Only large hotels could take advantage of the economies of scale inherent in modern machinery for generating heat, steam, ice, and other technologically determined amenities.[27] The logic of large-scale operations drove hotels—especially luxury hotels—to grow, but this growth created new problems of organization and coordination. Fortunately, hotel operators found, many of these additional problems were amenable to further technological and organizational innovation.

Back-of-the-house technologies, including the unglamorous ones for keeping records and handling information, were crucial to the successful workings of the hotel as machine. Stocks and provisions had to be sorted in specialized bins, shelves, and receptacles for quick access and to make inventory accounting easier. Time stamps were employed to keep track of when things such as orders for supplies or mail and telegraph message deliveries took place. The hotel restaurant—traditionally a sinkhole for wasting goods and materials, given their perishable nature—even adopted machines to cut or shape food in standardized portions.[28]

Perhaps the most important technology of control at hand for hotel managers was the telephone and related communications devices. No modern hotel could operate without the most up-to-date communications system. Business travelers expected to keep in touch while on the road. Leisure travelers, removed from their normal physical surroundings, were living in a liminal space while at the hotel, and although liminality might be liberating, it could also be threatening. Being connected via the technologies of the day—the telephone, most notably—was not a luxury in these cases. Indeed, assiduous managers made sure that clerks, telegraphers, and telephone switchboard operators were drilled in the importance of getting messages to the guests as soon as possible and with the greatest accuracy possible. Nothing could more quickly damage a hotel's reputation than a missed appointment due to careless handling of messages. Hotels were to be nodes of connection with the rest of the world, not refuges from them. [fig. 15]

Communications also helped to run a large-scale operation. The imposing physical size of hotels, even in space-precious New York, was simply too great to handle on foot alone. Lobby clerks kept in touch with floor clerks by internal telephone. Guest bills arrived from the accounting office via pneumatic tubes, cutting the wait at checkout time. The head housekeeper used an internal teleautograph (an electrical device that reproduced writing at a distance) to track the flow of linens

top:
[fig. 13]
En route service, Savoy-Plaza Hotel, New York (McKim, Mead & White, 1927), 1928

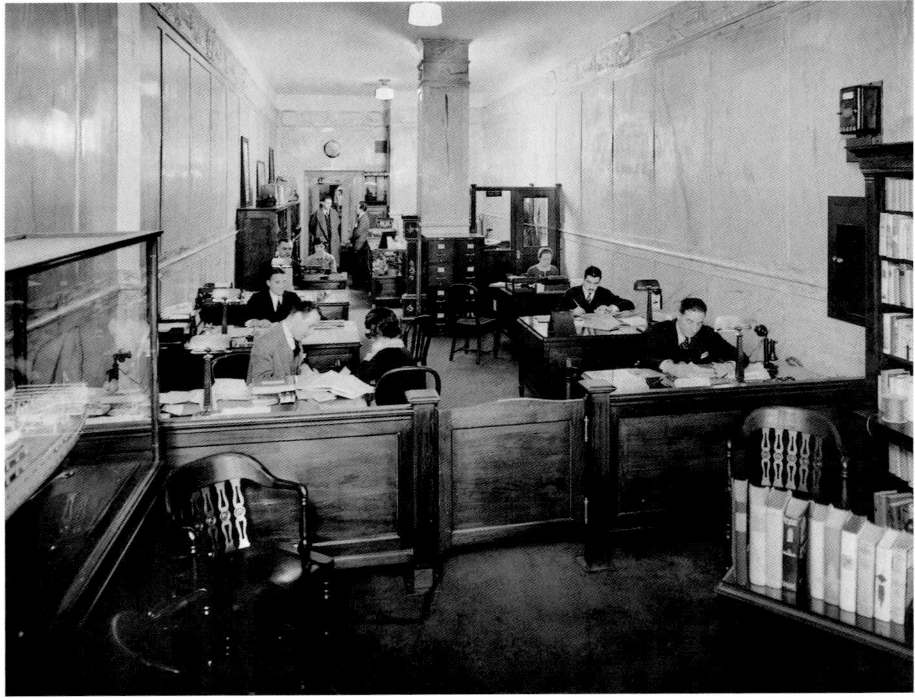

above:
[fig. 14]
Barbershop, Waldorf-Astoria Hotel, presentation drawing, ca. 1930
The large, modern hotel, with its array of consumer services such as the Waldorf's barbershop, created a self-contained world of luxury for its guests, a city within a city.

opposite:
[fig. 15]
Poster, *"I'm So Glad I Telephoned First,"* ca. 1930

"I'm so glad I
TELEPHONED
FIRST"
This is the season
for such timely
suggestions as
"CALL AHEAD for
RESERVATIONS
-KEEP in TOUCH
WITH HOME BY
TELEPHONE"

[fig. 16]
Switchboard operators, Waldorf-Astoria Hotel, from *Behind the Scenes at the Waldorf-Astoria* (ca. 1939)
Hotels were information and communication hubs. This switchboard, with its crew of operators, matched the size and volume of city telephone exchanges of the time.

from laundry to cupboard, to chambermaid cart back to laundry, so that there was never a shortage. Patrons called for room service or used automatic dial systems that ordered cabs, ice, shoe-shines, laundry service, and other amenities, which workers delivered silently and quickly once the order was received. [fig. 16]

Had simplification and system been all there was to hotel management, then the perfect application of Henry Ford's rationalized production policies would have ensured the seamless operation of the large-scale hotel. But even as they advocated order and rationalization, hotel owners and managers saw a danger if these values were taken too far. As even the strongest advocate of system, Lucius Boomer, warned, "there will remain many problems which cannot be settled in the light of fixed policies"; for managers, the sad fact was that "a hotel is not a factory turning out standardized machine parts."[29] Rooms as "uniform as cells" would never do in a high-class establishment. Instead, the astute manager sought an edge over the competition by simplifying in ways "not manifest to the customer."[30] Rational design allowed for speed of operations on a large scale while showing proper deference to guests' sense of style and aesthetics. Hotels, in short, did not adopt Ford's methods but rather adapted them. They straddled the gulf between rigid simplification and utter chaos. Management, control, training, and professionalism would produce a rational system, sufficiently simple to be efficient and sufficiently differentiated and flexible to give guests that sense of luxury and individualism they craved.

A good architect was crucial in creating this balanced environment. Leonard Schultze recognized that "No two structures need be, nor are they likely to be, the same," since there were so many different conditions, from the land plot to the purpose of the hotel, that could vary depending on city and local codes and on the customers to whom the hotel was to appeal. Still, simplicity in design, if not rigorous standardization, offered sizeable economies. Simplicity was "the first essential," wrote Schultze, and good materials with a minimum of ornament the most effective approach.[31] Certain features, notably the floor plan, could be fairly standard, with a small number of different room types. Other features, such as the ballroom or shops, had to be changeable to accommodate shifting consumer preferences.[32] [fig. 17] Methodical planning, combined with the adoption of certain materials and

[fig. 17]
Ballroom, Waldorf-Astoria Hotel, presentation drawing, rendered by Lloyd Morgan, 1929

construction methods such as steel framing, permitted flexibility in designing both the building's footprint and the internal spaces of the hotel.

It was especially on the interior that architects had to adapt their design ideas to the business and technological imperatives of the modern hotel. "The essence of the hotel plan is, after all, its usefulness as a service machine," wrote W. Sydney Wagner.[33] Architects laid out plans that would make it easier to clean and repair equipment, provide for adequate ventilation, and minimize the clanging and banging of heating systems. They inked in space for dumbwaiters to transport food quickly from the central kitchen to guest and function rooms. They included commodious elevators to move guests up and down the skyscraper. They used basements and subbasements to provide sufficient space and structural support for large steam plants, refrigerators, and laundry machines.

In their design for the Waldorf-Astoria, Schultze & Weaver paid special attention to space for crucial machinery. They had no choice, as the hotel—perched above the tracks of the New York Central Railroad—had only a small basement area. The layout of equipment in the basement they solved by use of "templates," or small drawings of the machinery, fit together like a jigsaw puzzle.[34] Horace Leland Wiggins, a vice president of United Hotels Company, recognized the value of such a meticulous approach to even the unseen parts of the building: "In planning the service portions of the hotel architects should keep constantly in mind that too much study cannot be given to the economical arrangement of the various working parts."[35] Architects, for example, had to make a thorough study of what went on in kitchens, taking as models the layout of galleys in steamboats and railroad dining cars or other places where space was at a premium. The economics of urban real estate markets, where "every cubic foot of construction has to be paid for," were relentless.[36]

In the smaller-scale hotels and inns of the early nineteenth century, guests might expect to interact with the establishment's proprietor. The scale of the large urban hotel made this impossible. As with the city itself, scale and diversity bred anonymity, which could be exciting or off-putting. In the late nineteenth century, hotel clerks were infamous for their rudeness and arrogance. Hotels themselves guarded their reputations, which were threatened by the potentially disreputable behavior of their guests. Women traveling alone presented special problems, particularly in the highly masculine public space of the hotel lobby, the restaurant, and the bar. Rudeness, reputation, and deportment were addressed in the twentieth-century skyscraper hotel through a combination of technology and systemization.[37]

Hotel manager Boomer laid greater stress on management: it was the coordination of human and technological resources through a central director, not any one piece of technology, that made the hotel work. In this, Boomer was adopting an attitude of professionalism and service, the progressive business values of the 1920s. Ford seemed to be suggesting that system would reduce humans to mere cogs in machines. His contemporary, the father of scientific management Frederick Taylor, advocated using harsh carrot-and-stick methods to motivate workers. But by the 1920s, a kinder, gentler form of labor management had come into vogue. Managers stressed serving the customer in a dignified, refined, professional way over pure profit-making or even the entrepreneurial transformation of the economic landscape.

This new managerial philosophy fit the hotel business much better than did strict Fordism. As Boomer and others noted, despite the incipient growth of hotel chains and attempts to standardize management practices and customer experience, there were simply too many variables in the urban landscape, too much fickleness in taste and fashion, to permit this. The key was to find out where economies through standardization were possible, so that profits might still flow while providing more costly personalized attention.

[fig. 18]
Wake-up call, Waldorf-Astoria Hotel, from *Behind the Scenes at the Waldorf-Astoria* (ca. 1939)
Personalized service relieved the technological monotony of the large-scale hotel.

Experts of hotel management such as Boomer, Statler, and Bowman explored various options in the 1910s and 1920s. Statler's version was perhaps the most highly standardized, but all of the most insightful thinkers on the hotel offered similar answers. Certain back room operations could be handled through a combination of new technology and more systematic worker training. Well-trained clerks would assure maximized revenue by offering each patron the highest priced room he or she might desire, while using specialized technologies such as the room rack, to keep track of which rooms were rented to whom. Cash registers and other machines for recording transactions fed financial data to back office accountants and controllers and monitored, as well, the fiduciary duties of the staff. Floor clerks catered to guests' wishes while coordinating with the front desk to anticipate the resources that might need to be marshaled for each room at any time. A system of bells, enunciators, internal telephones, and the like kept guest, floor staff, kitchen, and front desk in constant communication. This not only gave guests the option of personalizing their service but also allowed hotel management to know the desires of their patrons almost as soon as the wish formed in their minds. Speed of information meant not only speed of service but cost-efficient service as well.

Professionalization assured that employees worked well with the ordered system that was the modern hotel. A mark of the growing professionalization of the hotel staff was to be found in the technical skills mastered by the manager. He was now seen as not only an impresario of the grand spectacle and a paterfamilias to employees but as an expert in a number of scientific and technical fields of endeavor: air conditioning and accounting, dietetics and banking, music, mathematics and insurance, refrigeration, sanitation, psychology, and, of course, "effective methods of preventing and eliminating vermin."[38] New external institutions helped in the shift to this more professional outlook; Cornell University opened its school of hotel management in 1921, and the American Hotel Association was founded in 1924.[39]

Still, efficiency and standardization alone were not enough when it came to service. As hotels achieved "mechanical perfection," they were "obliged to seek distinction" by returning into the inns of old, by offering greater "*personal service*."[40] In fact, the American hotel, despite its technological wizardry, had more staff per patron than did European hotels. This may have reflected the American desire for speed of service, but it also showed that hotel technology could not completely eclipse the essential human touch.[41] Service had to be provided in a way that was profitable and also did not undermine the sense of luxury and exclusiveness a high-end establishment offered. What was more impressive, the seventy thousand morning wake-up calls made by Waldorf-Astoria operators each year, or the fact that in each case they had to call the guest by name? [fig. 18]

One way hotel operators strove for both efficiency and personal service was by recruiting women into staff and management positions. Lucius Boomer was a strong believer in employing women not only for lower-level functions but as floor managers and heads of housekeeping departments. Women, Boomer believed, were naturally adapted to these tasks. In part, his staffing choices reflected his shrewd assessment that hotels could expand their market by appealing to women traveling alone, which became more common and more respectable in the liberated 1920s. Parlors and separate ladies' restaurants were some of the amenities he advocated to appeal to female patrons. Female staff would create the homelike qualities threatened by the magnitude of the skyscraper hotel.[42]

Good service also depended on a special type of building design. Just as the financial imperatives of hotels occupying prime urban real estate required static efficiency in the layout of space, so too they necessitated dynamic efficiency in the flow of people through space. Profit required moving guests quickly through registration and into their rooms. As architectural critic Kenneth Murchison pointed out, an inefficient service layout "can easily ruin a hotel."[43] Good service, what every high-end hotel thought distinguished it from the run-of-the-mill establishment, was practically defined by smooth flow.[44]

As with so much else, the Waldorf-Astoria provided Schultze & Weaver with a supreme canvas on which to deploy all their skills and experience in this aspect of hotel design. Murchison noted how the plans of the first floor showed an appreciation for circulation, from the entrance lobby to lounges to the main lobby, "where you dig up your last simolean to pay the bill."[45] Elevators were liberally sprinkled around the lobbies to maximize movement. Schultze & Weaver, wrote Murchison, "know that the merchandise they sell is service and they make it possible for the hotel operator to sell service to his patrons with the minimum of expense and with the least possible waste of time."[46] [fig. 19]

Food service provided an opportunity to connect with guests at the most basic level, while a slip-up could leave a hungry guest vowing never to return. Since the central kitchen of the skyscraper hotel had to serve transient guests, permanent residents, and restaurant patrons alike, its internal organization, as well as location, in the flow of hotel services was vital. Ideally the kitchen would be as square as possible for maximum layout flexibility. Sufficient space had to be provided for augmenting technologies—conveyers to carry dirty dishes from, and clean dishes to, various dining rooms; lines of broilers and fryers against the walls; workspaces in the center; bake shops and confectionary sections on one side; fruit pantry on another; vegetable preparation in still another section; all neatly subdivided but

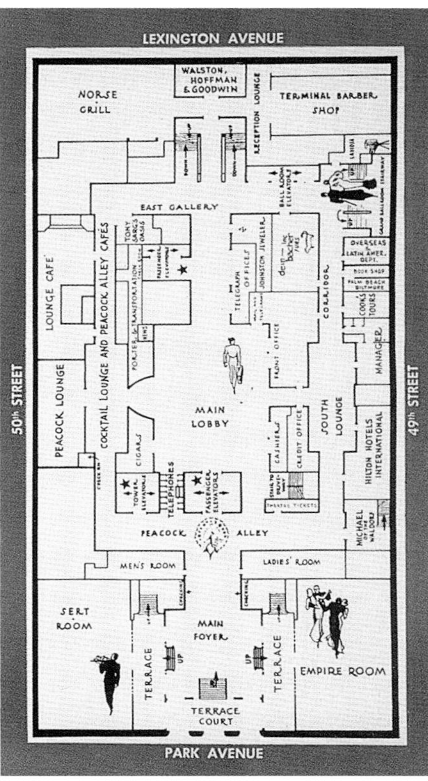

[fig. 19]
Lobby floor plan, Waldorf-Astoria Hotel, from *Facts About the Waldorf-Astoria* (ca. 1939)

[fig. 20]
Home Cooking in the Waldorf-Astoria (1938)

arranged to bring those parts requiring close contact together and all food out the door as fast as possible.[47] The strength of the Waldorf-Astoria's kitchen was not only in its shape but in how its "octopuslike tentacles, in the form of service pantries"[48] extended in all directions. [fig. 20]

Henry Ford may have been the hero of his age, but he was not, by the early 1920s, the most successful motor car maker. That banner had passed to his chief competitor, General Motors. And the well-known reason for Ford's relative decline so soon after his moment of triumph was his refusal to abandon mass production and standardization as his chief, indeed only, value. In place of the rigid product standardization of Ford's Model-T, General Motors began to offer a variety of products of different shape, design, color, and price. So, too, with the hotel. If, as Boomer wrote, "people's tastes in food were identical, or everybody liked the same rooms and furnishings, and employees could be secured who would always do the same thing in the same way, the perfect hotel might be developed."[49] But rather than seeking the perfect hotel, architects, hotel managers, and financiers instead sought a practical alternative, one that reflected the realities of changing tastes, uncertain demand, fluctuating real estate values, and the political debates over zoning. Like much American industry, even after Ford, local conditions, fickle consumer fashions, and unpredictable market conditions worked against rigid standardization. Industries producing glass, ceramics, furniture, and other wares that were part of the hotel's material life could be profitable and highly progressive in their use of technology and organization. They did so, however, by maintaining flexibility in their deployment of specialized skills and craft techniques. Hotels, too, had to be sites of "flexible specialization," not standardization.[50] The hotel became a place between modernity and tradition, between the machinelike efficiency of mass production and the familial, republican space of the old civic hotel.

Schultze & Weaver were perhaps the finest practitioners of this balancing act. "Using modern skyscraper construction techniques, but embellishing these... with traditional ornamental forms," they perfected a hotel model that was financially profitable and technologically sophisticated, yet sufficiently distinguished to command premium prices from upper-class patrons.[51] They combined enough traditional decorative elements to make each of their buildings distinctive and produced them using adequate standardization to assure that each building would turn a profit. The architects worked closely with engineers, urban planners, renowned chefs, and new practitioners of the science of hotel management to make their buildings both attractive in traditional terms and useful in modern technological and managerial terms. The result was a hotel that could deploy modern values of professionalism, service, and management to maintain an important tradition of personal service.

The model of the hotel perfected by Schultze & Weaver fell apart on the rocky shoals of the Depression era. In the post-war period, a greater variety of hotel types that served a more differentiated market appeared. After World War II, architects no longer could, as Schultze & Weaver had, conceive of the grand urban hotel as all things to all (middle-class) people. In this sense, the hotel practice of Schultze & Weaver was a transitional moment, partaking of the mass consumption emerging in an industrial America of mass production but not yet reduced to just another form of business enterprise, as the post-war hotel industry would be.

HOME COOKING
IN
The Waldorf-Astoria
MENU SUGGESTIONS

NOTES

ESCAPE AND CONTINUITY

1 According to an account kept by the firm, the cost of all the projects it completed through 1931 (almost all of these begun before the stock market crash of October 1929) totaled $91.3 million. Out of this sum, resorts, hotels, and private clubs accounted for $65.1 million, or a little over 70 percent. Leonard Schultze & Associates, Architects, "History of the Firm," October 5, 1942, Appendix I ("Volume of Work by Years"), unpublished typescript, Schultze & Weaver collection, The Wolfsonian–FIU.

2 Kenneth Murchison, "The Drawings for the New Waldorf-Astoria," *American Architect* 139 (January 1931): 30.

3 James S. Warren, "The Present Status of the Hotel Business," *Architectural Forum* XXXIX, no. 5 (November 1923): 714.

4 See Molly Winger Berger, "The Modern Hotel in America, 1829–1929" (Ph.D. dissertation, Case Western Reserve University, 1997), especially Chapter 8; Susan Braden, *The Architecture of Leisure: The Florida Resort Hotels of Henry Flagler and Henry Plant* (Gainesville: University Press of Florida, 2002), 310–13; Lisa Pfueller Davidson, "Early Twentieth-Century Hotel Architects and the Origins of Standardization," *Journal of Decorative and Propaganda Arts* 25 (2005): 9–37.

5 Leonard Schultze, "The Architecture of the Modern Hotel," *Architectural Forum* XXXIX, no. 5 (November 1923): 204.

6 John McEntee Bowman, "Good Architecture, a Modern Hotel Requisite," *Architectural Forum* XXXIX, no. 5 (November 1923): 195.

7 The biographical information on Schultze comes, unless otherwise noted, from two sources: the typescript "History of the Firm," cited in n. 1; and his obituary, "L. Schultze Dead; Architect was 73," *The New York Times*, 26 August 1951.

8 Masqueray also served as chief of design for the 1904 Louisiana Purchase Exposition in St. Louis, Missouri, which emulated the 1893 Chicago Exposition's "White City" with its own expansive beaux-arts fairgrounds. Among his other significant American buildings was the Cathedral of St. Paul in Minnesota. See Erik Mattie, *World's Fairs* (New York: Princeton Architectural Press, 1998), 119–20; and "Noted Architect Dead," *The New York Times*, 27 May 1917.

9 See, for example, *The American Renaissance* (New York: Brooklyn Museum of Art, 1979); and, Robert A. M. Stern, Gregory Gilmartin, and John Montegue Massengale, *New York 1900: Metropolitan Architecture and Urbanism* (New York: Rizzoli, 1983), 21–22.

10 Dates in parentheses after hotels or other structures indicate the public opening of the establishments.

11 Leonard Schultze, "The Waldorf-Astoria Hotel," *Architecture* LXIV, no. 5 (November 1931): 252.

12 "Major Weaver Dead; Park Ave. Builder," *The New York Times*, 2 January 1939; "Architects' Appendix," *Upper East Side Historic District* (New York: Landmarks Preservation Commission, 1981), 1339.

13 "Another Big Hotel for Park Avenue," *The New York Times*, 7 September 1922.

14 "Maj. Weaver Gives a Costume Ball," *The New York Times*, 22 November 1924; "'Crazy Costume' Ball Held," *The New York Times*, 22 August 1925; "Major S. Fullerton Weaver Host," *The New York Times*, 7 October 1926; "Lillian L. Howell Weds S. F. Weaver," *The New York Times*, 18 June 1929; "Major and Mrs. Weaver Hosts," *The New York Times*, 9 May 1930; "The S. F. Weavers Hosts at Reception," *The New York Times*, 1 December 1933; "Costume Dance Given by the S. F. Weavers," *The New York Times*, 16 May 1934; "Major Weaver Dead."

15 "Leonard Schultze is Host," *The New York Times*, 15 December 1931.

16 *Who's Who in New York* (New York: Who's Who Publications, 1929), 1506.

17 Except where otherwise noted, the information about Morgan's career is taken from a curriculum vitae included in a notebook labeled "Morgan Firm History, 1/14/62," Schultze & Weaver collection, The Wolfsonian–FIU.

18 Morgan's prize-winning entry was a design for a civic exhibition and assembly hall. See "Paris Prize, Goal of Architects, Won by Ex-Office Boy," *The New York Times*, 23 August 1921.

19 *Who Was Who in America*, vol. IX, 1985–89 (Wilmette, Ill.: Marquis Who's Who, 1989), 256.

20 "Worldly Known Lloyd Morgan is Praised as Architect-Teacher-Humanitarian," *AIA Journal*, October 1970, 13.

21 Braden, *The Architecture of Leisure*, 11–14, 87, 117–18, 124.

22 See Seth Bramson, "A Tale of Three Henrys," *Journal of Decorative and Propaganda Arts* 23 (1998): 132–33; Edward N. Akin, *Flagler: Rockefeller Partner and Florida Baron* (Gainesville: University Press of Florida, 1991), 166; Nicholas N. Patricios, *Building Marvelous Miami* (Gainesville: University Press of Florida, 1994), 31–33; and Mark S. Foster, *Castles in the Sand: The Life and Times of Carl Graham Fisher* (Gainesville: University Press of Florida, 2000), 160–71.

23 Foster, *Castles in the Sand*, 194–97.

24 "New York Architects Here for Conference on New Beach Hotel," *Miami Daily Metropolis*, 6 March 1923. I am grateful to Michael Hughes and Carolyn Klepser for bringing this article to my attention.

25 "Bowman Adds Two Hotels to Holdings," *The New York Times*, 6 May 1918.

26 Patricios, *Building Marvelous Miami*, 34–35; Samuel D. LaRoue, Jr., and Ellen Uguccioni, *The Biltmore Hotel: An Enduring Legacy* (Miami: Arva Parks & Company and Centennial Press, 2002), 14–18, 27–32.

27 Braden, *Architecture of Leisure*, 319.

28 Beth Dunlop, "Inventing Antiquity: The Art and Craft of Mediterranean Revival Architecture," *Journal of Decorative and Propaganda Arts* 23 (1998): 192–93.

29 Leland M. Roth, *American Architecture: A History* (Boulder: Westview Press, 2001), 347; "Arts Gratia Artis… .The Story Behind One of the West's Cultural & Artistic Masterpieces—The Los Angeles Biltmore Hotel," brochure published for the Los Angeles Biltmore; text reprinted by the University of Southern California Information Services Division website, http://www.usc.edu/isd/archives/la/pubart/Downtown/figueroa/Pershing_Square_History/biltmore_decor_history.html.

30 LaRoue and Uguccioni, *The Biltmore Hotel*, 29, 31; *The Biltmore Revisited* (Coral Gables, Florida: Metropolitan Museum & Art Center, 1981), 35.

31 *The Miami Biltmore* (New York: John McEntee Bowman, 1926), unpaginated.

32 LaRoue and Uguccioni, *The Biltmore Hotel*, 44–48.

33 "New Breakers Architectural Gem Gleaned from Italian Renaissance Villa Period," *Palm Beach Daily News*, 19 December 1926.

34 "Architects Guide," *Palm Beach Daily News*, 19 December 1926.

35 Ibid.

36 Ibid.

37 Leonard Schultze & Associates, Architects, "History of the Firm."

38 "Another Big Hotel for Park Avenue," *The New York Times*, 7 September 1922; "Park Av. Changes Made in a Decade," *The New York Times*, 9 November 1924.

39 "Park Av. Changes Made in a Decade."

40 Advertisement, "The Lexington—Ready Tomorrow," *The New York Times*, 14 October 1929.

41 The quotation comes from Max Page, *The Creative Destruction of Manhattan, 1900–1940* (Chicago: University of Chicago Press, 1999), 5; See also pages 23–29 for more description of these changes.

42 Andrew S. Dolkart, "Millionaires' Elysiums: The Luxury Apartment Hotels of Schultze & Weaver," *Journal of Decorative and Propaganda Arts* 25 (2005): 13–14; Paul Groth, *Living Downtown: The History of Residential Hotels in the United States* (Berkeley: University of California Press, 1994), 27–32.

43 Dolkart, "Millionaires' Elysiums," 13; Steven Ruttenbaum, *Mansions in the Clouds: The Skyscraper Palazzi of Emery Roth* (New York: Balsam Press, Inc., 1996), 99–100.

44 Ruttenbaum, *Mansions in the Clouds*, 99.

45 Lucius Boomer, *Hotel Management: Principles and Practice*, second ed. (New York and London: Harper & Brothers Publications, 1931), XVII–XVIII.

46 R. W. Sexton, *American Apartment Houses, Hotels, and Apartment Hotels of Today: Exterior and Interior Photographs and Plans* (New York: Architectural Book Publishing Company, Inc., 1929), 7–8.

47 Martin Clary, *Mid-Manhattan: That Section of the Greater City of New York Between Washington Square and Central Park and the East and North Rivers in the Borough of Manhattan* (New York: Forty-Second Street Property Owners and Merchants Association, Inc., 1929), 81.

48 Andrew Dolkart's "Millionaires' Elysiums," provides very good descriptions of these hotels and has been a valuable source—along with other works cited—for the section that follows.

49 "Hotel Netherland Closes its Doors," *The New York Times*, 10 May 1925; "36-Story Hotel to Replace the Netherland on Fifth Av.," *The New York Times*, 25 May 1926.

50 "Modern Appointments for New Netherland," *The New York Times*, 20 June 1926; "New 5th Av. Hotel in Boomer Chain," *The New York Times*, 8 March 1927; "Hotel Netherland Tower Ablaze 38 Stories Above Fifth Avenue," *The New York Times*, 13 April 1927.

51 James M. Dennis, *Karl Bitter: Architectural Sculptor, 1867–1915* (Madison: University of Wisconsin Press, 1967), 19, 23–24; "Sherry-Netherland Ready," *The New York Times*, 25 September 1927.

52 *The Sherry-Netherland* (New York: n.p., n.d.), 3–4, 12.

53 Christopher Matthew, *A Different World: Stories of Great Hotels* (New York and London: Paddington Press Ltd., 1976), 131–33.

54 "Pierre Hotel to Rise on Gerry Home Site," *The New York Times*, 9 February 1929.

55 Sarah Bradford Landau and Carl W. Condit, *Rise of the New York Skyscraper* (New Haven: Yale University Press, 1986), 340.

56 Walter Rendell Storey, "Making the Hotel More Homelike," *The New York Times*, 14 December 1930.

57 "Hotel Pierre, New York City," *Architecture* LXIII, no. 1 (January 1931): 23–32; "Hotel Pierre, New York City," *Architecture and Building*, LXII, no. 11 (November 1930), 310–11, 319–23.

58 Storey, "Making the Hotel Room More Homelike"; see also, "Hotel Pierre, New York City," *Architecture*; "Hotel Pierre, New York City," *Architecture and Building*: 311, 322.

59 Alan Gowans, *The Comfortable House: North American Suburban Architecture 1890–1930* (Cambridge, Mass.: MIT Press, 1986), 144. See also Braden, *Architecture of Leisure*, 73; and Samuel G. White, *The Houses of McKim, Mead & White* (New York: Rizzoli International Publications, 1998), 236.

60 Display advertisement, *The New York Times*, 26 October 1930; "R. L. Gerry Jr. Gives Bachelor Dinner," *The New York Times*, 22 April 1934.

61 "Straus Loan Placed on Hotel Lexington," *The New York Times*, 2 May 1928; "Hotel Lexington, New York City," *Architecture and Building* LXII, no. 2 (February 1930): 35.

62 Robert A. M. Stern, Gregory Gilmartin, and Thomas Mellins, *New York 1930: Architecture and Urbanism Between the Two World Wars* (New York: Rizzoli, 1987), 212.

63 "The Lexington—Ready Tomorrow," *The New York Times*, 14 October 1929.

64 Horace Sutton, *Confessions of a Grand Hotel: The Waldorf-Astoria* (Harry Holt and Company, 1951), 40–44; Frank Crowninshield, ed., *The Unofficial Palace of New York: A Tribute to the Waldorf-Astoria* (New York: Hotel Waldorf-Astoria Corporation, 1939), 1; "40-Story Waldorf to Rise in Park Av.," *The New York Times*, 9 March 1929; "New Waldorf Gets Own Rail Siding," *The New York Times*, 8 September 1929; "Huge Organ For Waldorf," *The New York Times*, 20 May 1930; "Gold-Plated Doorknobs for the New Waldorf-Astoria," *The New York Times*, 2 July 1930; "New Waldorf to Get $200,000 Radio Plant," *The New York Times*, 9 August 1930; "Huge Phone System for New Waldorf," *The New York Times*, 10 August 1930.

65 Paul Goldberger, *The Skyscraper* (New York: Alfred A. Knopf, 1982), 97–98.

66 Murchison, "The Drawings for the New Waldorf-Astoria," 32.

67 Leonard Schultze, "The Plan," *Building Investment* VII, no. 5 (January 1932): 26.

68 Schultze, "The Plan," 27; Schultze, "The Waldorf-Astoria Hotel," 276.

69 Schultze, "The Plan," 27; Schultze, "The Waldorf-Astoria Hotel," 271–75, 278–80; Francis A. Lenygon, "Furnishing and Decoration," in *The Unofficial Palace of New York*, 35, 38.

70 Schultze, "The Waldorf-Astoria," 264, 266, 295–97; Lenygon, "Furnishing and Decoration," 34; Edward Alden Jewell, "Art," *The New York Times*, 27 September 1931.

71 Decorators included Sir Charles Allom; Barton, Price & Wilson, Inc.; W. & J. Sloane; Jacques Bodart, Inc.; R. T. H. Halsey; Arthur S. Vernay, Inc.; and Mrs. Charles H. Sabin.

72 Schultze, "The Plan," 27; Schultze, "The Waldorf-Astoria," 276–77, 286–87; Lenygon, "Furnishing and Decoration," 40–41, 43–45.

73 Lewis Musmford, "The Skyline: Unconscious Architecture," *New Yorker*, 13 February 1932, reprinted in *Sidewalk Critic: Lewis Mumford's Writings on New York*, ed. Robert Wojtowicz (New York: Princeton Architectural Press, 1998), 70.

74 Sutton, *Confessions of a Grand Hotel*, 50–51, 53; Annabel Wharton, "Two Waldorf-Astorias: Spatial Economies as Totem and Fetish," *Art Bulletin* LXXXV, no. 3 (September 2003): 539.

75 "Hotel Pierre Files Bankruptcy Plea," *The New York Times*, 8 March 1932; "Hotel Pierre Bankrupt," *The New York Times*, 30 April 1939; "Hotel Lexington in Receiver's Hands," *The New York Times*, 11 March 1932; "Miami Biltmore Closed," *The New York Times*, 13 March 1929; LaRoue and Uguccioni, *The Biltmore Hotel*, 65; Pfueller-Davidson, "Early Twentieth-Century Hotel Architects," 33.

76 Information about the firm's projects in the years after 1931 comes from the document prepared by Lloyd Morgan, "Historical Background of the Firm" (January 1962), Schultze & Weaver collection, The Wolfsonian–FIU.

1 Anthony Trollope, *North America* (1862; reprinted New York: Alfred A, Knopf, 1951), 480.

2 Henry James, *The American Scene* (1907; reprinted New York: Horizon, 1967), 102.

3 The most useful sources on hotel history include Elaine Denby, *Grand Hotels: Reality and Illusion* (London: Reaktion Books, 1998); Christopher Matthew, *A Different World: Stories of Great Hotels* (New York & London: Paddington Press Ltd., 1976); Brian McGinty, "America Invents the Hotel," in *The Palace Inns: A Connoisseurs Guide to Historic American Homes* (Harrisburg: Stackpole Books, 1978); Hilary Rubinstein, *Hotels and Inns* (Oxford: Oxford University Press, 1984); David Watkin, *Grand Hotel: The Golden Age of Palace Hotels: An Architectural and Social History* (New York: Viking Press, 1984); Arthur White, *Palaces of the People: A Social History of Commercial Hospitality* (New York: Taplinger Publishing Company, 1968); and David B. Wolinski, *Historic Hotels of America* (Washington, D.C.: Preservation Press, National Trust for Historic Preservation, 1994). The classic text on the history of hotels in America is Jefferson Williamson, *The American Hotel* (1930; reprinted New York: Arno Press, 1975).

In addition, several dissertations on historic hotels examining their social, economic, and technological functions, have appeared in recent years. They include Molly Winger Berger, "The Modern Hotel in America, 1829-1929" (Ph.D. dissertation, Case Western Reserve University, 1997); Lisa Pfueller Davidson, "Consumption and Efficiency in the 'City within a City': Commercial Hotel Architecture and the Emergence of Modern American Culture, 1890-1930" (Ph.D. dissertation, George Washington University, 2003); and Andrew K. Sandoval-Strauss, "For Accommodation of Strangers: Urban Space, Travel, Law, the Market, and Modernity at the American Hotel, 1789-1908" (Ph.D. dissertation, University of Chicago, 2002).

4 E. L. Potter, "Operating American Resort Hotels," *Hotel Management,* January 1923, 26.

5 White, *Palaces of the People*, 130.

6 William Havard Eliot, *A Description of the Tremont House* (Boston: Gray and Bowden, 1830), 1–2.

7 Russell Lynes, *The Taste-Makers* (New York: Harper & Brothers, 1954), 83. For further discussion of the Tremont and its architect, Isaiah Rogers, see Elizabeth Fizpatrick Jones, "Hotel Design in the Work of Isaiah Rogers and Henry Whitestone," in *Victorian Resorts and Hotels*, ed. Richard Guy Wilson (Philadelphia: Victorian Society in America, 1982), 33–37; and Henry F. Wilthey and E. R. Wilthey, *Biographical Dictionary of American Architects* (Los Angeles: New Age Publishing Company, 1956), 522.

8 Lynes, *The Taste-Makers*, 85, 86.

9 See *Godey's Ladies Book and Magazine 60* (May 1860): 465. See also Berger, "The Modern Hotel," 136-47. The Continental Hotel became the premier hotel in Philadelphia after its opening. A branch of the hotel was showcased at the 1876 Centennial Exhibition in Philadelphia as an example of the latest modern hotel design. See *Harper's Weekly,* Jan. 1, 1876, n.p.

10 For more on the Palmer House, see Catherine Cocks, *Doing the Town: The Rise of Urban Tourism in the United States, 1850–1915* (Berkeley: University of California Press, 2001), 79; Leslie Dorsey and Janice Devine, *Fare Thee Well* (New York: Crown Publishers, Inc., 1964); and Wallace Rice, *Palmer House, Old and New* (Chicago: R. R. Donnelly and Sons Company, 1925).

11 *Frank Leslie's Illustrated Newspaper* 45 (1878). See also "American Hotel Luxury," *Harper's Weekly,* May 8, 1875, n.p.; Berger, "The Modern Hotel," 182–210; Denby, *Grand Hotels*, 36; Lynes, *The Taste-Makers*, 85.

12 "Astor House," *Home Journal,* April 7, 1849, quoted in Carolyn Brucken, "In the Public Eye: Women and the American Luxury Hotel," *Winterthur Portfolio* 31:4 (1996): 203–20, 219.

13 For further discussion of gender and hotel spaces, see especially Berger, "The Modern Hotel"; Brucken, *In the Public Eye*; Davidson, *Consumption and Efficiency*; Katherine C. Grier, *Culture and Comfort: People, Parlors and Upholstery, 1850–1930* (Amherst: University of Massachusetts Press, 1988), 29–38.

14 H. J. Hardenbergh, "Hotel," in Russell Sturgis, *A Dictionary of Architecture and Building, Biographical, Historical, and Descriptive*, vol. 2 (New York: The Macmillan Co., 1902), 410; also quoted in Berger, "The Modern Hotel," 288.

15 A 1905 article in *Architectural Record* stated that the Waldorf-Astoria "indicated the main lines of the design of a hotel 'sky-scraper'" and went on to claim that the Waldorf was the origin of "the design of the contemporary American hotel." *See* Arthur C. David, "Three New Hotels," *Architectural Record* 17 (March 1905): 168; and William Hutchins, "New York Hotels, II," *Architectural Record* 12 (November 1902): 626.

For further discussion of the original Waldorf-Astoria, see Berger, "The Modern Hotel"; Davidson, "Consumption and Efficiency," 1–13; Denby, *Grand Hotels*, 222–26; Dorsey and Devine, *Fare Thee Well,* 108–28; and Williamson, *American Hotel,* 70-75. For contemporary accounts, see Frank Crowninshield, ed. *The Unofficial Palace of New York: A Tribute to the Waldof-Astoria* (New York: Hotel Waldorf-Astoria Corporation, 1939); Edward Hungerford, *The Story of the Waldorf-Astoria* (New York: Knickerbocker Press, 1925); Henry B. Lent, *The Waldorf-Astoria* (New York: Hotel Waldorf-Astoria Corporation, 1934); Ward Morehouse, III, *The Waldorf-Astoria: American's Gilded Dream* (New York: M. Evans and Company, Inc., 1991).

16 Article about the Waldorf-Astoria from *Scientific American* (1897), quoted in Dorsey and Devine, *Fare Thee Well,* 120, 111.

17 Hardenbergh, quoted in Nikolaus Pevsner, *A History of Building* Types (Princeton: Princeton University Press, 1976), 181.

18 Cocks, *Doing the Town,* 84.

19 Brown, *The Plaza*, 15–18; "The Plaza of New York," *Hotel Monthly* 15, no. 176 (November 1907): 18.

20 Dorsey and Devine, *Fare Thee Well*, 137–39. A night at the Plaza cost $2.50 to $4 for rooms without a private bath; $3 to $6 for rooms with a bath; $6 to $10 for double rooms; $12 to $20 for suites; and $16 to $25 for suites with a parlor, two bedrooms and two baths. See Brown, *The Plaza,* 32.

21 David, "Three New Hotels," 183; Wolinski, *Historic Hotels of America*, 64.

22 As social theorist Dean MacCannell explained, tourism is the process of commodifying therapeutic experience. See MacCannell, *The Tourist: A New Theory of the Leisure Class* (1976; reprinted Berkeley: University of California Press, 1999), 39–46.

23 Charles E. Funnell, *By the Beautiful Sea: The Rise and High Times of that Great, American Resort, Atlantic City* (New York: Alfred A. Knopf, 1975), 3–4.

24 Jeffrey Limerick, Nancy Ferguson, and Richard Oliver, *America's Grand Resort Hotels* (New York: Pantheon Books, 1979), 27–28.

25 Cindy S. Aron, *Working at Play: A History of Vacations in the United States* (New York: Oxford University Press, 1999), 105–06.

26 Aron, *Working at Play*, 188; and Bryant Simon, *Boardwalk of Dreams: Atlantic City and the Fate of Urban America* (New York: Oxford University Press, 2004), 19–21.

27 Frank M. Butler, *The Book of the Boardwalk* (Atlantic City: The 1954 Association, 1952), 1–14; Vicki Gold Levy and Lee Eisenberg, *Atlantic City: 125 Years of Ocean Madness* (Berkeley, Calif.: Ten Speed Press, 1979), 17–25; and William McMahon, *So Young . . . So Gay* (Atlantic City: Press Publishing, 1970), 100–01.

28 McMahon, *So Young . . . So Gay*, 100–01.

29 Levy and Eisenberg, *Atlantic City*, 28–37.

30 *The New York Times,* 18 December 1901.

31 Limerick et al., *America's Grand Resort Hotels*, 161. For a thorough discussion of William L. Price and his changing design ideals, see George E. Thomas, *William L. Price: From Arts and Crafts to Modern Design* (New York: Princeton Architectural Press, 2000).

32 William T. [sic] Price, "The Possibilities of Concrete Construction from the Standpoint of Utility and Art," published by the American Portland Cement Manufacturers Association as "Bulletin #2," reprinted in *American Architecture and Building News* 89, no. 1579 (March 24, 1906): 120.

33 William L. Price, quoted in Thomas, *William L. Price,* 135.

34 Ibid., 2.

35 George Edgell, *The American Architecture of Today* (New York: Charles Scribner's Sons, 1928), 342. See also *Architectural Record* 27 (November 1917): 119–23, for a positive reaction to the Traymore.

36 Limerick et al., *America's Grand Resort Hotels*, 161. See also Richard Guy Wilson, "Nineteenth Century American Resorts and Hotels," in *Victorian Resorts and Hotels* (Philadelphia: Victorian Society in America, 1982), 19.

37 A. Hyatt Verrill, *Romantic and Historic Florida* (New York: Dodd, Mead & Company, 1935), 66.

38 Funnell, *By the Beautiful Sea*, 5.

39 Susan R. Braden, *The Architecture of Leisure: The Florida Resort Hotels of Henry Flagler and Henry Plant* (Gainesville: University Press of Florida, 2002), 135–42, 145–78; Denby, *Grand Hotels* (London: Reaktion Books, 1998), 229; and Limerick et al., *America's Grand Resort Hotels*, 82–86.

40 Braden, *Architecture of Leisure*, 157–73; and Limerick et al., *America's Grand Resort Hotels*, 82–86. See also the advertising brochures for the Florida East Coast Railway, especially *FEC Railroad and Hotels* (St. Augustine, Fla.: FEC Railway Company, 1902–03); and *Resume of the Famous Luxurious East Coast Hotels* (St. Augustine, Fla.: FEC Railway Company, 1904).

41 Braden, *Architecture of Leisure*, 208–22; Limerick et al., *America's Grand Resort Hotels*, 95–97; Theodore Pratt, *That Was Palm Beach* (St. Petersburg, Fla.: Great Outdoors, 1968), 19–38; and "The Industrious Time Killers," *Hotel Monthly*, May 1922, quoted in Norman S. Hayner, *Hotel Life* (Chapel Hill: University of North Carolina Press, 1936), 136.

42 James, *The American Scene,* 449.

43 Pratt, *That Was Palm Beach*, 24.

44 Braden, *Architecture of Leisure*, 319; Limerick et al., *America's Grand Resort Hotels*, 177.

45 Braden, *Architecture of Leisure,* 321–29.

46 *Cocoanut Grove by Biscayne Bay: The Land of Perpetual June*, published by the Cocoanut Grove Development Company (1910), courtesy of Richter Library Special Collections, University of Miami. Other promotional materials highlighted the benefits of sunshine, including C. H. Ward, *The Lure of the Southland: Miami and Miami Beach, Florida* (Miami: s.n., 1915); and *Miami by the Sea: The Land of Palms and Sunshine* (Miami: Chamber of Commerce, 1919).

47 *Cocoanut Grove*, n.p.

48 For further discussion of George Merrick and Coral Gables, see Roberto M. Behar and Maurice G. Culot, eds., *Coral Gables: An American Garden City* (Paris: Norma Editions, 1997); *Coral Gables: A Brief History* (Coral

Gables: Department of Historic Preservation, 1989); and *Coral Gables: Florida's Most Beautiful and Finest Developed Suburb at Miami* (Coral Gables: G. E. Merrick, 1924).

49 Quoted in David B. Wolinksi, ed., *Historic Hotels of America* (Washington, D.C.: Preservation Press, National Trust for Historic Preservation, 1994), 78.

50 *The Miami Biltmore* (New York: John McEntee Bownan, 1926), 5. For further discussion of the Coral Gables Biltmore, see *The Biltmore Revisited* (Coral Gables: Metropolitan Museum and Art Center, 1981); and Samuel D. LaRoue, Jr., and Ellen J. Uguccioni, *The Biltmore Hotel: An Enduring Legacy* (Miami: Arva Parks & Company Centennial Press, 2002).

51 Mark S. Foster, *Castles in the Sand: The Life and Times of Carl Graham Fischer* (Gainesville: University Press of Florida, 2000), 44, 55, 75–79; Howard Kleinberg, *Miami Beach: A History* (Miami: Centennial Press, 1994), 27–36; Abraham D. Lavender, *Miami Beach in 1920* (Charleston, S.C.: Arcadia Publishing, 2002); J. N. Lummus, *The Miracle of Miami Beach* (Miami: Miami Post Publishing Company, 1952); Helen Muir, *Miami, U.S.A.* (1953; reprinted Miami: Pickering Press, 1990); Polly Redford, *Billion-Dollar Sandbar: A Biography of Miami Beach* (New York: E. P. Dutton and Co., 1970), 54–64; and F. Page Wilson, *Miami, From Frontier to Metropolis* (Miami: Historical Association of Southern Florida, 1956), 27–28.

52 Foster, *Castles in the Sand,* 146.

53 Redford, *Billion-Dollar Sandbar*, 15. See also, "First Polo in Florida on Beach Grounds Today," *Miami Metropolis*, 20 February 1919.

54 *Miami Metropolis*, quoted in Redford, *Billion-Dollar Sandbar,* 68.

55 *Miami Metropolis*, 6 January 1920.

56 Redford, *Billion-Dollar Sandbar*, 124.

57 Indian Creek Drive, postcard, Florida Postcard Collection, Archives and Special Collections, Otto G. Richter Library, University of Miami.

58 Montmartre Hotel, postcard, Florida Postcard Collection, Archives and Special Collections, Otto G. Richter Library, University of Miami.

59 "Beautiful Flamingo is Opened Formally with New Year's Eve Party," *Miami Metropolis*, 4 January 1921; Jean-François Lejeune and Allan T. Shulman, *The Making of Miami Beach, 1933–1942: The Architecture of Lawrence Murray Dixon* (Miami Beach: Bass Museum of Art and Rizzoli, 2000), 17.

60 Redford, *Billion-Dollar Sandbar*, 127.

61 Ibid., 126–27.

62 "Naturalist Brings Flamingo to Beach," *Miami Herald*, 18 October 1921. See also, Kleinberg, *Miami Beach*, 60. Fisher also hired childrens' book illustrator N. C. Wyeth to decorate the lobby and other public rooms at the Flamingo, marking another collaboration between Price and McLanahan and Wyeth (Wyeth also decorated the childrens' playroom at the Traymore). See Thomas, *William L. Price*, 166.

63 Kleinberg, *Miami Beach*, 61; "Beautiful Flamingo is Opened," *Miami Metropolis*, 4 January 1921.

64 Redford, *Billion-Dollar Sandbar*, 127.

65 Lavender, *Miami Beach*, 88–89.

66 Quoted in Barbara Baer Capitman, ed., *Time Present, Time Past: The Art Deco District* (Miami Beach: Miami Design Preservation League, 1980), 9.

67 See "Miami Herald Personals," *Miami Herald*, beginning in 1921, for lists of balls, charity functions, and guests at Miami and Miami Beach hotels.

68 "Tea Dance at the Nautilus," 1925, postcard, Florida Postcard Collection, Archives and Special Collections, Otto G. Richter Library, University of Miami. See also, "Nautilus Tea Dance Opens Quaint Garden," *Miami Herald*, 1 February 1924.

69 From *Dade County, Florida Deed Book*, vol. 112, 88, March 19, 1914, quoted in Kleinberg, *Miami Beach*, 52.

70 *Miami Metropolis*, 2 January 1921.

71 Redford notes that, while many people recount their memories of the "No Jews or Dogs" signs, she could not find evidence of them. She does say that there was an apartment in the 1930s near 43rd Street that featured a sign reading "Gentiles Only. No Dogs." Redford, *Billion-Dollar Sandbar*, 214. See advertising brochures for Miami Beach hotels that were "Restricted" or "For Gentiles Only" in the Mark F. Boyd Collection, Florida Promotional Materials, #37, series 6, Archives and Special Collections, Otto G. Richter Library, University of Miami. For further discussion of anti-Semitism in South Florida, see Raymond A. Mohl, *South of the South: Jewish Activists and the Civil Rights Movement in Miami, 1945–1960* (Gainesville: University Press of Florida, 2004), 20–25; and Deborah Dash Moore, *To the Golden Cities: Pursuing the American Jewish Dream in Miami and L.A.* (Cambridge, Mass.: Harvard University Press, 1994), 48, 154–55, 167–71.

72 Kleinberg, *Miami Beach*, 74–76; Redford, *Billion-Dollar Sandbar*, 211–15.

73 "Million in Realty Sold in Nineteen Days," *Miami Herald*, 24 January 1924.

74 Letter from Carl Fisher to John LaGorce, 4 December 1920, quoted in Kleinberg, *Miami Beach*, 60–61.

75 Limerick et al., *America's Grand Resorts*, 97.

76 Simon, *Boardwalk of Dreams*, 68–69.

77 Braden, *Architecture of Leisure*, 128; Limerick et al., *America's Grand Resorts*, 86.

78 For discussion of the impact Jewish migrants had on reshaping the character of Miami Beach, see Kleinberg, *Miami Beach*, 117, 128; Lejeune and Shulman, *Making of Miami Beach*, 32–34; Moore, *To the Golden Cities*, 53–92; Redford, *Billion-Dollar Sandbar*, 204–15.

79 Allan Shulman, "Miami Beach as Urban Assemblage: A Unique Culture of Housing," *The New City 3: Modern Cities* (New York: Princeton Architectural Press, 1996), 25–49.

80 Lejeune and Shulman, *Making of Miami Beach*, 40–72.

THE SKYSCRAPER AND THE CITY

1 "Mr. Murchison of New York Says," *The Architect* 12 (May 1929): 219.

2 Edwin H. Spengler, "Land Economics," *American Economic Review*, supplement, 19 (March 1929): 52.

3 "Lexington Avenue Changing Rapidly," *The New York Times*, 6 May 1928; "Trend Toward Apartment House Living in American Cities," *Monthly Labor Review* 26 (June 1928): 61.

4 "Park Avenue Fights Trade Invasion," *The New York Times*, 3 March 1929.

5 "Artistic Buildings for Lexington Avenue," *The New York Times*, 3 January 1932; "Park Avenue Apartment Area Continues to Expand Northward," *The New York Times*, 7 September 1930; *Julius Forstmann v. Joray Holding Company*, 244 N.Y. 22 (1926); "French Shop Type on Fifth Avenue," *The New York Times*, 29 May 1928; Louis G. Kibbe, "Present Status of Cooperative Apartment Promotion and Finance," *Architectural Forum* XXXXVIII, no. 1 (January 1928): 117, 118.

6 Ethel M. Smith, "America's Domestic Servant Shortage," *Current History* 26 (May 1927): 214.

7 "The Passing of the Household Servant," *Literary Digest* 74 (July 8, 1922): 19, 20.

8 "Hired Girl Now Almost Extinct," *The New York Times*, 14 October 1923; "Predicts General Shortage of Labor," *The New York Times*, 8 October 1922; "Immigration Restriction and the 'Scarcity' of Domestic Servants," *Monthly Labor Review* 25 (July 1927): 1, 4–5.

9 "Domestic Service Put on Eight-Hour Basis," *The New York Times*, 14 June 1925; I. M. Rubinow, "The Problem of Domestic Service," *The Journal of Political Economy* 14 (October 1906): 512.

10 Smith, "America's Domestic Servant Shortage," 215.

11 Ibid., 216.

12 "Servants Offered by Society Women," *The New York Times*, 2 May 1927.

13 "Park Avenue Changes Made in a Decade," *The New York Times*, 9 November 1924; "Growth of Cooperative Movement Shown by Demand and Building," *The New York Times*, 14 September 1924.

14 Matlack Price, "The Latest Type of American Hotel Apartment," *Arts and Decoration* 21 (September 1924): 41.

15 "Park Avenue Changes Made in a Decade."

16 Ibid. Serving pantries also solved a legal difficulty faced by architects in New York City. Buildings with kitchens were technically tenements and were subject to the height restrictions of the 1901 Tenement Law limiting buildings to 1.5 times the width of the widest street they fronted. Buildings with serving pantries were subject to the more liberal height limits of the 1916 zoning ordinance (see n. 31). Architects could thus design very tall residential buildings on higher priced land. Kibbe, "Present Status of Cooperative Apartment Promotion and Finance," 118, and "$100,000,000 Hotels Halted by Deegan," *The New York Times*, 20 June 1929.

17 "As Per Schedule!" advertisement for the Sherry-Netherland, *The New York Times*, 14 April 1927.

18 "Real Estate Transaction 1—No Title," *The New York Times*, 13 March 1927.

19 "Boxing Titled Settled in Sherry-Netherland," *The New York Times*, 19 February 1928.

20 "Pierre Hotel to Rise on Gerry Home Site," *The New York Times*, 9 February 1929.

21 "5th Av. Hotel Gets a $6,500,000 Loan," *The New York Times*, April 18, 1929; "Sees Society Trend Back to Fifth Av.," *The New York Times*, 15 July 1930.

22 "Sees Society Trend Back to Fifth Av."

23 "Charles Pierre, Hotel Man, Dead," *The New York Times*, 9 October 1934.

24 "Louis Sherry Dies: Famous Caterer," *The New York Times*, 10 June 1926.

25 Ibid.

26 Ibid.

27 Arthur C. David, "The St. Regis—The Best Type of Metropolitan Hotel," *Architectural Record* 15 (June 1904): 552–600; "The Hotel Astor," *Architects' and Builders' Magazine* 6 (November 1904): 49–71, 61; "The Hotel Knickerbocker," *Architects' and Builders' Magazine* 8 (December 1906): 89-102.

28 "Novel Features in the New Zone Hotel," *The New York Times*, 14 October 1929.

29 Ibid.

30 Leonard Schultze, "The Architecture of the Modern Hotel," *Architectural Forum* XXXIX, no. 5 (November 1923): 202.

31 Schultze, "The Architecture of the Modern Hotel," 204, 199. On the zoning ordinance, see Keith D. Revell,

"Law Makes Order: The Search for Ensemble in the Skyscraper City, 1890–1930," in *The American Skyscraper: Cultural Histories*, ed. Roberta Moudry (New York: Cambridge University Press, 2005). Carol Willis, "Zoning and *Zeitgeist*: The Skyscraper in the 1920s," *Journal of the Society of Architectural Historians* 45 (March 1986): 47–59.

32 Commission on Building Districts and Restrictions, *Final Report* (New York: Board of Estimate and Apportionment, Committee on the City Plan, 1916), 237.

33 Ibid., 262–63.

34 "New 5th Avenue Hotel in Boomer Chain," *The New York Times*, 8 March 1927.

35 "Skyscraper Ban on Upper Fifth Avenue Lifted by Court," *The New York Times* 6 November 1923; *Matter of Palmer v. Mann*, 237 N.Y. 616 (1924).

36 "World's Tallest Hotel Built on Stilts Over Railway," *Popular Mechanics* 56 (December 1931): 979–80.

37 Mary Fanton Roberts, "A New Ideal in City Living," *Arts and Decoration* 35 (October 1931): 50–51.

38 "Oscar of Waldorf Dead at Age of 84," *The New York Times*, 8 November 1950.

THE HOTEL MACHINE

1 Steven Millhauser, *Martin Dressler* (New York: Vintage Books, 1997), 24.

2 Molly Winger Berger, "The Modern Hotel in America, 1829–1929" (Ph.D. dissertation, Case Western Reserve University, 1997). Catherine Cocks, *Doing the Town: The Rise of Urban Tourism in the United States, 1850–1915* (Berkeley: University of California Press, 2001).

3 J. Otis Post, "Efficient Planning for Economical Operation," *Architectural Forum* LI, no. 6 (December 1929): 667–68.

4 Ibid.

5 Lucius Boomer, *Hotel Management: Principles and Practice* (New York: Harper Brothers, 1931), 318.

6 Clyde R. Place, "Wheels Behind the Scenes," in *The Unofficial Palace of New York: A Tribute to the Waldorf-Astoria,* ed. Frank Crowninshield (New York: Hotel Waldorf-Astoria Corporation, 1939), 57–67.

7 Kenneth Murchison, "Architecture," in *Unofficial Palace of New York*, 19–22.

8 Albert E. Merrill, "The Planning and Equipment of Hotel Kitchens," *Architectural Forum* XXXIX, no. 5 (November 1923): 234.

9 Ibid.

10 James S. Warren, "The Present Status of the Hotel Business," *Architectural Forum* LI, no. 6 (December 1929): 711–14.

11 Boomer, *Hotel Management*, 8.

12 Daniel Ritchey, "Economics of the Hotel Project," *Architectural Forum* XXXIX, no. 6 (November 1923): 220.

13 Boomer, *Hotel Management*, 1.

14 Lisa Pfueller Davidson, "Early Twentieth-Century Hotel Architects and the Origins of Standardization," *Journal of Decorative and Propaganda Arts* 25 (2005): 74.

15 Parker Morse Hooper, "The New Hotel," *Architectural Forum* XI, no. 6 (December 1929): 583–601.

16 Ibid., 583.

17 As architect Kenneth Murchison noted, Schultze & Weaver were among a small group practicing the increasingly complex art of hotel design. Kenneth M. Murchison, "The Drawings for the New Waldorf-Astoria," *American Architect* 139 (January 1931): 30.

18 Andrew Dolkart, "Millionaires' Elysiums: The Luxury Apartment Hotels of Schultz and Weaver," *Journal of Decorative and Propaganda Arts* 25 (2005): 12–14.

19 W. Sydney Wagner, "The Hotel Plan," *Architectural Forum* XXXIX, no. 5 (November 1923): 218.

20 Post, "Efficient Planning for Economical Operation," 667.

21 Ibid.

22 David Hounshell, *From the American System to Mass Production, 1800–1932* (Baltimore: Johns Hopkins University Press, 1984); Lindy Biggs, *The Rational Factory: Architecture, Technology, and Work in America's Age of Mass Production* (Baltimore: Johns Hopkins University Press, 1984).

23 Wagner, "The Hotel Plan," 211–18.

24 Boomer, *Hotel Management*, 30, 152.

25 John J. Phillips, "The Hotel Laundry," *Architectural Forum* XXXIX, no. 5 (November 1923): 235.

26 L. M. Boomer, "How We Fitted Ford's Principles to Our Business," *System* 44, no. 4 (October, 1923): 423–24; Boomer, *Hotel Management*, 30.

27 The machines that ironed hotel laundry looked like they came out of a modern textile mill, with massive rollers turned by gears and belts. The cylindrical washing machines and water extractors looked like small electric turbines from a power plant, stacked in double rows in the basement. Phillips, "The Hotel Laundry," 235–37.

28 For example, there was a specified number of butter pats per pound. See Boomer, *Hotel Management*, 89, for more. On the importance of information in business and tools for managing it, see JoAnne Yates, *Control Through Communication: The Rise of System in American Management* (Baltimore: Johns Hopkins University Press, 1989).

29 Boomer, *Hotel Management*, 9, 169.

30 Boomer, "How We Fitted Ford's Principles," 421.

31 Leonard Schultze, "The Architecture of the Modern Hotel," *Architectural Forum* XXXIX, no. 5 (November 1923): 204.

32 William Hull Stangle, "Planning the Hotel for Maximum Flexibility and Utility," *Architectural Forum* XI, no. 6 (December 1929): 723–27.

33 Wagner, "The Hotel Plan," 218.

34 Place, "Wheels Behind the Scenes," 57.

35 Horace Leland Wiggins, "Service and Administration Requirements," *Architectural Forum* XXXIX, no. 6 (November 1923): 241.

36 Ibid.

37 A. K. Sandoval-Strausz and Daniel Levinson Wilk, "Princes and Maids of the City Hotel: The Cultural Politics of Commercial Hospitality in America," *Journal of Decorative and Propaganda Arts* 25 (2005): 161–85.

38 Boomer, *Hotel Management*, 232.

39 The Waldorf-Astoria's opening night featured a speech telephoned in by President Herbert Hoover. It was a symbolic choice, for Hoover's brand of moderate Republicanism emphasized science, efficiency, and professional competence.

40 J. Leslie Kincaid, "Popular Features that Sell Hotel Service," *Architectural Forum* XXXIX, no. 5 (November 923): 197. Emphasis in the original.

41 Boomer, *Hotel Management*, 96.

42 Ibid., 295.

43 Murchison, "Architecture," 24.

44 Post, "Efficient Planning for Economical Operation," 669.

45 Murchison, "The Drawings for the New Waldorf-Astoria," 30.

46 Ibid.

47 Albert E. Merrill, "The Planning and Equipment of Hotel Kitchens," *Architectural Forum* XXXIX, no. 5 (November 1923): 227–32.

48 Murchison, "Architecture," 26.

49 Boomer, *Hotel Management*, 169.

50 Philip Scranton, *Endless Novelty: Specialty Production and American Industrialization, 1865–1925* (Princeton: Princeton University Press, 1997); Regina Blaszczyk, *Imagining Consumers: Design and Innovation from Wedgwood to Corning* (Baltimore: Johns Hopkins University Press, 2000).

51 Dolkart, "Millionaires' Elysiums," 11.

THE HOTELS OF SCHULTZE & WEAVER

LOS ANGELES BILTMORE HOTEL

Los Angeles, California, 1922–23

Commissioned by John McEntee Bowman

Constructed by Scofield Engineering Construction Company

Opened to the public on October 1, 1923

Currently the Millennium Biltmore Hotel, Los Angeles, operated by Millennium Hotels and Resorts

In November 1923, Leonard Schultze's article "The Architecture of the Modern Hotel" appeared in *Architectural Forum*'s hotel issue with photographs of the newly completed Los Angeles Biltmore. The hotel shared many of the attributes of the New York Biltmore Hotel, built a decade earlier by Warren & Wetmore, for which Schultze served as design director.

Like the New York Biltmore, the Los Angeles Biltmore was part of John McEntee Bowman's growing chain. In the early 1920s, Los Angeles was undergoing a tremendous surge in development. Drawn by the sunshine, the booming oil industry, and the glamour and opportunities of Hollywood, Americans from all over the country were flooding into Southern California. The population of Los Angeles grew by an average of one hundred thousand people each year during the 1920s, reaching 2.2 million by 1930. This kind of growth made Los Angeles an attractive place for Bowman to build his first hotel outside of the northeastern United States.

The first large-scale commercial hotel by Schultze & Weaver, the Los Angeles Biltmore was lauded as the biggest hotel west of Chicago. Each of its 1,112 bedrooms had a private bath. Two commercial kitchens and five pantries accommodated over twenty-five hundred diners at a time, including 650 in the grand ballroom. Among the other dining facilities were a men's lounge, grill room, formal dining room, palm room, and supper room, as well as several private dining rooms.

Composed of three massive towers separated by courts on a three-story neoclassical base, the hotel was constructed of steel and reinforced concrete. The towers were finished in light red brick with terra cotta trim; the base, in granite and limestone.

The hotel's entrance, located at the center of the main facade on Olive Street facing Pershing Square, featured a Palladian motif of a classical arch flanked by paired Ionic columns forming an entrance loggia. The massive entrance portal consisted of an ornate cast-iron framework with glass. Bas reliefs of Ceres, goddess of agriculture, and Neptune, god of the sea, and portraits of Christopher Columbus and Vasco Núñez de Balboa were set into the entrance facade.

The main lobby on the ground floor was three stories high with deep barrel vaulting and a gilded, coffered ceiling. Paired corbels decorated with masks projected from the ribs of the ceiling. The focal point of the lobby was a dramatic staircase,

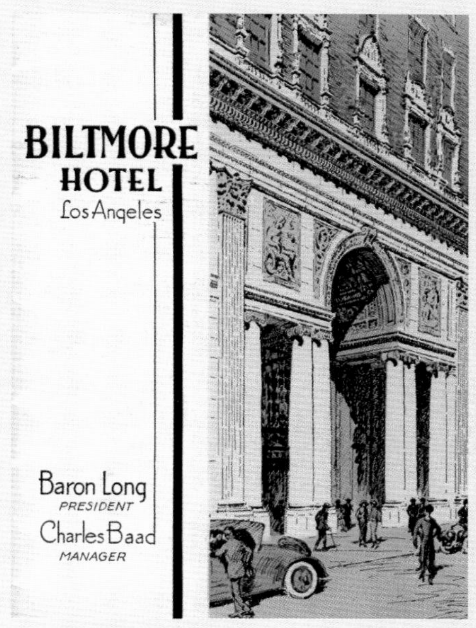

above:
Brochure for the Los Angeles Biltmore Hotel, ca. 1935
This brochure highlights the Biltmore Bowl, the 140- by 107-foot entertainment center where the Academy Awards ceremonies were held beginning in 1935.

opposite:
Entrance facade of the Los Angeles Biltmore Hotel, fronting South Olive Street, ca. 1935

above:
Menu cover for the hotel, after 1923
The Renaissance-inspired design of this piece derives from the ballroom ceiling by Giovanni Smeraldi.

right:
Detail of the main entrance, ca. 1923
Symbols of Los Angeles, Ceres, goddess of agriculture, and Neptune, god of the sea, flank the entrance to the hotel.

opposite:
Detail of the main entrance, from *Architectural Forum* XXXIX, no. 5 (November 1923)

the form of which was derived from the early sixteenth-century staircase in the Burgos Cathedral in Spain. The long gallery entrance to the main ballroom echoed the hotel's main entrance; in this iteration, however, the design featured richly ornamented columns.

Another distinguishing feature of the hotel was the Gallery, a long, through-block passage running the width of the building on the mezzanine level. Decorated in a clever combination of classicism and California lore, it mixed pictures of ancient ruins and goddesses with American Indian scenes. Its ceiling, along with that of the main lobby, was painted by Giovanni Smeraldi, an Italian-born artisan working in Los Angeles.

Nearly one quarter of the $8 million construction budget was spent on the interiors of the hotel. Marble, stone, and plaster finishes on the walls, floors, and ceilings were richly embellished with silk damask upholstery fabrics, crystal chandeliers, and bronze metalwork.

—M.L.

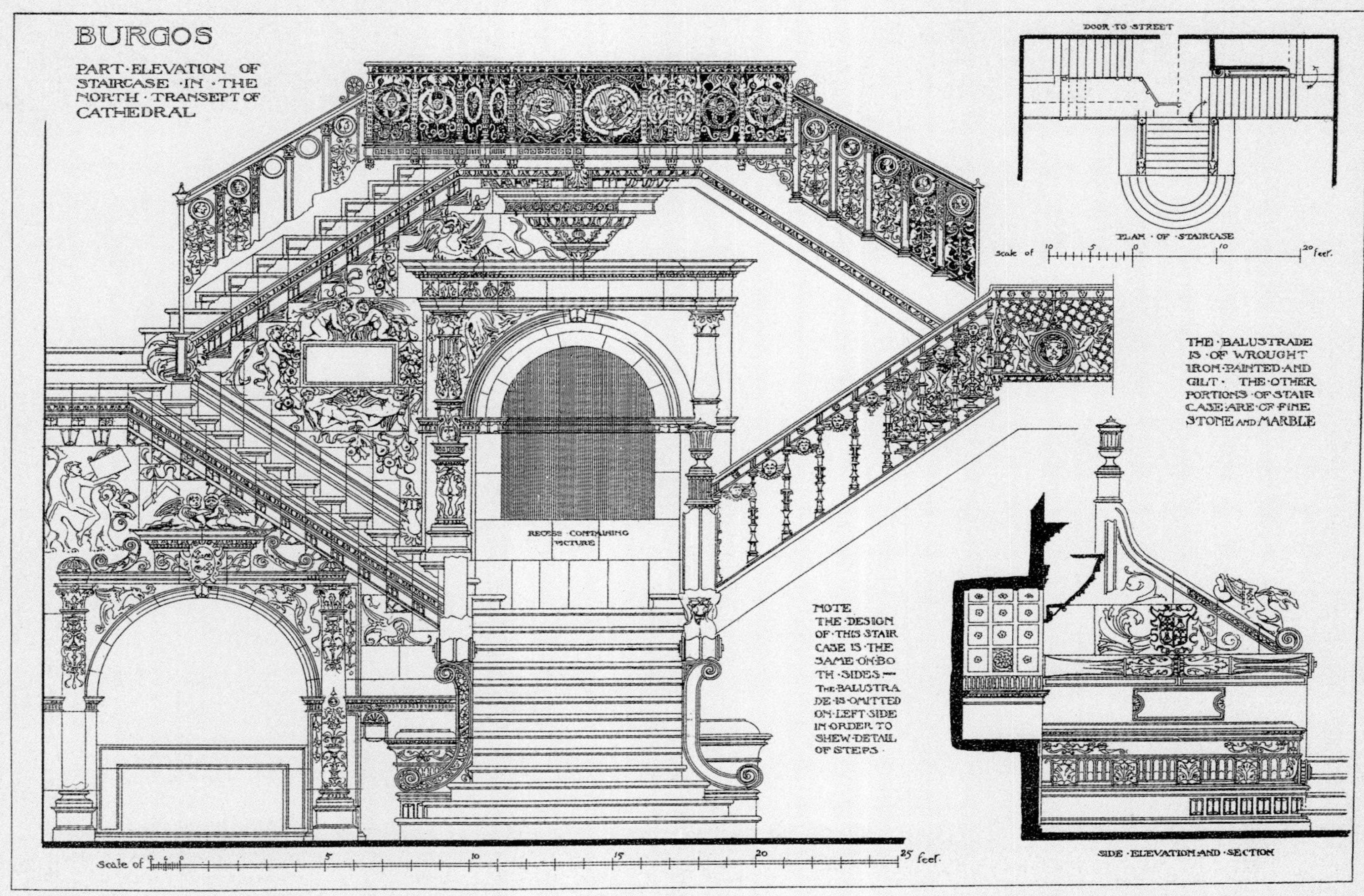

Partial elevation of staircase in Spain's Burgos Cathedral, from Andrew N. Prentice, *Renaissance Architecture and Ornament in Spain* (Washington, D.C.: The Reprint Company, n.d.)

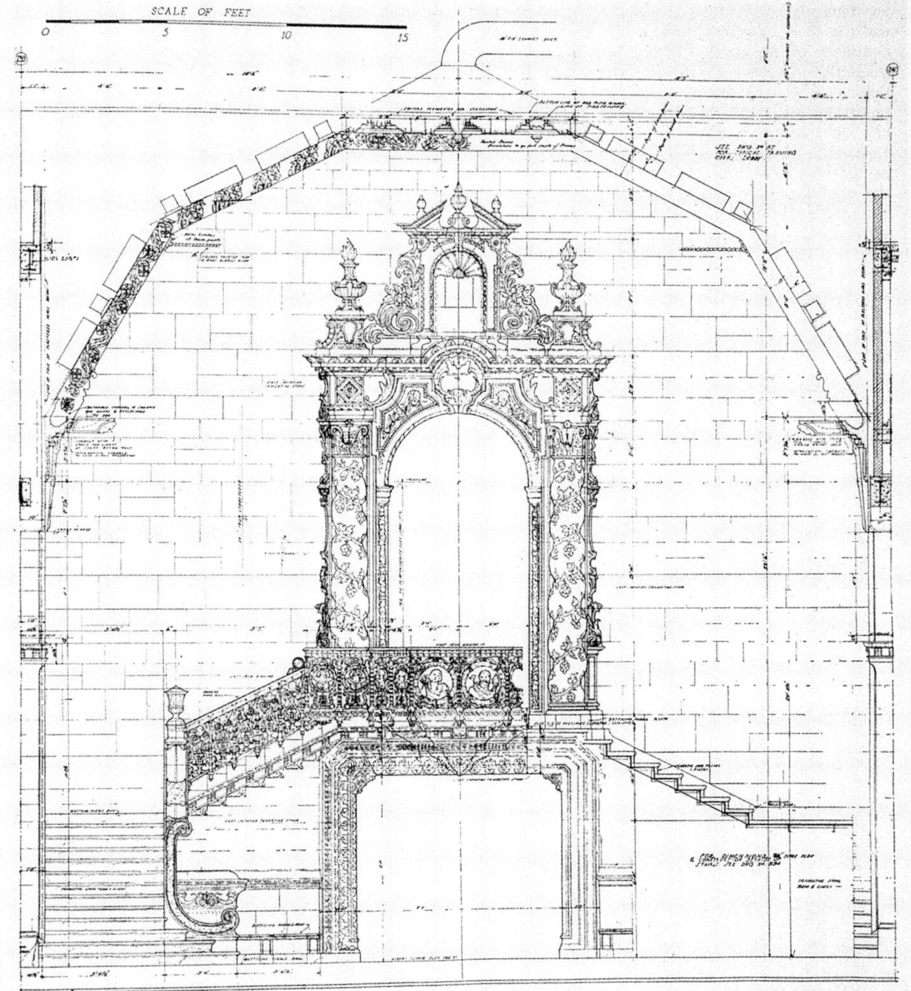

above:

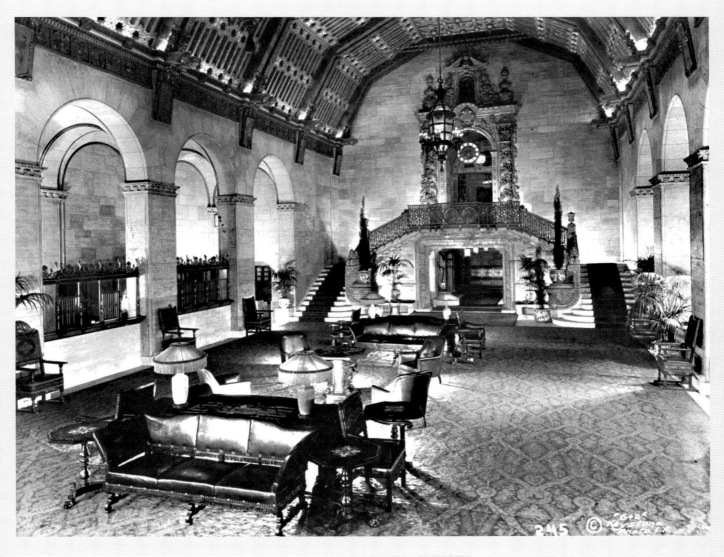

Main lobby, Olive Street, ca. 1923

left:

Plan for lobby staircase, from *Architectural Forum* XXXIX, no. 5 (November 1923)

top:
The Long Gallery, from *Architectural Forum* XXXIX, no. 5 (November 1923)
From this gallery, which ran the length of the hotel on the mezzanine level, guests could enter the ballroom foyer (and through it, the ballroom), the music room, and several large and small dining rooms.

bottom:
Supper room looking into Palm Room, from *Architectural Forum* XXXIX, no. 5 (November 1923)

Ballroom of the Los Angeles Biltmore Hotel, ca. 1923

right:
Detail of the painted ballroom ceiling panels, from *Architectural Forum* XXXIX, no. 5 (November 1923)

opposite:
Los Angeles Biltmore ballroom, from *Architectural Forum* XXXIX, no. 5 (November 1923)

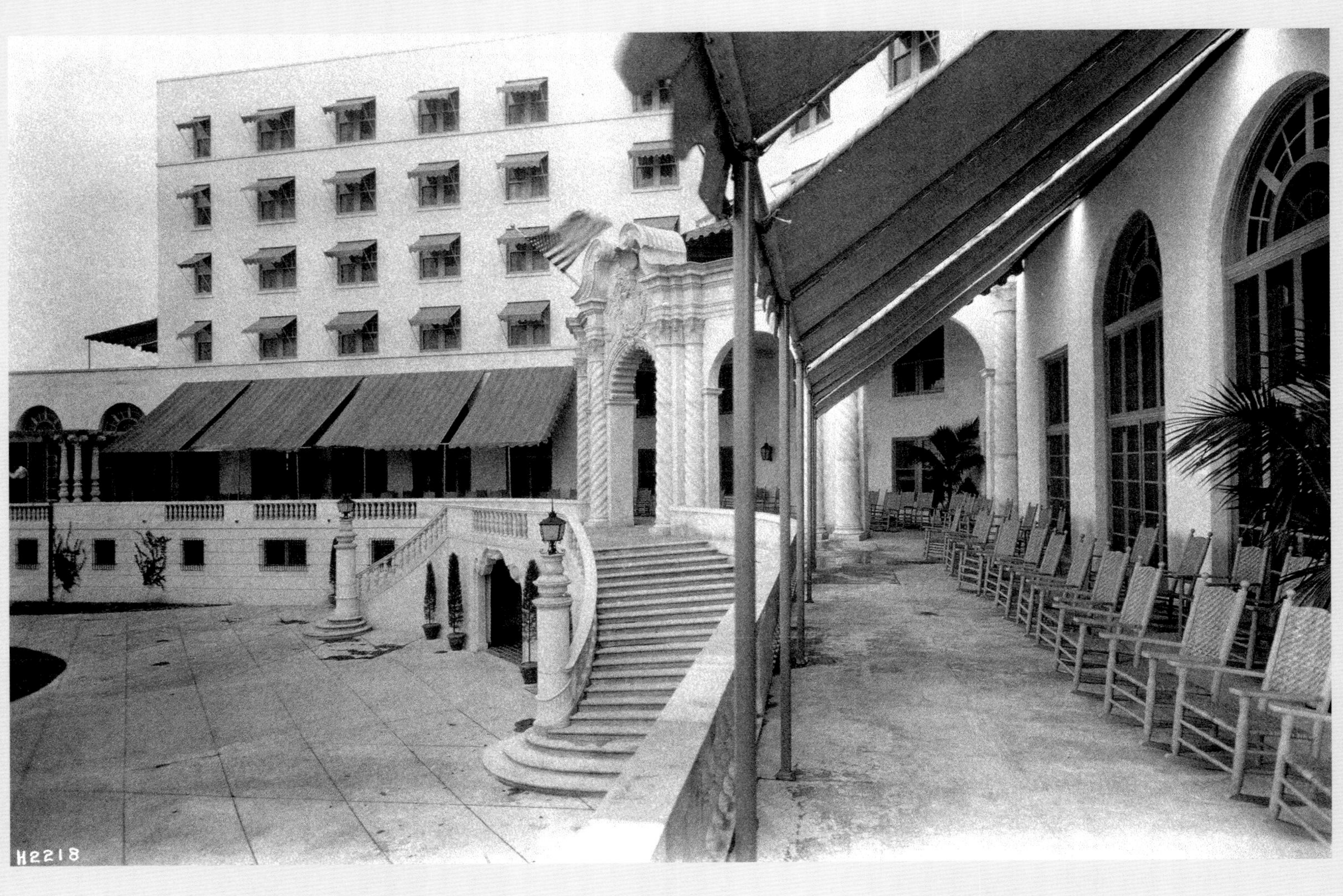
H2218

NAUTILUS HOTEL

Miami Beach, Florida, 1923–24

Commissioned by the Bay Shore Corporation

Constructed by the George A. Fuller Company

Opened to the public on January 15, 1924

Converted to a hospital during World War II and demolished in 1968

In 1923 Schultze and Weaver traveled to Miami Beach to present their plans for the Nautilus Hotel to Carl G. Fisher and Otis M. Fowler, the principal investors in the Bay Shore Corporation. A notice in the *Daily Metropolis* noting that S. Fullerton Weaver was "one of the leading hosts of the winter of 1921 at the Flamingo hotel" may explain why Schultze & Weaver were engaged by Fisher. At that time the firm was already working on several projects for John McEntee Bowman's Biltmore chain, including hotels in Atlanta, Los Angeles, and Havana. The Nautilus commission would be Schultze & Weaver's first resort hotel and their first project in South Florida.

Soon after the Collins Bridge (1913) linked Miami Beach to Miami proper, Fisher built two hotels on the island: the Lincoln Hotel (1917), a small, two-story building with only thirty-five rooms on Lincoln Boulevard, the beach's main east-west artery; and the Flamingo Hotel (1920) on Biscayne Bay, the beach's first large resort hotel with over one hundred and fifty rooms. Intended as the anchor for Fisher's new real estate development, known as the Nautilus subdivision, the new hotel would be located just north of Forty-first Street, far from the city's public amenities—the Lummus Park beach between Fifth and Fifteenth streets and the commercial district clustered below Twenty-third Street. Adjacent to Fisher's Polo Grounds and surrounded by residential properties, the hotel provided guests with transportation to area golf courses and the beach.

The six-story hotel had four fan-shaped arms extending in right angles from each end of a main central building, forming an X. The central portion was surmounted by two matching towers. The hotel's overall massing and layout were similar to Warren & Wetmore's Westchester-Biltmore Country Club (1920–21) in Rye, New York, built during Schultze's tenure with the firm. Its plain stucco surfaces, scalloped gables, and paired towers were inspired by eighteenth- and nineteenth-century Spanish mission architecture found in California and the Southwest, popularized at the 1915 Panama-California Exposition in San Diego. The portico over the hotel's entrance, which projected outward in a semicircle and was supported on twisted columns, shows the influence of Spanish baroque architectural forms.

The exterior staircase and upper gallery of the terraces were framed by a classical balustrade. Although reduced in size, the overall form of the decorative

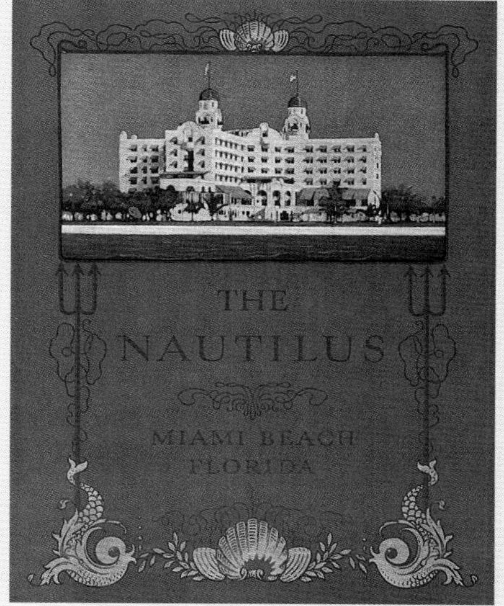

above:
Brochure for the Nautilus Hotel (1924)

opposite:
Rear porch and stairs of the hotel, where guests could enjoy the view of Biscayne Bay, ca. 1924

above:
Postcard with an aerial view of the hotel, after 1929
The Nautilus had no swimming pool when it opened. The pool and cabanas were added to the small island in Biscayne Bay in the late 1920s.

opposite top:
Postcard showing an afternoon tea dance at the Nautilus Hotel, 1924

opposite bottom:
Postcard of the lounge, after 1924

staircase resembled that grand feature in the three-story lobby of Schultze & Weaver's Los Angeles Biltmore Hotel.

With approximately two hundred guest rooms and 140 baths, the Nautilus surpassed the capacity of Fisher's Flamingo Hotel. Its principal public rooms were limited to a large dining room, which boasted seating for 750 patrons, and a lounge accommodating three hundred. Both rooms faced onto Biscayne Bay.

The dining room's Renaissance-inspired decor included a beamed plaster ceiling painted with floral and heraldic ornamentation, supported by paired corbels terminating in grotesque sculptural masks. At the westernmost end of the room, a rounded bay of windows was adorned with upright wooden supports carved with male figures. With an open terrace on its western front and a profusion of tall, glass-paned doors, the dining room combined the lightness and airiness of a garden pavilion with the staid demeanor of a luxurious palace.

The lounge was decorated in a more restrained classical idiom. A large fireplace on the south wall displayed a combination of neoclassical and Renaissance motifs. The room's maple floor and informally arranged furnishings, including both wicker and gaily upholstered seating pieces, gave the room a restrained but comfortable ambience.

The Nautilus relied on African Americans to staff many hotel functions. Floor plans show that the Nautilus, like other Florida hotels, enforced segregation through separate dining facilities for black and white employees.

—M.L.

©J. N. Chamberlain, Miami, Fla.

Postcard showing the Nautilus Hotel from Biscayne Bay, 1924
The gondoliers hired by the Nautilus Hotel provided guests not only with transportation but also with a sense of the exotic.

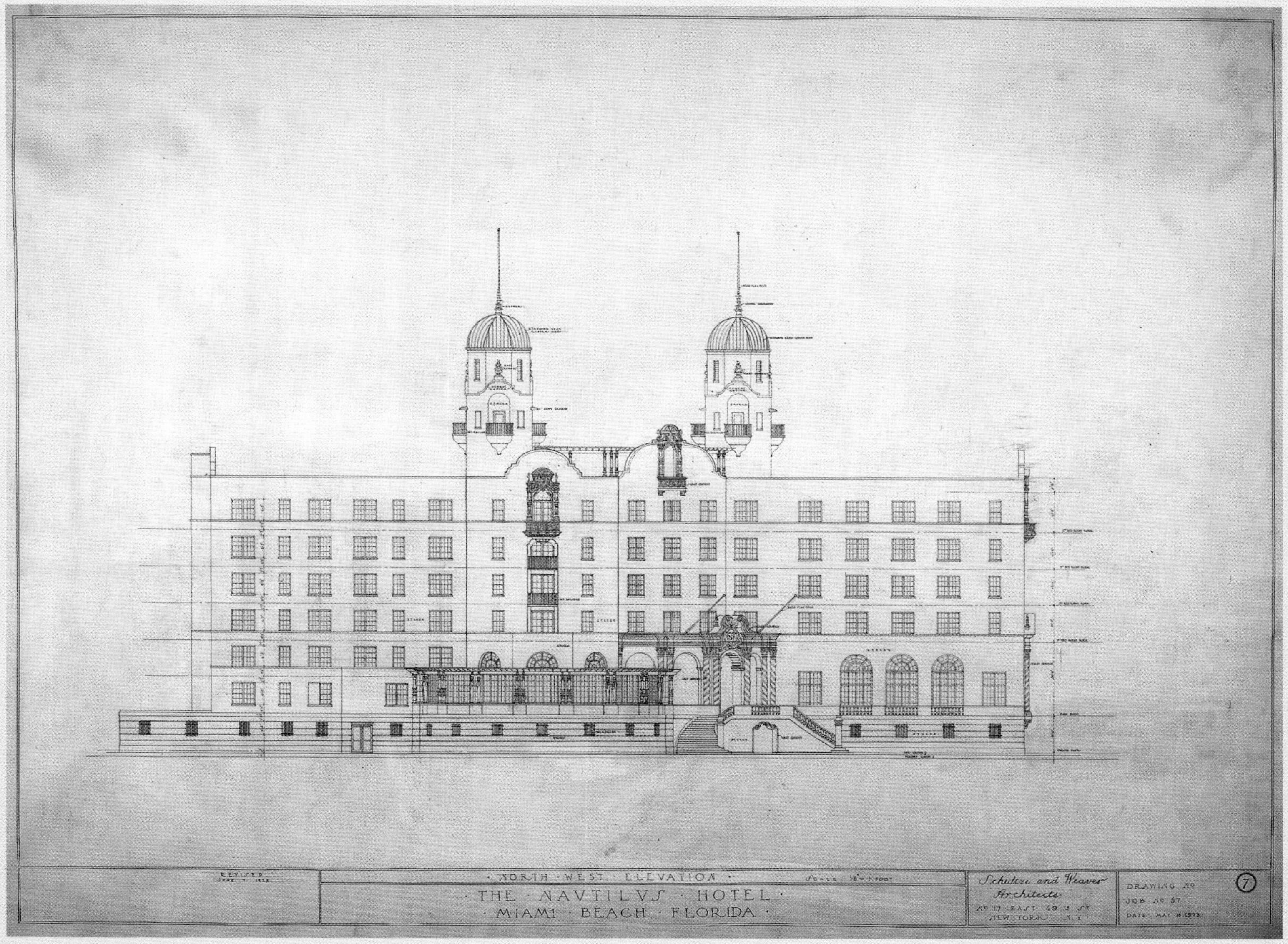

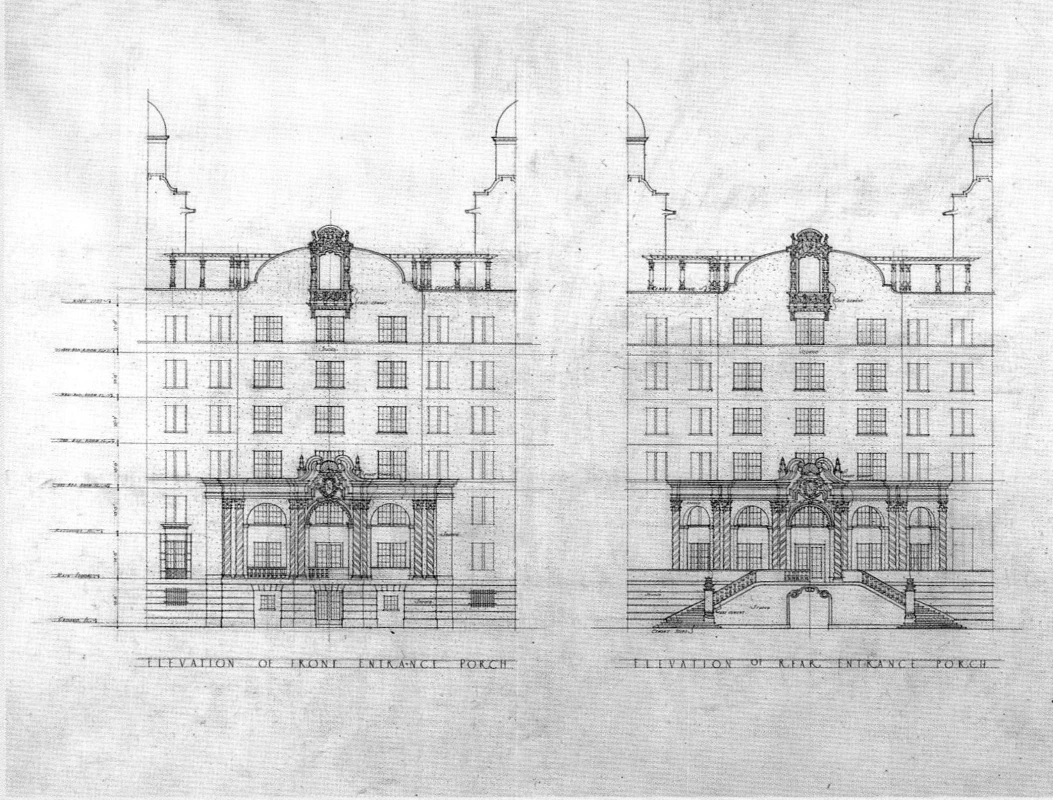

above:
Northwest elevation of the hotel, 1923

left:
Detail of elevations showing the hotel's entrance porches, 1923
From the rear entrance porch (to the right), guests descended the double flight of stairs to a garden facing Biscayne Bay. From the front entrance of the hotel (on the left), guests entered on the ground floor and climbed a flight of steps to the main lobby.

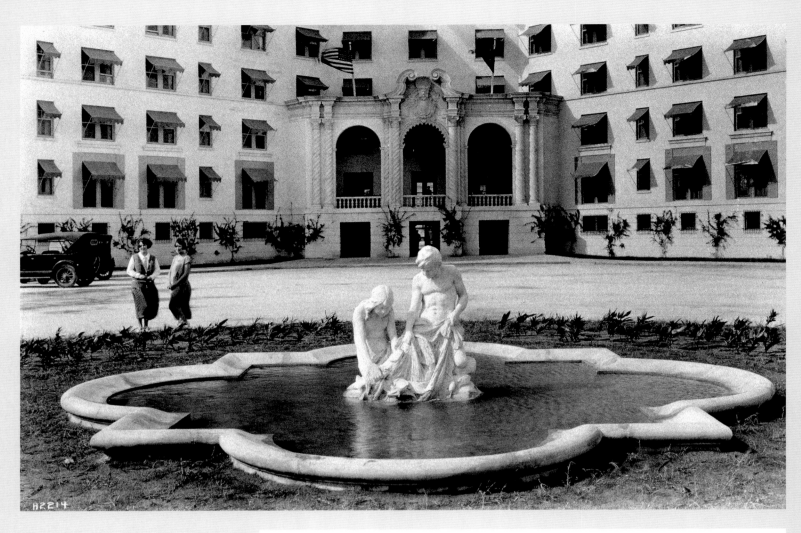

above:
Fountain in front of the main entrance, ca. 1924

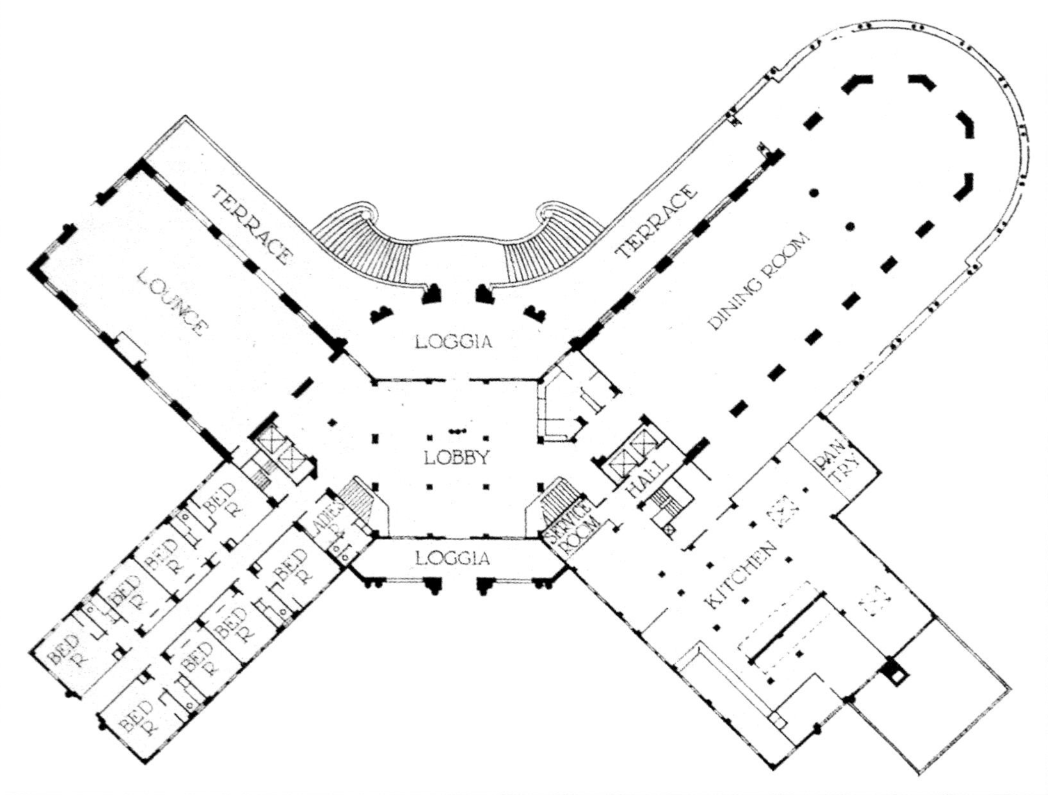

right:
First-floor plan of the Nautilus Hotel, from *Architectural Forum*, XXXIX, no. 5 (November 1923)
The main public rooms on the first floor—the dining room and lounge—were adjacent to terraces overlooking Biscayne Bay. There was no provision in the plan for a ballroom, though dances were held out of doors, on the garden patio.

opposite:
Elevation and section of the towers, 1923

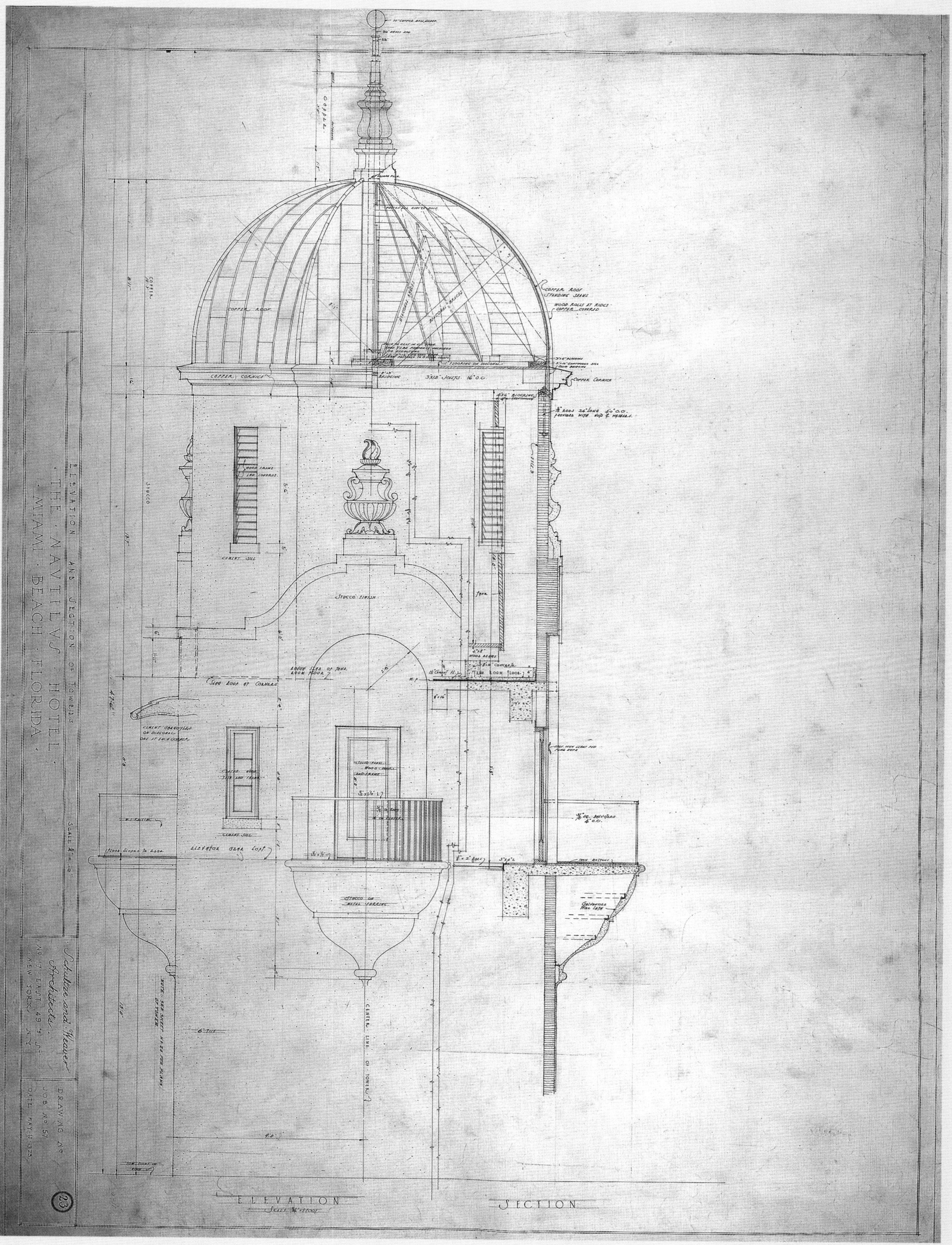
ELEVATION AND SECTION OF TOWERS
THE NAUTILUS HOTEL
MIAMI BEACH FLORIDA
Schultze and Weaver
Architects
COPPER ROOF
COPPER CORNICE
STUCCO
STUCCO FINISH
CEMENT SILL
CENTER LINE OF TOWER
ELEVATION
SECTION

right:
Detail of a plan showing features of the hotel's facade, 1923
The elaborate ornamentation of the roof-level balcony, like all of the ornament on the hotel's facade, was cast from cement.

opposite top:
Nautilus Hotel lounge, ca. 1924

opposite bottom:
Dining room of the hotel, ca. 1924

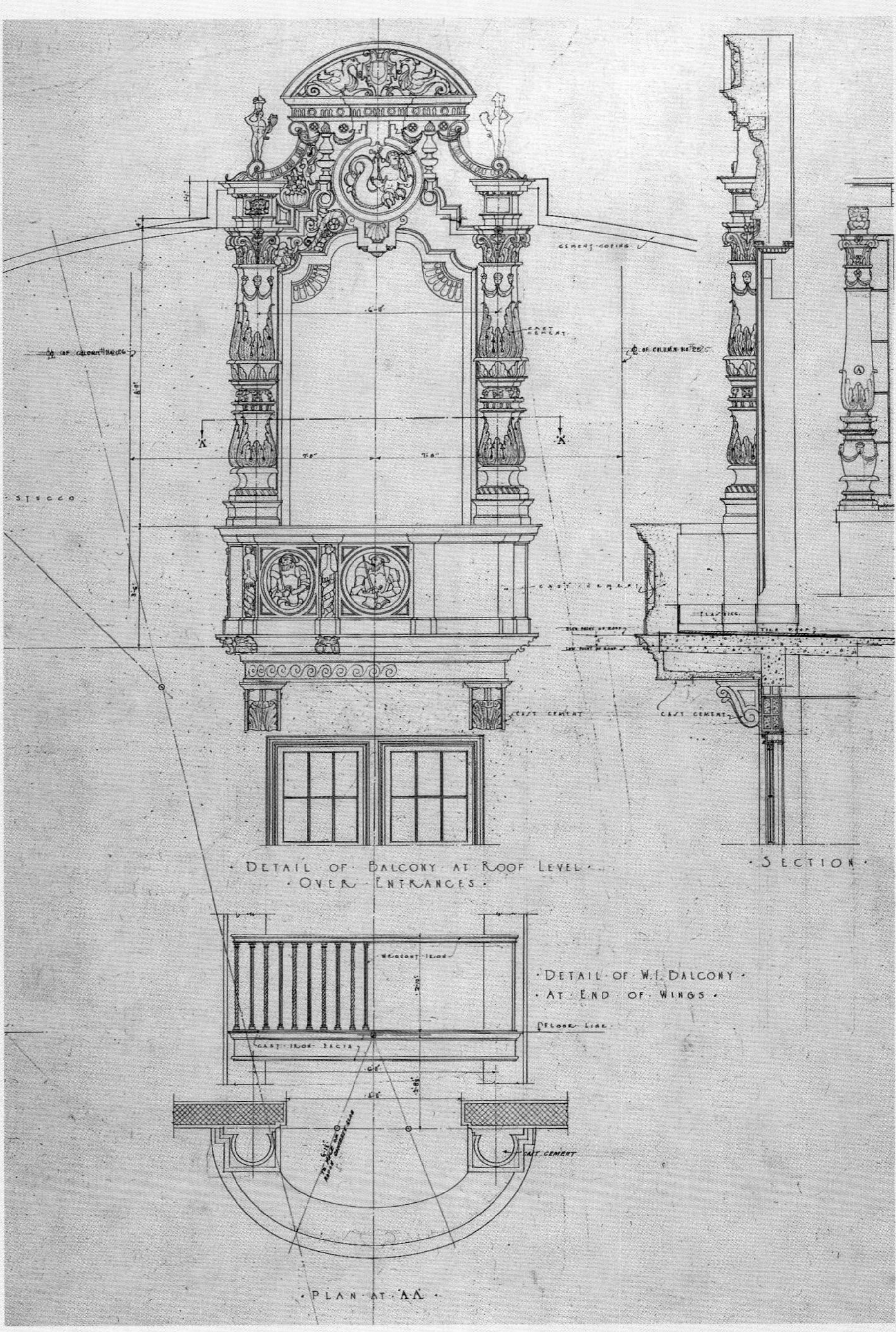

2212

HE213

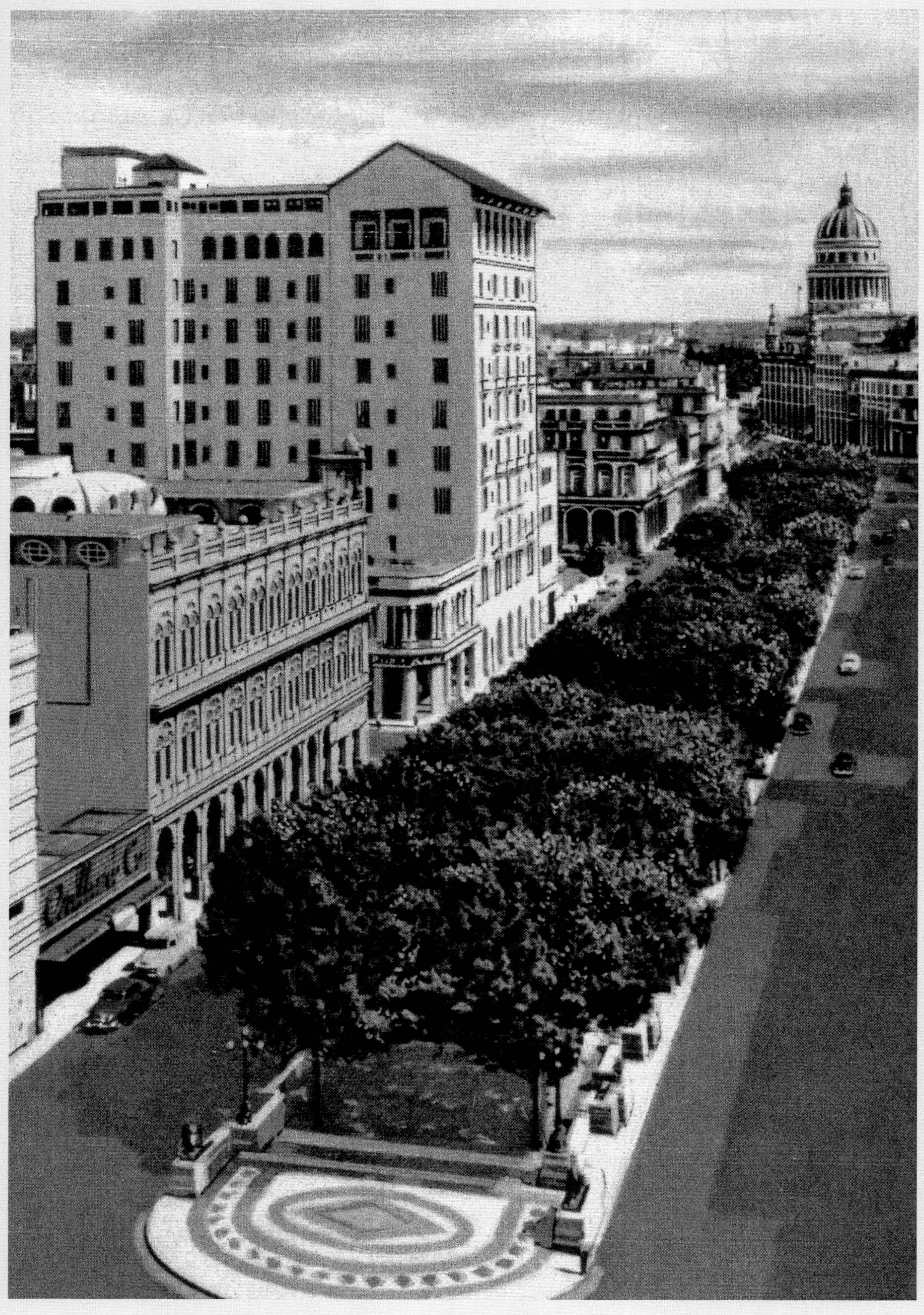

SEVILLA BILTMORE HOTEL (addition)

Havana, Cuba, 1922–24

Commissioned by John McEntee Bowman

Addition opened to the public January 30, 1924

Currently the Sevilla Hotel, operated by Sofitel Accor Hotels and Resorts

In the boom years of the 1920s, Havana became a favorite winter destination for wealthy American tourists. On January 28, 1923, *The New York Times* reported that John McEntee Bowman, president of the Bowman-Biltmore Hotels Corporation, would build an extensive addition to the Sevilla Hotel, which he had acquired several years earlier. Already at work on hotels in Los Angeles and Atlanta for Bowman, the Schultze & Weaver firm was given the job.

Set in the business and hotel center of Havana, the original, four-story Sevilla Hotel was built in 1908 by architects Arellano y Mendoza. Its main entrance on Calle Trocadero, with its Moorish-style pointed horseshoe arches forming its street arcade and ornate polylobed window treatments, reflected the then-current taste for Spanish *modernismo*. Schultze & Weaver's ten-story addition was conceived in a classical, Italianate style, a reflection of a broad shift in taste from exoticism to beaux-arts classicism. Interior treatments combined Spanish, Italian, and Cuban features. Set at a right angle to the original building, the new hotel opened onto the Paseo del Prado, Havana's grand north-south promenade that led from the Gulf of Mexico to the national capitol. According to an early hotel brochure, the Prado was "fashionable Havana's parade ground," a place for locals and tourists alike to see and be seen.

The building's exterior arcade was comprised of five rounded arches made of limestone surmounted by a mezzanine with slender columns and arches set in front of windows. The street arcade was a typical feature along the Paseo del Prado—one that was required by the building code for major avenues developed in Havana at the turn of the century. The tower block's plain stucco facade was punctuated by windows with alternating triangular and segmental pediments and limestone coins. The hotel's steep roof with deep eaves housed the renowned Roof Garden lounge and restaurant, which afforded its guests spectacular views of the Morro Castle, the Capitol, and the Presidential Palace.

The new addition was narrow—barely one hundred feet wide—and contained two hundred guest rooms, each with a private bath. A long passage on the ground floor led from the street arcade through a vaulted foyer into an interior courtyard, which brought light into the building's core. Schultze & Weaver

above:
Luggage label for the Sevilla Biltmore Hotel, after 1924

opposite:
Postcard of the Sevilla Biltmore, after 1924
The hotel was just a short walk along the grand Paseo del Prado from the national capitol, shown here in the background.

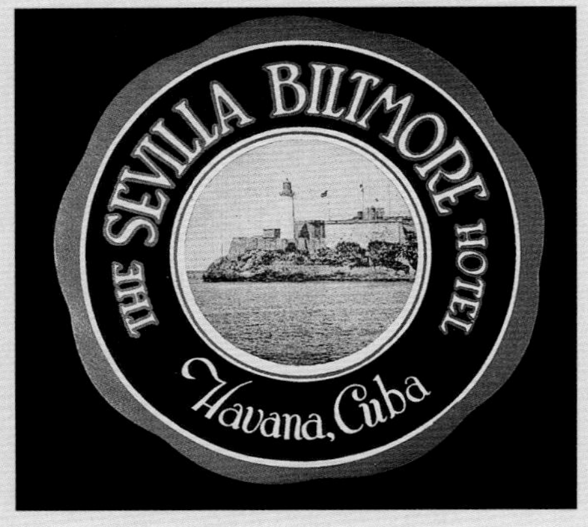

above:
Luggage label, after 1924

right:
Menu for the gala opening of the hotel, January 1924

also incorporated two light wells—one on the north and one on the south—to provide ventilation and light.

Ten shops, including a beauty parlor on the ground floor, provided services for hotel guests and for the general public. Areas such as the patio/café, the passageway between the old and new buildings, and the foyer of the Roof Garden were decorated with Spanish faience tiles, wrought-iron gates and window grilles, wooden beamed ceilings, and *persianas* (or typical wooden window louvers), all of which contributed to the hotel's Spanish colonial atmosphere.

The Roof Garden boasted accommodations for three hundred diners. The rich, dark palette of the foyer leading into the main dining room was a dramatic foil to the spectacular dining room itself, the neoclassical features of which included a painted plaster ceiling, fluted pilasters topped with ornate, gilded capitals, and a series of classical balustrades around the room's perimeter that created a room within a room. The central dance floor was used for patron dancing as well as floor shows.

—M.L.

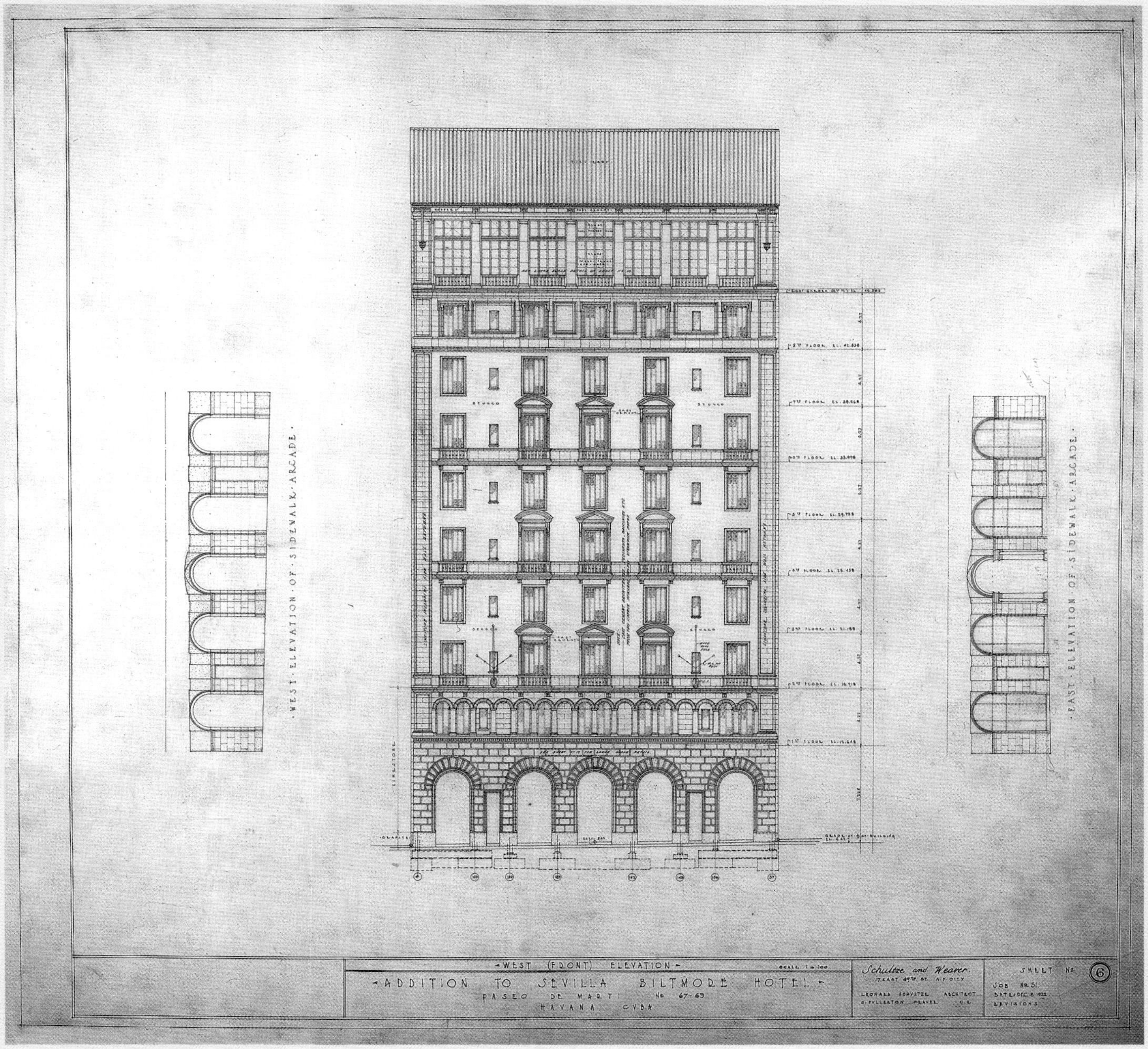

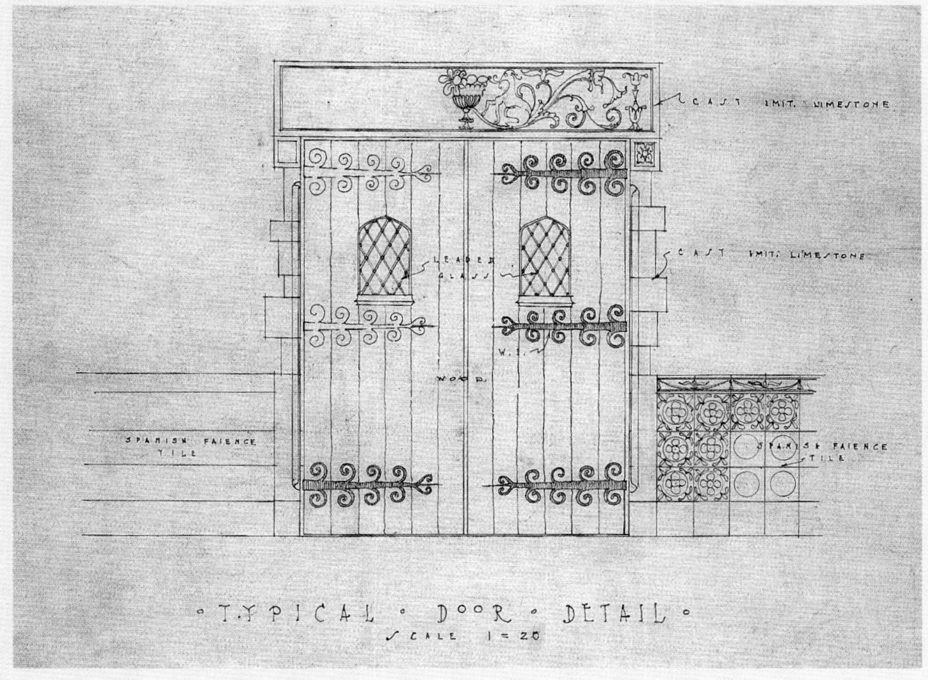

above:
Elevation drawing of the main facade, 1922
This was the second of two elevations prepared by Schultze & Weaver for the front of the hotel. The earlier plan had a much more elaborate cornice under the roof garden and a more steeply pitched roof.

left:
Detail of a plan for alterations to the existing patio, showing door design, ca. 1922

.14665
Fountain in Patio

above:
Foyer leading to the roof garden, from the photo album "Hotel Sevilla-Biltmore, Habana Cuba" (ca. 1924)

opposite:
Fountain in the patio, from "Hotel Sevilla-Biltmore, Habana, Cuba" (ca. 1924)

above:
Arcade of the hotel, 1924
The hotel's ground-floor arcade housed a variety of shops that catered to guests and the general public.

opposite top:
Patio, from "Hotel Sevilla-Biltmore, Habana, Cuba" (ca. 1924)

opposite bottom:
Roof garden, from "Hotel Sevilla-Biltmore, Habana, Cuba" (ca. 1924)

ATLANTA BILTMORE HOTEL

Atlanta, Georgia, 1922–24

Commissioned by the Atlanta-Biltmore Hotel Co.

Opened to the public on April 19, 1924

Currently an office building, operated by the Novare Group

The brainchild of John McEntee Bowman and Coca Cola heir William Candler, the Atlanta Biltmore Hotel was conceived as a convention facility. As a period advertisement boasted, its location was "convenient to the business section but just enough removed to be among the trees and have full sweep of Georgia's wondrous air."

The eleven-story building boasted six hundred guest rooms. The architects used a formal vocabulary based on the refined neoclassicism of late-eighteenth-century England and Colonial America. Popularly known as the Georgian style after the kings who ruled Britain in the eighteenth century, this kind of architecture and decoration was widely used in the American colonies, including Georgia. Georgian-inspired features, such as the two-story entrance portico with paired columns, the roof gallery with a neoclassical balustrade and ornamental urns, and the scrolling swan's neck pediments over the doors, were intended to convey "Southern hospitality" to the hotel's guests. The two-story main lobby was decorated with tall pilasters of black and gold marble and mahogany woodwork. The dining room and ballroom exploited classical elements such as fluted columns and pilasters, niches, and balustrades. The ceilings featured intricate plasterwork designs painted in a soft palette, in the style of eighteenth-century Scottish architect Robert Adam.

This massive, modern hotel catered to guests' every need. Each guest room had a private bath, circulating ice water, and an electric fan. Accommodations varied from single bedrooms to multi-room suites. The latter had private serving pantries, replete with refrigerator, electric plate-warmer, cupboard, and sink. Dining facilities included the formal main dining room, private rooms, quaint tea rooms with the "cheer of old colonial days," and an ultra-modern coffee shop with counter service.

—M.L.

above:
Postcard showing an aerial view of the hotel, 1931
WSB, Atlanta's first radio station, moved its studios and broadcasting towers to the Atlanta Biltmore in 1925, shortly after the hotel opened.

opposite:
Garden front of the Atlanta Biltmore Hotel, from *Architectural Forum* LI, no. 6 (December 1929)
The Atlanta Biltmore's long portico opened onto a garden terrace where tea and dinner dances were held.

right:
Brochure for the Atlanta Biltmore, ca. 1925

opposite top:
Main lobby, from *Architectural Forum* LI, no. 6 (December 1929)

opposite bottom:
Ballroom of the hotel, ca. 1924

Another
Great Reason for
Coming to Atlanta

top:
Dining room, ca. 1924

bottom:
Entrance to the dining room, from *Architectural Forum* LI, no. 6 (December 1929)

Detail of the dining room, ca. 1924

PARK LANE HOTEL

New York, New York, 1922–24

Commissioned by 299 Madison Avenue, Inc.

Constructed by the George A. Fuller Company

Opened to the public on September 27, 1924

Demolished in 1965

The Park Lane was Schultze & Weaver's first hotel commission. Built along an upscale section of Park Avenue between Forty-eighth and Forty-ninth streets, the massive thirteen-story building covered an entire eastside block. At the rear of the hotel, an eponymous street was created to accommodate the hotel's service functions. The new street and the building's H-shaped plan assured all apartment dwellers of ample light and air. Available in two- to six-room configurations, apartments featured a living room and one or more bedrooms as well as an entrance foyer, a serving pantry with refrigeration and electric plate warmers, spacious closets, and, in some of the larger units, a maid's room.

The building's facade was based on Italian Renaissance palace architecture and was executed in limestone and tapestry brick—so-called because its surfaces have been roughened by cutting a thin slice off the brick's face with a wire. The contemporary press consistently referred to the hotel's classical features as "Louis Seize," after the eighteenth-century French ruler who favored similar neoclassical forms, "marked by elegance, formality, and classic simplicity." During his tenure at Warren & Wetmore from 1903 to 1921, Leonard Schultze was the chief designer on several important New York hotels, including the Biltmore (1912–13) and the Commodore (1918–19). The Park Lane shared many features with these earlier buildings, such as a multi-story stone base, brick towers with prominent stone coins, and classical ornamentation around windows and doors.

The residential entrance to the hotel was on Park Avenue off Forty-eighth Street, where an entrance foyer led to the richly finished lobby with travertine walls and a wood-beamed ceiling. The Park Lane's most distinctive characteristic was its central portion on Park Avenue, designed as a two-story arcade with patterned columns separating five large windows. The composition was enriched by a Renaissance-inspired frieze with putti and floral swags and a classical balustrade on the roof above. The hotel's dining room occupied the interior of this space. Open to residents and the public, this luxurious room featured a classical balustrade that encircled the room forming a balcony, tall windows adorned with twisted columns and ornamental capitals, and an ornate, coffered ceiling. Seventeenth-century Flemish tapestries and period-style furnishings completed the decor.

above:
Screen in the ballroom suite, from *Architectural Forum* LI, no. 6 (November 1924)
This gold and polychrome screen closed off the ballroom suite (which had its own entrance) from the lobby and the other public rooms of the hotel. The Park Lane was designed so that activities in the ballroom would not interfere with the comfort of permanent guests.

opposite:
Exterior of the building from Park Avenue, from *Architectural Forum* LI, no. 6 (November 1924)

right:
Plans of the first floor and typical apartments, from *Architecture* LX, no. 4 (October 1929)

opposite top:
Ballroom, from *Architectural Forum* LI, no. 6 (November 1924)

opposite bottom:
Dining room, from *Architectural Forum* LI, no. 6 (November 1924)

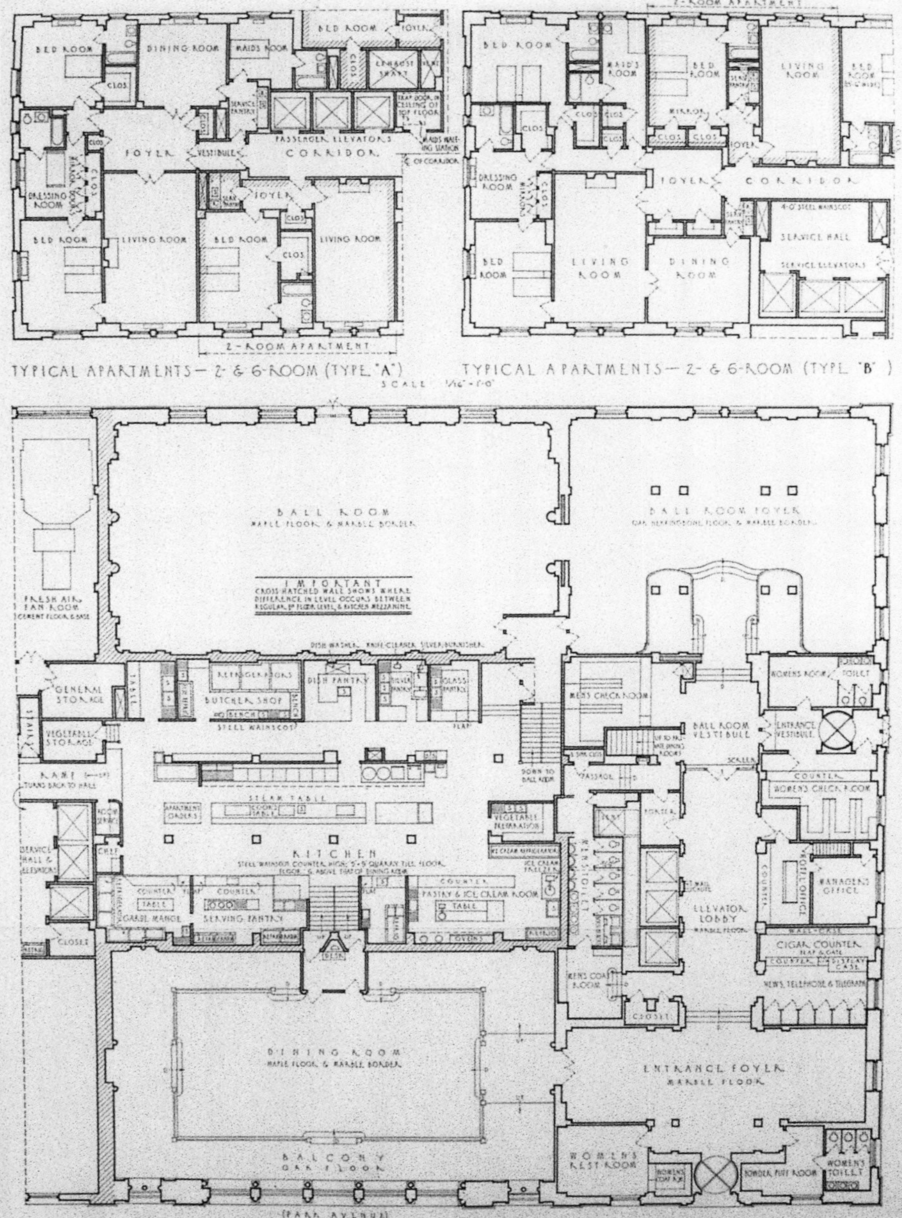

The mirrored ballroom was reached through a separate entrance on Forty-eighth Street, assuring that residents would not be disturbed by transitory guests. Because of the hotel's public and private functions, the interior architecture was critical for maintaining the privacy of the residents. Commercial functions such as the hotel office, telephone/telegraph room, and cigar shop/newsstand were creatively set off by screening devices. In the main entrance foyer, three steps set within an arched architectural framework created what one critic for *Architecture* magazine called "a restraining psychological effect," which prevented dining room guests from wandering into the residential areas.

—M.L.

MIAMI BILTMORE HOTEL

Coral Gables, Florida, 1924–26

Commissioned by the Coral Gables Corporation and the Bowman-Biltmore Hotels Corporation

Opened to the public on January 15, 1926

Currently the Biltmore Hotel, operated by Seaway Group

The city of Coral Gables was the brainchild of one man: George Merrick. The developer planned the new town according to the principles of the City Beautiful movement, making extensive use of winding boulevards, scenic vistas, plazas, and parks. Like Carl Fisher in Miami Beach, Merrick understood the value of using a hotel and country club to anchor his real estate development, and he created the elaborate Miami Biltmore to serve the purpose.

In February 1924, Merrick revealed his plans for the new hotel. Local architect Martin L. Hampton presented a design that had a distinct Spanish touch, incorporating a modified version of the Giralda tower from the Cathedral of Seville in Spain. Several months later, Merrick announced that he would partner with John McEntee Bowman, president of the Bowman-Biltmore Hotels Corporation, to build the Miami Biltmore. Bowman asked Schultze & Weaver, architects of Biltmore hotels in Los Angeles, Atlanta, and Havana, to design the new hotel.

In Schultze & Weaver's design, four wings extended from a central block surmounted by a 315-foot tower. The plan was similar in its overall massing and layout to the Westchester-Biltmore Country Club in Rye, New York (1920–21), produced while Schultze was employed by Warren & Wetmore. The varying heights of the tower, central block, and wings contributed to the spatial complexity of the composition, which gave the impression of separate but interconnected buildings similar to a Renaissance hill town. At the core of the building, a sunken courtyard with open loggias or arcades on three sides created an enclosed Italian Renaissance-style portico.

Often used for dining and dancing, the southernmost end of the portico, which faced onto the golf course, was one of the most photographed features of the hotel. Another spectacular element of the hotel's plan was the 250-foot-long swimming pool on the western side of the building. The pool was framed on one side by a colonnaded porch and on the other by the classical facade of the Biltmore Country Club. At the time it was built, it was the largest pool in America.

The main entrance on the north side of the building was reached by a graded ramp lined with a classical balustrade that rose to the second-floor level. Passing through an ornate portal that ascended nearly four stories, guests entered the hotel lobby. Extending lengthwise on the east-west axis, the magnificent room featured

above:
Program for a fashion show (1926)
Among the festivities accompanying the hotel's opening was a fashion review featuring ten models and attended by more than fifteen hundred spectators

opposite:
Miami Biltmore Hotel and service building, from *The Miami Biltmore* (1926)

Postcard of the Miami Biltmore Hotel at night, after 1926

two aisles of columns and a large, hooded fireplace on the east wall. The huge columns adorned with floral capitals of cast concrete and the ribbed vaulted ceiling painted dark blue with golden stars gave the impression of a Romanesque chapel. Ornamental metalwork, ceramic pots, and area rugs contributed to the luxurious ambience.

In the west pavilion, a lounge opened onto a large terrace overlooking the swimming pool on one side and the interior courtyard on the other. Rough, hand-finished plaster covered the walls; the coffered plaster ceiling was painted rich hues of red, blue, and gold; and the oak floor was covered with a patterned carpet. As in the lobby, an enormous hooded fireplace was centered on one wall. In the opposite pavilion, on the east side of the courtyard, was the dining room. The barrel-vaulted ceiling was painted by Giovanni Smeraldi, the Los Angeles painter who decorated the rooms at the Los Angeles Biltmore Hotel. Oak wainscoting, polychrome chandeliers with colored glass pendants, and a richly patterned, Spanish-inspired carpet gave the large room warmth and texture.

The hotel's four hundred guest rooms and tower suites were each equipped with a private bath and a telephone. Most of the bedrooms had a distinctly Spanish feel, with custom-designed beds in walnut with gold trim and carpeting that resembled antique floor tiles. Newspapers reported that one million dollars were invested in authentic Spanish, Italian, and Moorish furniture, draperies, and rugs, which augmented locally made furniture created in Spanish and Italian styles.

—M.L.

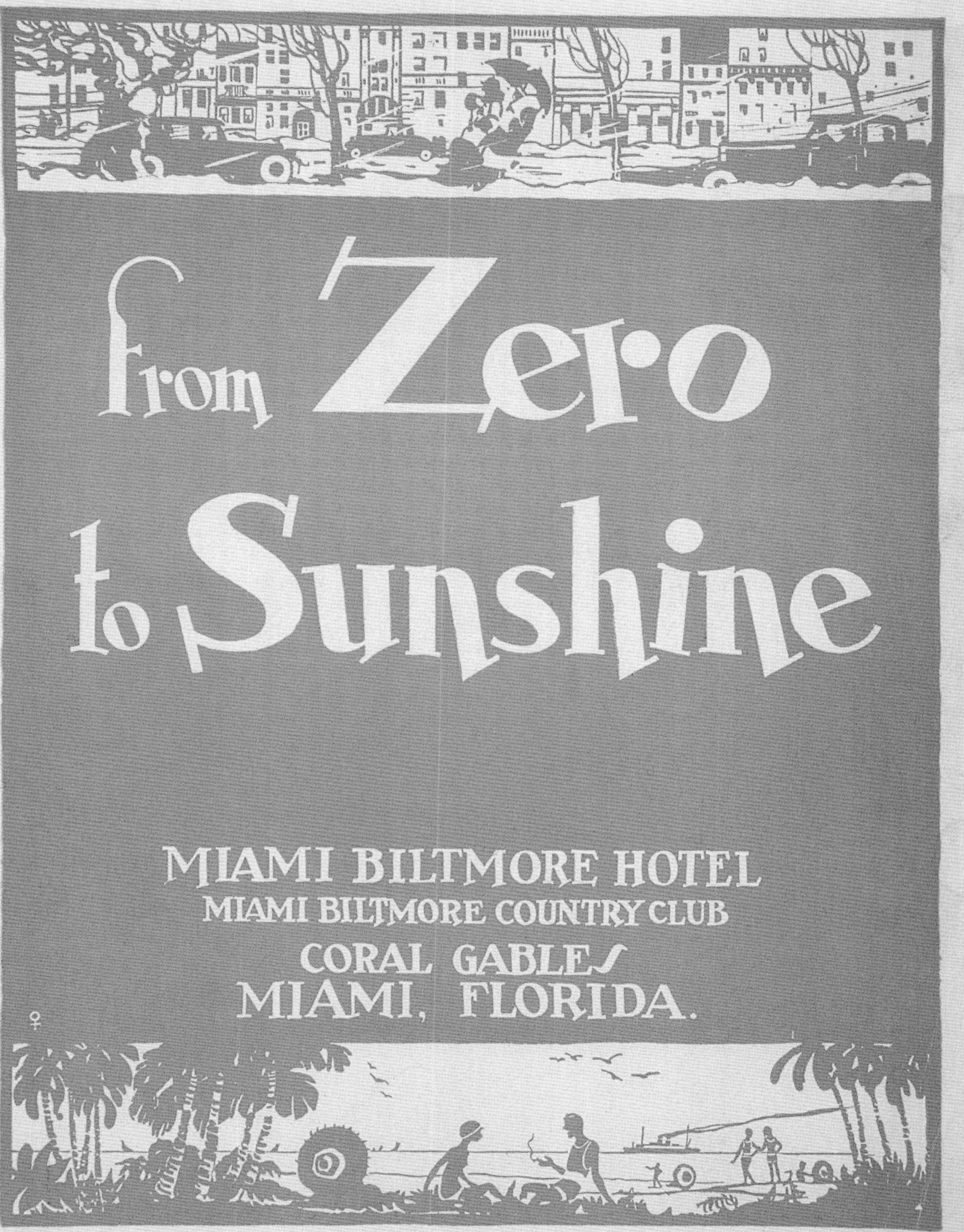

Brochure for the Miami Biltmore Hotel (ca. 1930)
This brochure promotes the hotel as an escape from the frigid northern winter.

top:
Postcard of the patio, after 1926

bottom:
Swimming pool and the end of the club house, from *The Miami Biltmore Hotel* (1926)

opposite:
Terrace over the patio, ca. 1926

M4144

above:
Lobby of the hotel, ca. 1926
The Biltmore's lobby, like other public rooms in the hotel, was furnished with antique pieces (some purchased in Europe) and a profusion of rich textiles. Its opulent ceiling was painted a deep blue with gold stars to mimic the night sky.

opposite:
Interior corridor of the hotel, ca. 1926

above:
On the green at the eighteenth hole of the Miami Biltmore Open, 1937

opposite:
Early postcard featuring horseback riders in front of the Miami Biltmore Hotel, after 1926

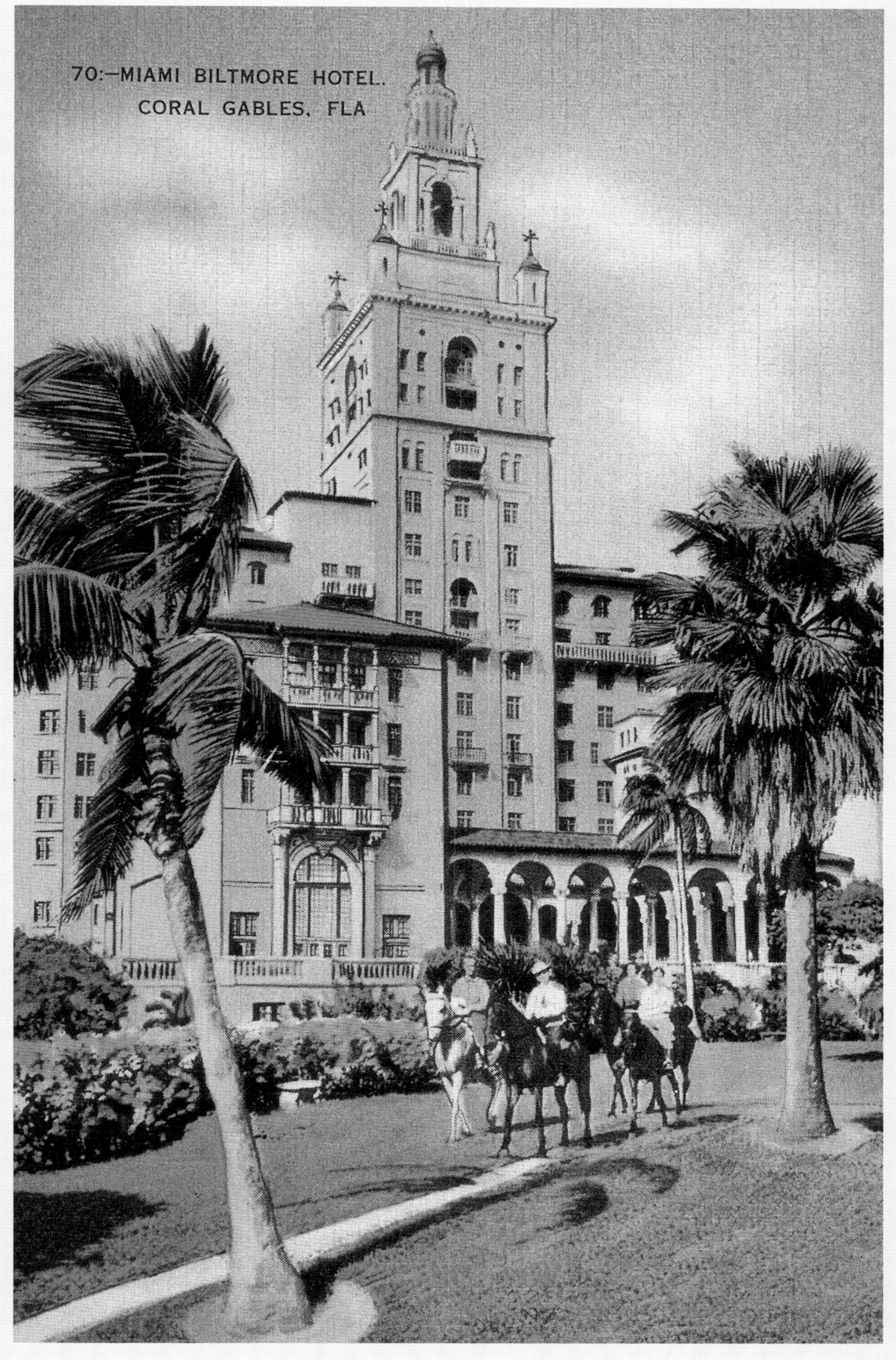
70:—MIAMI BILTMORE HOTEL.
CORAL GABLES, FLA

RONEY PLAZA HOTEL

Miami Beach, Florida, 1925–26

Commissioned by N. B. T. Roney

Constructed by the George A. Fuller Company

Opened to the public on February 6, 1926

Demolished in 1968

Newton B. T. Roney arrived in South Florida in the late 1910s and voraciously acquired property for commercial development in Miami and Miami Beach. In early 1925 he announced plans to build a grand hotel ...ld cover an entire city block on Collins Avenue from Twenty-third to ...rth streets in Miami Beach. Schultze & Weaver were chosen as the ... the new project, having just completed Carl G. Fisher's Nautilus ...ney Plaza opened in February 1926 against serious odds: during con... ...ailroad embargo delayed shipments of vital materials to Miami, and a ...hip capsized in the harbor, preventing goods from reaching port.

The hotel's site—within the urban grid and on the oceanfront—set it apart from Schultze & Weaver's other South Florida hotels, which were located within garden settings. The architects used these aspects to advantage. They placed shops along Collins Avenue and Twenty-third Street and a promenade on the oceanfront. They also created an enclosed garden and pool area on the north facade. Like Roney's recently completed Española Way—a "Spanish Village" with two hotels, sixteen apartment buildings, and shops—the Roney Plaza was a "community within itself," as the *Miami Daily News and Metropolis* branded it upon opening.

Richly ornamented and luxuriously appointed, the new hotel mixed service with theatricality. It rivaled all other properties on the beach at that time both in sheer size (boasting approximately three hundred guest rooms) and its range of amenities (including tower suites, over forty shops, formal and informal dining options, a swimming pool, and terraces and promenades for enjoying the outdoors). Catering to the wealthy, the hotel also offered a well-equipped service wing with one hundred and fifty rooms for valets, chauffeurs, maids, and housekeepers.

Schultze & Weaver chose a Spanish-inspired Mediterranean revival style for the new hotel. The building's most prominent feature was the tower at the Collins Avenue and Twenty-third Street corner, modeled after the Giralda, the Seville Cathedral's bell tower. (The architects also used this grandiose element on two other Miami projects conceived at the same time: the Miami Biltmore Hotel and the Miami News and Metropolis Building.) The building's plaster facade was enlivened with decorative elements, including cast concrete coats of arms evoking Spain in the age of King Ferdinand and Queen Isabella; sculptural lions holding

above:
Brochure for the Roney Plaza (ca. 1926)

opposite:
Bird's-eye view of the Roney Plaza Hotel and the Roman Pools and Casino, February 10, 1929
Built in 1920 by Carl Fisher, the Roman Pools and Casino provided bathing facilities for Roney Plaza guests prior to the construction of the hotel's pool in late 1929.

Postcard of the hotel, after 1926

shields, which were placed on top of the terrace gallery; and obelisks, which ornamented the summit of the tower. The soaring height of the main entrance on Twenty-third Street dwarfed visitors; the portal's base alone measured over four feet tall.

The hotel's vestibule featured a double staircase with ornately patterned Spanish tiles and a delicate wrought-iron balustrade. Public rooms had hand-finished plaster walls or wood wainscoting, terrazzo floors, and coffered or beamed ceilings. Renaissance-inspired furnishings and metalwork and striking carpets completed the regal look.

—M.L.

top:
Postcard featuring an aerial view of the hotel and its surroundings, after 1926

bottom:
The hotel's terrace restaurant, after 1926

right:
Twenty-third Street entrance and interior stairway, June 6, 1930
Visitors walked through the entrance into a vestibule, from where they could climb the stair to the hotel's main lobby or pass through the arch to a ground floor area opening onto shops and a garden beyond.

opposite top:
Twenty-third Street elevation, 1925

opposite bottom:
Detail of the plan for the main lobby showing the elevation toward the garden, 1925

TWENTY THIRD STREET ELEVATION
RONEY PLAZA HOTEL
TWENTY THIRD AND TWENTY FOURTH STREETS AND COLLINS AVENUE
MIAMI BEACH FLORIDA

Schultze and Weaver Architects

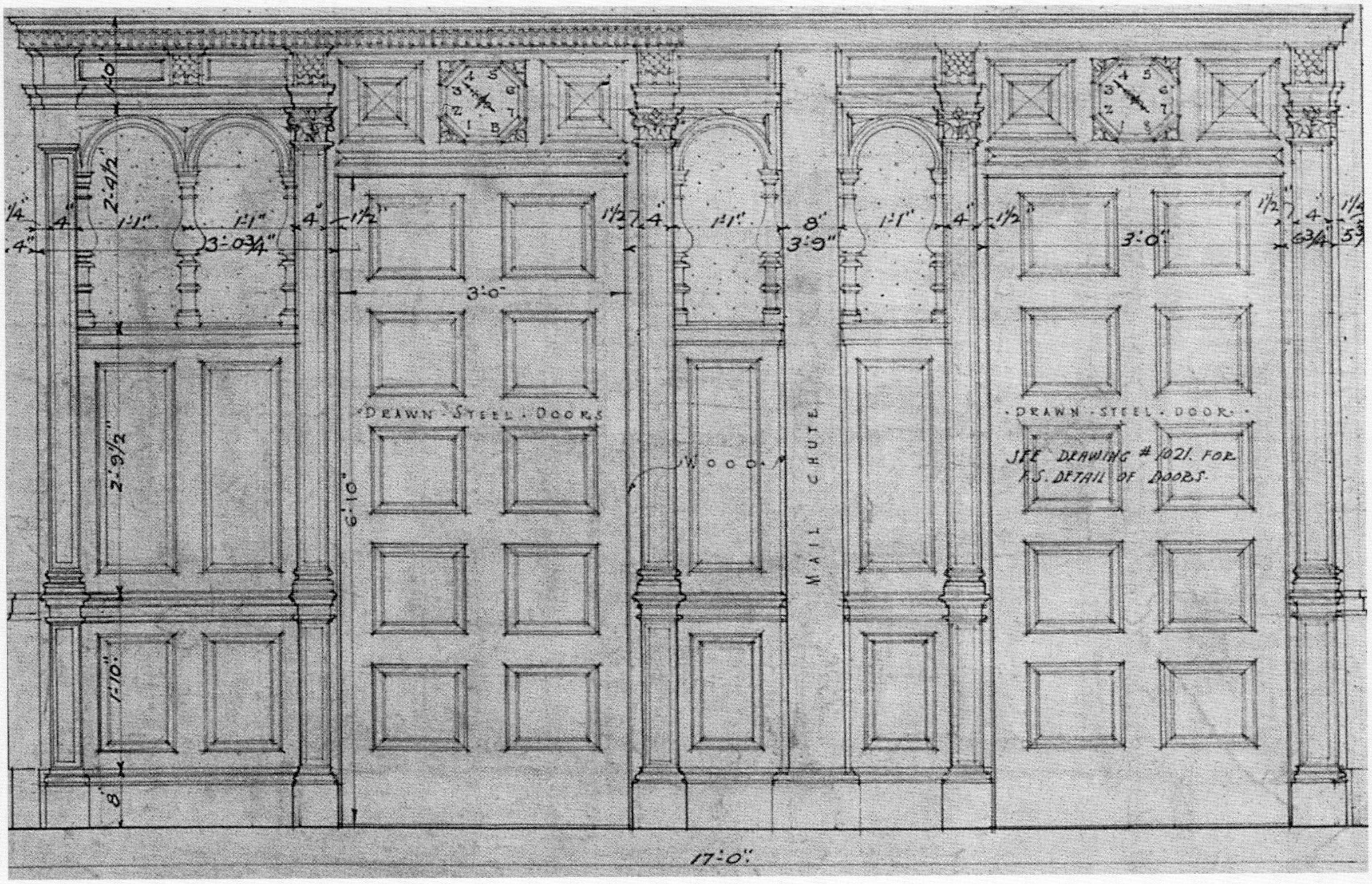

DRAWN STEEL DOORS

WOOD

MAIL CHUTE

DRAWN STEEL DOOR

SEE DRAWING #1021 FOR F.S. DETAIL OF DOORS

top:
Dining room, ca. 1926
The hotel's dining room, located on the main floor, overlooking the corner of Twenty-third Street and Collins Avenue.

bottom:
Lobby of the hotel, ca. 1926

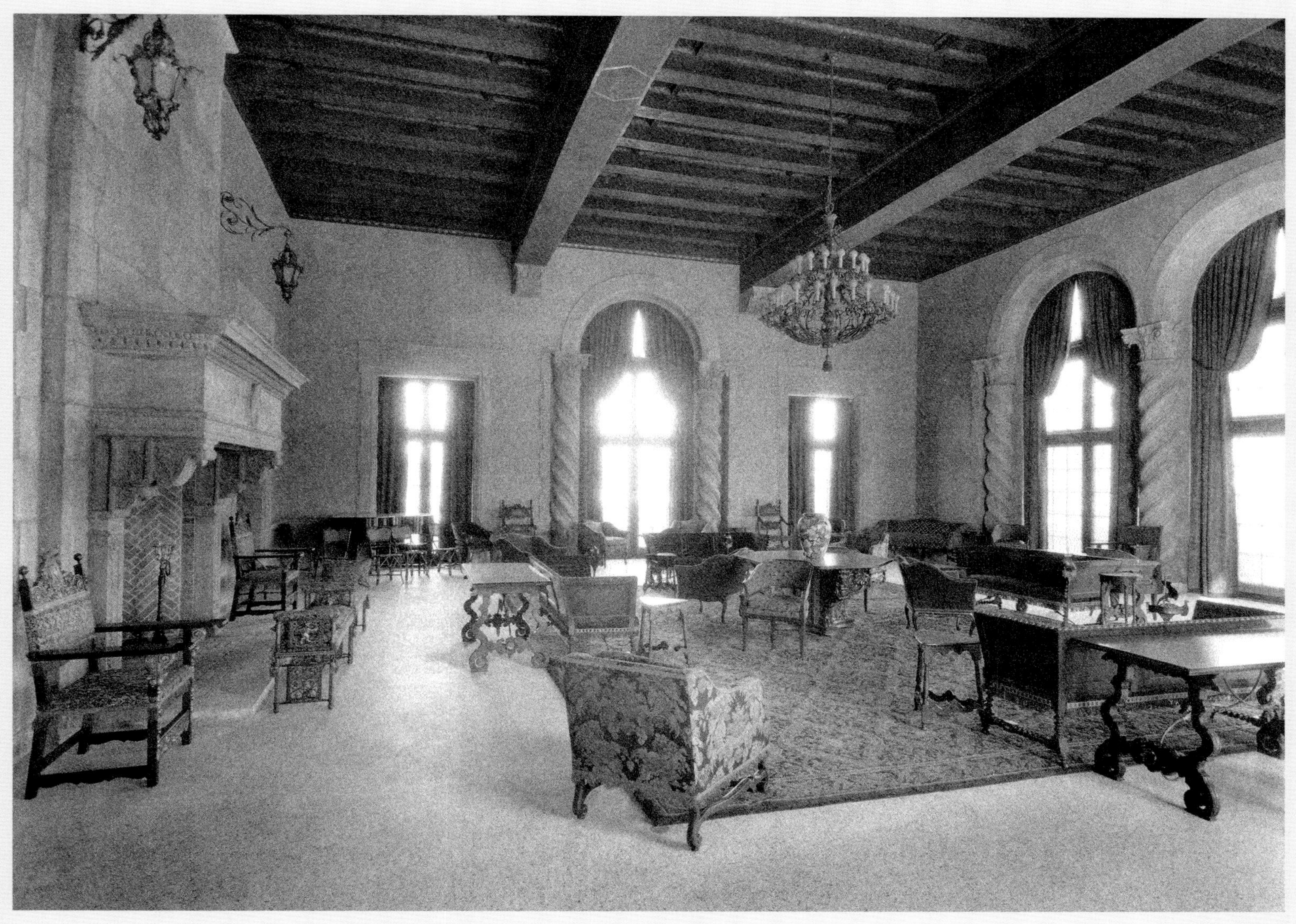

Lounge, ca. 1926
The lounge of the Roney Plaza had large windows overlooking the ocean, framed by cast imitation travertine columns. The beams on the ceiling were plaster, rather than wood, with painted ornament.

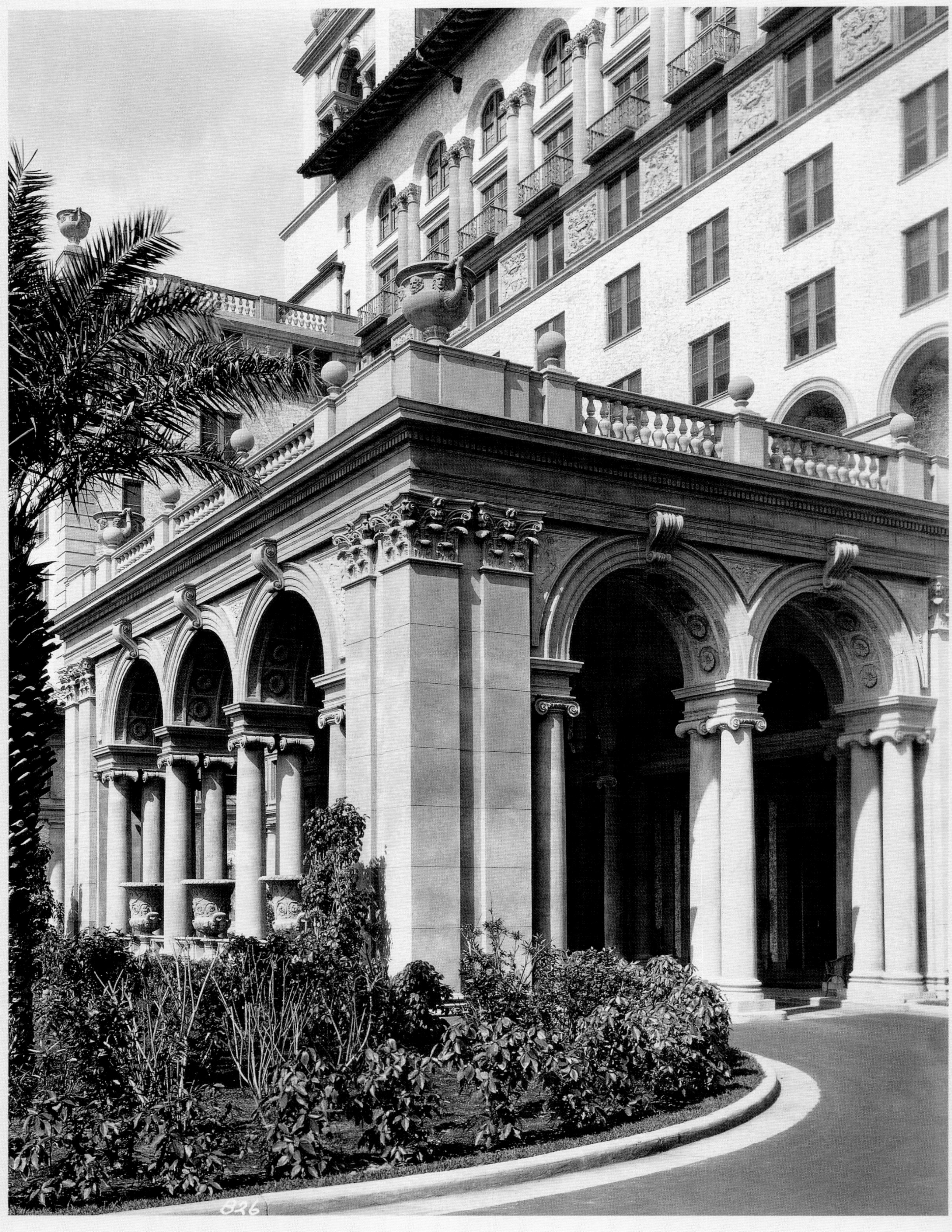

BREAKERS HOTEL

Palm Beach, Florida, 1925–26

Commissioned by the Florida East Coast Hotel Company

Constructed by the Turner Construction Company

Opened to the public in December 29, 1926

Currently owned by Flagler System, Inc.

Built by the heirs of Florida East Coast Railway magnate Henry Flagler to replace the old Breakers Hotel, which was destroyed by fire in March 1925, the new Breakers opened at the end of December 1926. When William R. Kenan, Jr., invited Schultze & Weaver to design the new hotel, the firm was working on the Roney Plaza in Miami Beach and the Biltmore in Coral Gables. Looking to distinguish the Breakers from the picturesque Mediterranean revival homes and clubs in Palm Beach, Kenan sent Schultze to Italy to gather ideas. The new hotel resembled an Italian Renaissance palazzo. Modeled after the sixteenth-century Villa Medici in Rome, it comprised two pavilions running east to west and a main pavilion running north to south, topped with twin towers rising 175 feet. The exterior was treated with rough-textured stucco enlivened by decorative stonework, tile roofs, ornamental iron balconies, and green painted window casings and sashes.

above:
Postcard of the Grand Loggia, after 1926
Overlooking the patio on one side and the Atlantic Ocean on the other, the Grand Loggia had marble floors and frescoes that were said to be inspired by a room in Genoa's Palazzo Imperiale.

opposite:
Entrance porch of the Breakers Hotel, after 1926
The hotel's imposing entrance incorporated a Renaissance-inspired portico with lavish decorative embellishments such as balustrades, urns, and bas-relief panels.

Guests approached the hotel from a wide, sumptuously planted lane and entered the building through a regal porte cochere comprised of three delicate arches and embellished with classical balustrades at the base and on the gallery above. Fashionable shops and a wheelchair porch were located in the southwest corner of the building, and services were clustered in the northwest corner, out of sight of the guests.

The hotel had over four hundred bedrooms with baths. Overlooking the ocean on each of the five bedroom floors were elaborate suites that occupied the full width of the pavilions. The hotel also provided two hundred and fifty rooms for hotel employees and fifty rooms for guests' servants. On the bedroom floors, strategically placed service facilities and two corridors—one for servants and the other for guests—ensured that guests received premium service. The doorways of guest rooms were fitted with two doors—one solid and one with wooden louvers—to allow for the circulation of air.

The architects bestowed great attention on the hotel's enormous public rooms on the main floor, each lavishly designed with references to Italian precedents. Known as the Great Hall, the 200-foot-long main lobby ran north to south, parallel to the Atlantic Ocean, and had travertine walls, marble floors, and an exquisitely painted, barrel-vaulted plaster ceiling. Its six two-story arched windows

faced onto a patio at the center of the hotel's plan, with a sunken garden reached on all four sides by short flights of stairs.

On the south end of the lobby running west to east was a loggia or Grand Promenade, a long passage leading to the South Lounge. Inspired by the ornate Renaissance interiors of the Doge's Palace in Venice, the South Lounge had a diagonally paneled, gilded plaster ceiling with a deep cornice that was painted with portraits of forty-four rulers and explorers of the New World, such as Ponce de Léon and Christopher Columbus. Flanking the central patio on the north side was the main dining room, which accommodated over five hundred guests. Two aisles of freestanding columns divided the 150-foot-long room into three spaces, which were ornamented with a Renaissance-inspired beamed and painted ceiling, oak wainscoting, and creamy travertine walls. In late 1928 a dramatic circular dining room was added to the hotel. Its thirty-foot-high ceiling was capped by a shallow domed skylight resembling a sunburst. According to Charles Lockwood, who wrote a history of the hotel, the musicians' gallery with its classical balustrade, located one story above the dining room, was said to have been used during Prohibition as a private dining room where alcohol could be enjoyed with impunity.

The Grand Loggia, running along the east end of the central patio, connected the North and South lounges and looked onto the Ocean Terrace. Over one hundred feet long, the room had windows on both the east and west walls that created the ambience of an open garden casino. The central panel of the ceiling was painted to represent the Florida sky on a sunny day.

—M.L.

above:
Postcard of the old Breakers Hotel (McGuire and McDonald, 1904), after 1904

top:
Schultze & Weaver's presentation drawing showing the hotel from the Atlantic Ocean, rendered by Lloyd Morgan, 1927
This plan shows proposed future development along the ocean side to the north and south of the main hotel building (at the center of the drawing).

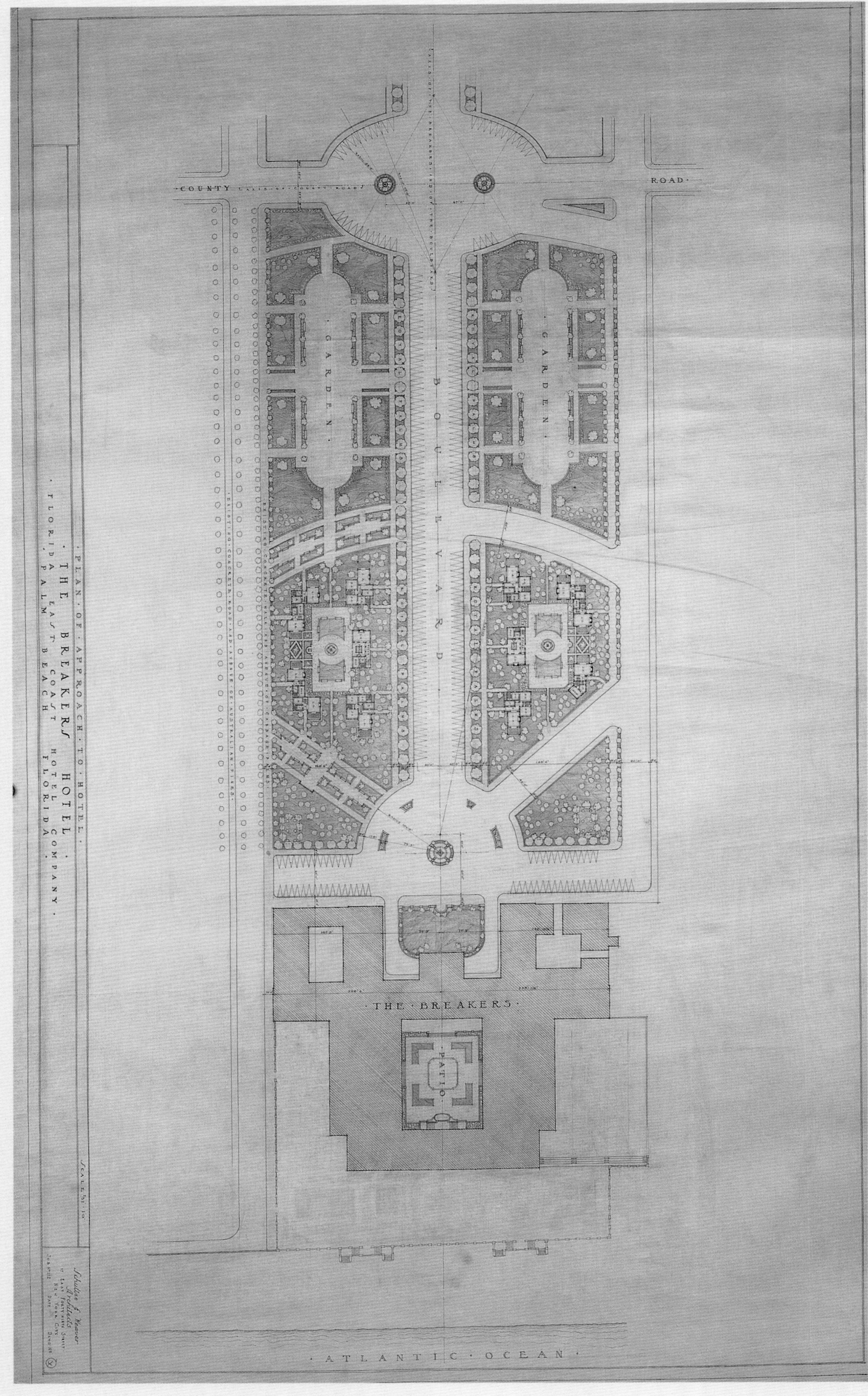

·PLAN·OF·APPROACH·TO·HOTEL·
·THE BREAKERS HOTEL·
·FLORIDA EAST COAST HOTEL COMPANY·
·PALM BEACH FLORIDA·
COUNTY
ROAD
GARDEN
GARDEN
BOULEVARD
THE BREAKERS
PATIO
ATLANTIC OCEAN

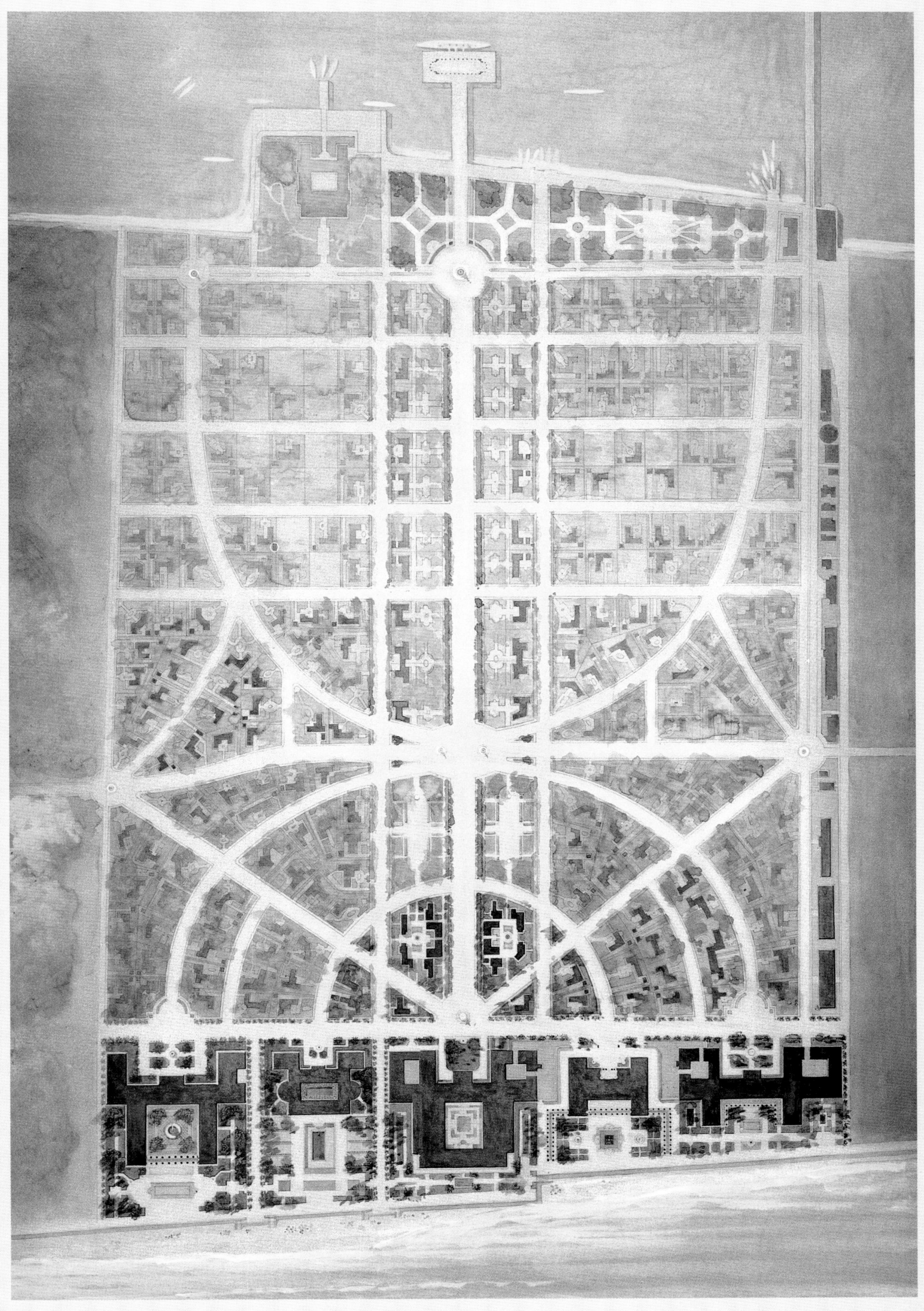

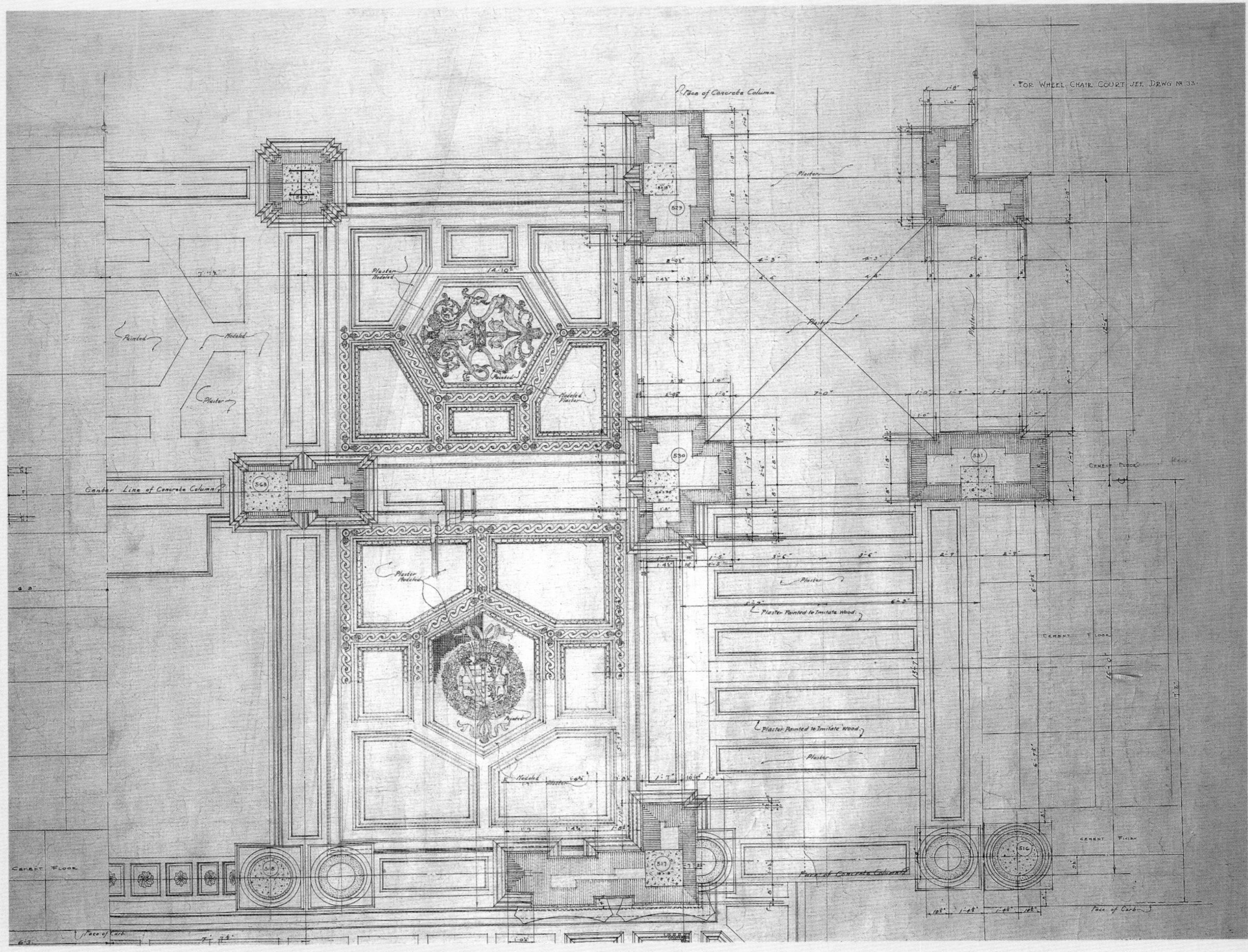

above:
Floor and ceiling plan of Loggia no. 1 (detail), 1926

opposite top:
West elevation showing the main entrance to the hotel, 1926

opposite bottom:
Main-floor plan of the hotel, 1926

previous spread
left:
Plan of the approach to the hotel, 1926
In keeping with the design scheme of a Renaissance villa, the hotel's landscape was arranged on axis with the hotel's entrance and its garden beds laid out in geometric patterns.

right:
General plan showing future development of property for the Florida East Coast Hotel Company, rendered by Lloyd Morgan, 1927
The structure shown at the western (top) edge of the plan is Whitehall, Henry Flagler's mansion, designed by Carrère & Hastings. Between the two properties are golf courses.

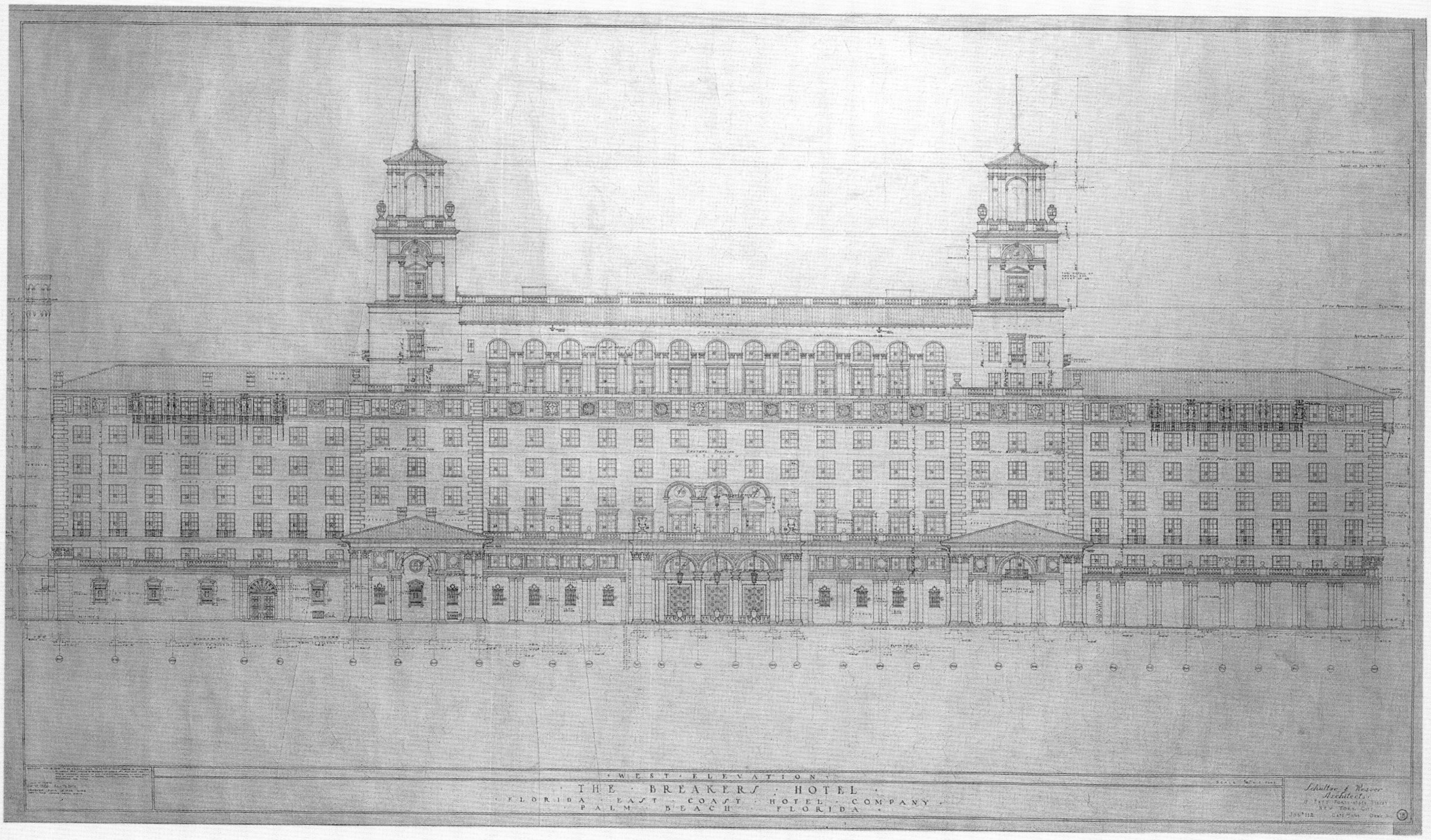
WEST ELEVATION
THE BREAKERS HOTEL
FLORIDA EAST COAST HOTEL COMPANY
PALM BEACH FLORIDA

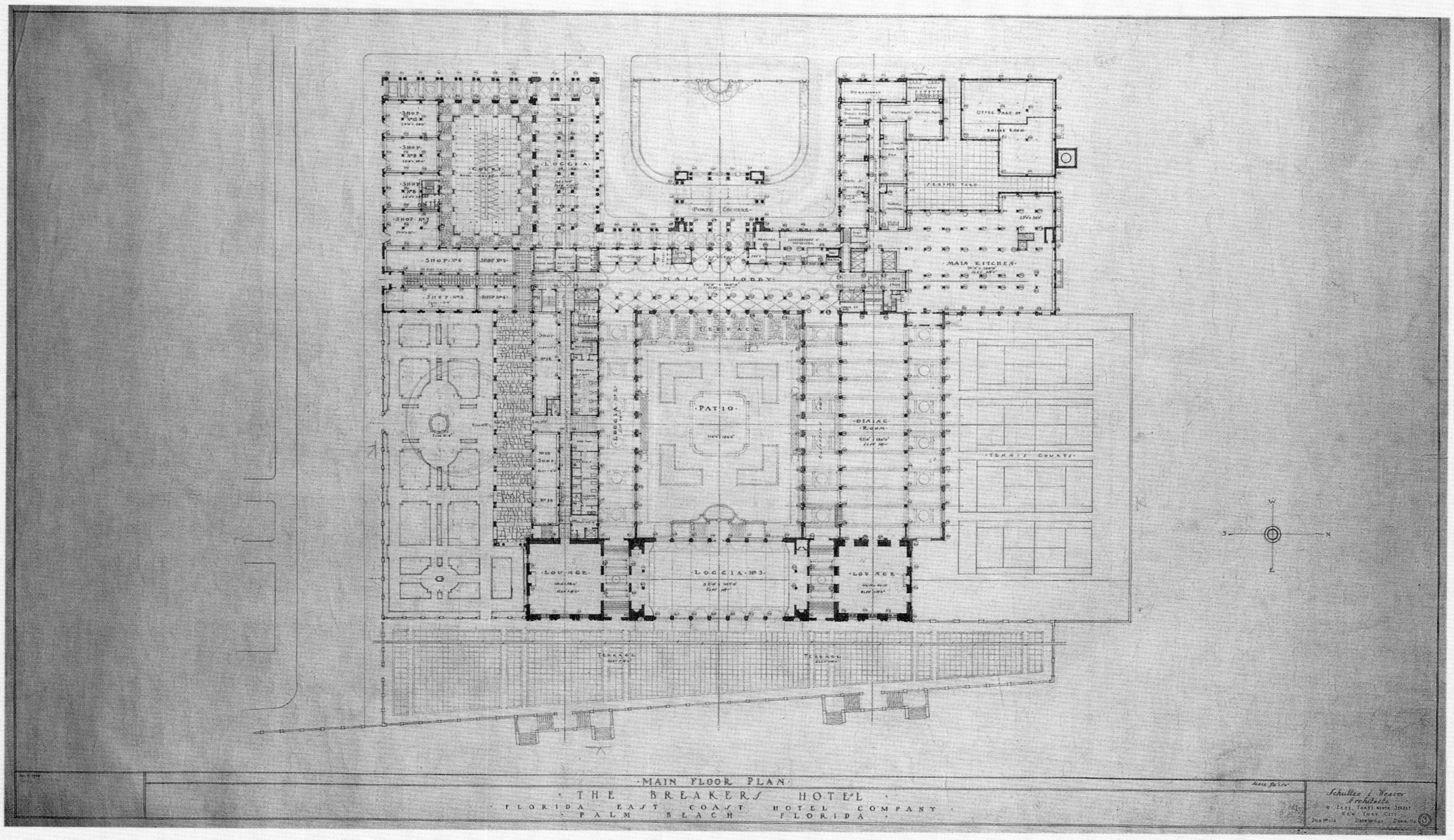
MAIN FLOOR PLAN
THE BREAKERS HOTEL
FLORIDA EAST COAST HOTEL COMPANY
PALM BEACH FLORIDA
PATIO
DINING ROOM
MAIN KITCHEN
MAIN LOBBY
LOGGIA
LOUNGE
TENNIS COURTS

top:
Postcard featuring the hotel's courtyard, after 1926
Surrounded on all sides by wings of the hotel, the courtyard featured a formal garden with terraces, walkways, balustrades, and a fountain.

opposite:
Postcard of the hotel lobby, after 1926
The lobby's ornate decorative scheme was attributed to the Great Hall of the Palazzo Carrega-Cataldi in Genoa, with furniture and frescoes replicated from the original.

E.J. Foley
Palm Beach

South Lounge, after 1926

right:
Rocking chair porch, after 1926

opposite:
Women standing under the hotel's entrance, ca. 1926
These fashionably dressed hotel guests are dwarfed by the height of the entrance portico.

2009
6-1-27

MONTAUK MANOR

Montauk Point, New York, 1926–27

Commissioned by the Montauk Beach Development Corporation

Opened to the public on June 1, 1927

Currently operated as the Montauk Manor Condominium Resort

In 1925 Miami Beach real estate tycoon and hotel developer Carl G. Fisher fixed his sights on the southeasternmost tip of New York's Long Island—Montauk Point. Conceived as a sporting retreat, Fisher's plan included three hotels, a gambling and bathing casino, polo fields, golf courses, and some thirty or forty houses. Although the area had been settled for nearly three centuries, Montauk remained remote and rugged: Fisher would provide the resources for public utilities such as roads and a water supply.

Construction at Montauk began in September 1926 and continued through the spring of 1927. By the time the first hotel opened in June 1927, Fisher had completed an eighteen-hole golf course, one polo field, and a half-mile driving track. The Mediterranean revival style that Schultze & Weaver had used to create picturesque Florida resorts must have seemed less appropriate for a northern setting like Montauk. Tudor revival, a nostalgic reference to England, provided the unifying style for Fisher's Long Island development, including Schultze & Weaver's new hotel. The H-shaped building featured steep gabled roofs and dormers, tall narrow windows with small panes, prominent chimneys, half-timbering, decorative brickwork, and slate roofs.

Inside the building, the main lobby ran lengthwise, with two long rows of rounded piers forming three aisles that served to separate public amenities and hotel services. A dining room, grill room, and a few commercial shops were located on the ground floor off the main lobby. Walls were finished in plaster or imitation stone, slate lined the floors, and wood beams supported the ceilings. In the dining room, the beams were painted with a grapevine motif. In the grill room, heavy wood-paneled doors and robust metalwork created a medieval feeling.

—M.L.

above:
Brochure for Montauk Beach (ca. 1926)

opposite:
Montauk Manor, Summer 1927

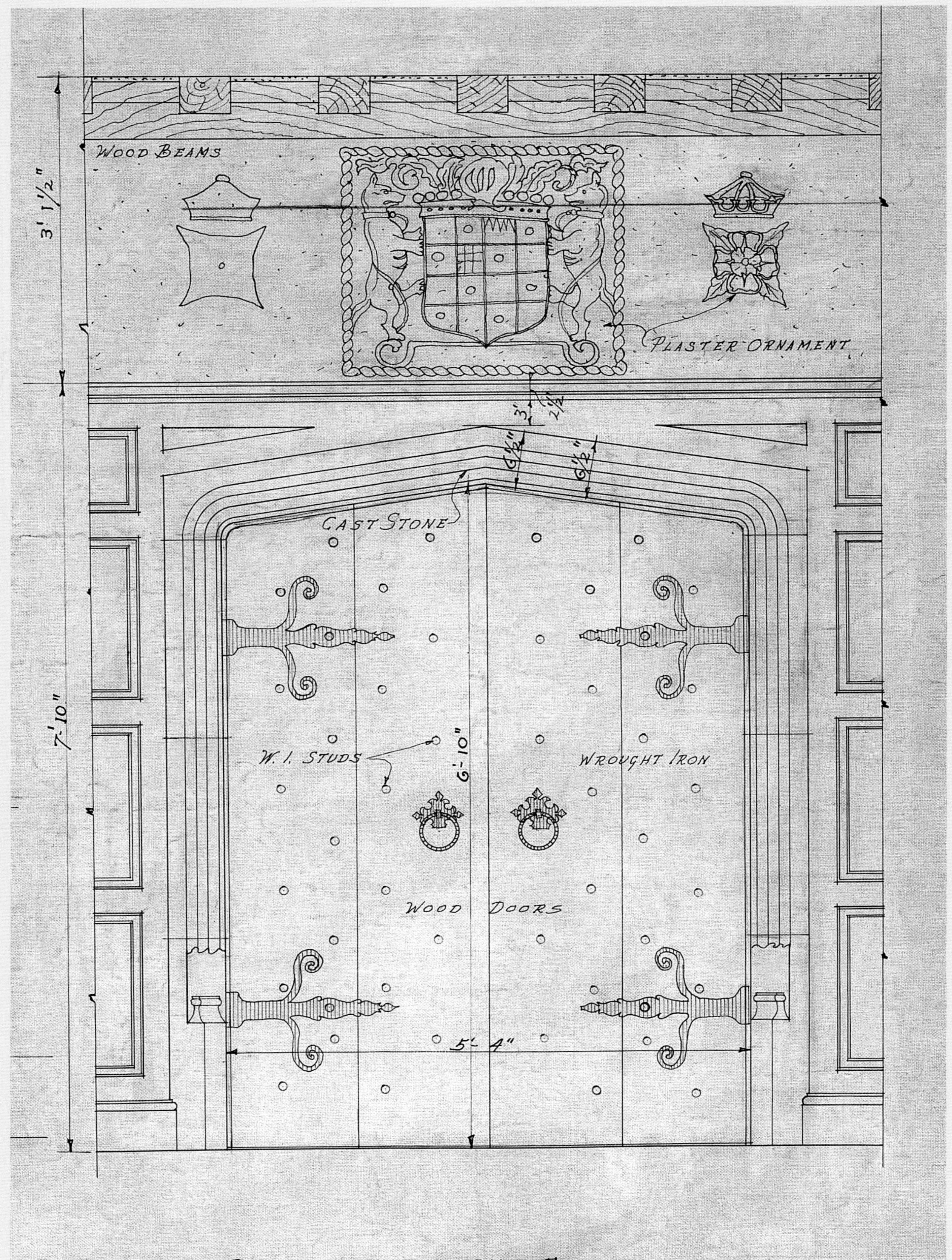
WOOD BEAMS
3' 1 1/2"
PLASTER ORNAMENT
3"
1 1/2"
6 1/2"
6 1/2"
CAST STONE
7'-10"
W. I. STUDS
6'-10"
WROUGHT IRON
WOOD DOORS
5'-4"
DETAIL OF ENTRANCE

above:
Detail showing south elevation of the hotel, 1926

left:
Aerial view of the hotel, from *A Noble Manor House* (ca. 1927)

opposite:
Detail from the plan for the grill room, showing an entrance, 1926
Details such as this wooden door in the grill room, with its wrought-iron hardware, stone frame, and plaster ornament, reinforced the Tudor revival atmosphere created by the hotel's architecture.

top:
Postcard showing the hotel's lobby, after 1927

bottom:
Views of Carl Fisher's Montauk Beach development, from *Montauk Beach on Long Island: The Miami Beach of the North* (ca. 1926)
Below two views of a proposed second hotel (never actually built) for Fisher's development is a sketch of the Montauk Manor. The Tudor revival style provides a unifying motif for the entire Montauk project.

opposite:
Montauk Manor, from *Montauk Beach: A Distinguished Summer Colony on the Slender Tip of Long Island* (1929)

GENERAL OGLETHORPE HOTEL
Savannah, Georgia, 1926–27

Commissioned by Citizen's Tourist Hotel Corporation

Opened to the public on October 17, 1927

Currently operated as the Wilmington Plantation Condominium Complex

The General Oglethorpe Hotel represents the end of Schultze & Weaver's resort hotel phase, which began with their 1923 plans for the Nautilus Hotel in Miami Beach. Located on the Wilmington River, rather than Biscayne Bay, the hotel shared the Nautilus's basic arrangement of four wings radiating from a central core. The wings were stepped back, allowing for several rooftop terraces. The white stucco facade, Spanish-tile roof, and metal balconies were loosely based on Italian or Spanish architectural forms. The principal entrance faced the water and was designed as a classical loggia with an open arcade.

The hotel's facilities were limited to a large dining room and a grand ballroom/lounge. Photographs reveal that the rooms were very stark, with stucco walls, imitation limestone piers and bases, cast-plaster capitals, and plaster-decorated ceilings. One wall of the dining room consisted of a series of tall, arched windows, which was matched on the facing wall by blind arches set with small clerestory windows. The painted plaster coffered ceiling and chandeliers added a touch of luxury to the room. The ballroom/lounge was similarly arranged with one wall of windows and the other of masonry. The decorative detailing was limited to a series of vaults above each window, terminating in decorative corbels. The kitchen and service rooms were separated from the main guest wings, but they were centrally located at the back of the building, providing easy access to both the dining room and lounge.

Adjacent to a golf course designed by the legendary Donald Ross in 1927, the Wilmington Island property featured a river-side pavilion that enclosed a swimming pool and other bath and changing facilities. The pavilion took the form of two neoclassical casinos with open arcades and a diving tower.

—M.L.

The
Savannah-Oglethorpe
Savannah, Georgia

above:
Brochure for the hotel, ca. 1927

opposite:
View from the Wilmington River back to the Oglethorpe Hotel, ca. 1927

Elevation drawing for the General Oglethorpe Hotel, 1926

THE SAVANNAH-OGLETHORPE HOTEL
"On the Enchanted Isle"
Savannah, Georgia

top:
Postcard of the hotel, 1940

bottom:
Postcard of the hotel, ca. 1929

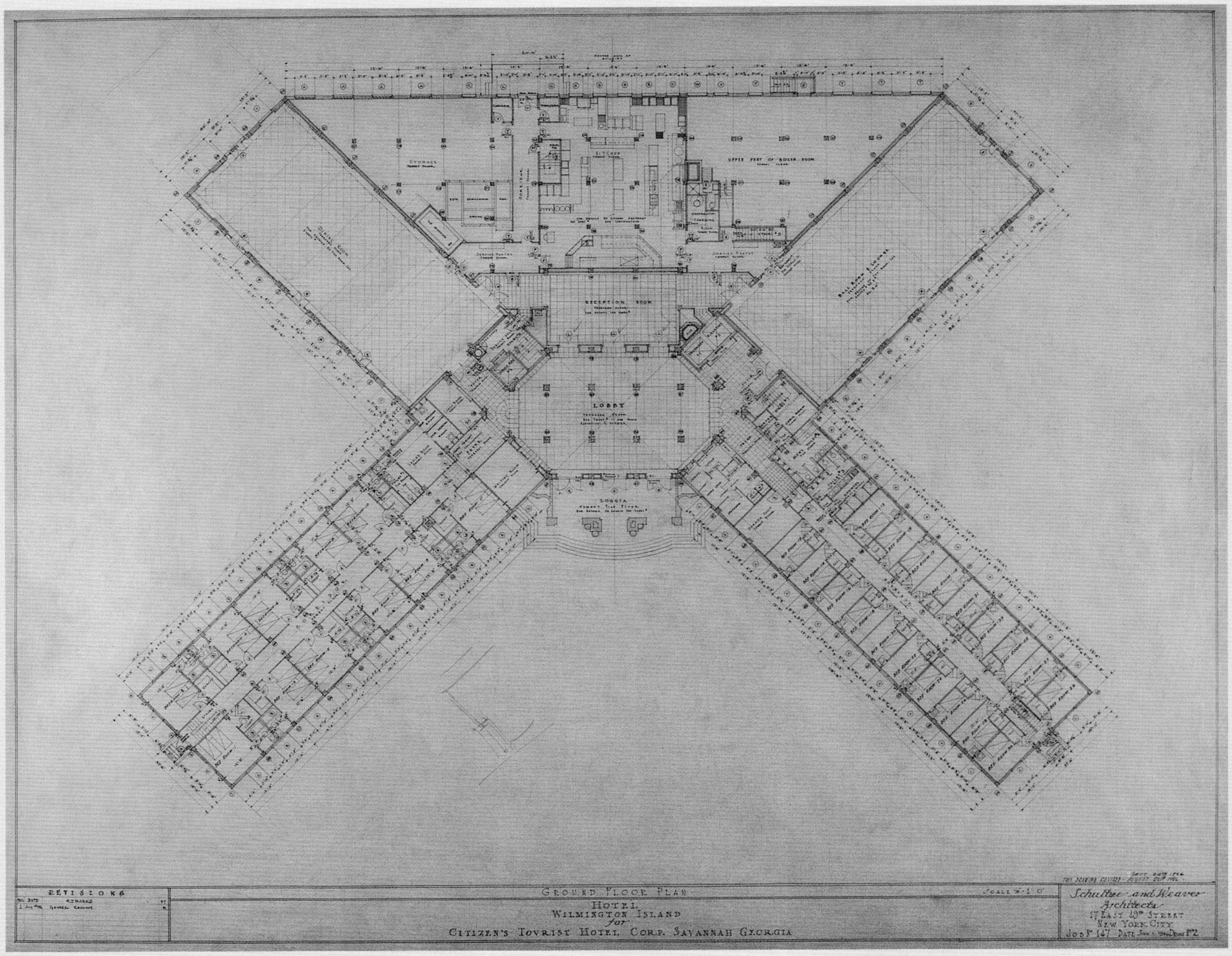

above:
Ground-floor plan, 1926

right:
Detail of the plan for the hotel's swimming pool and pavilions, 1927

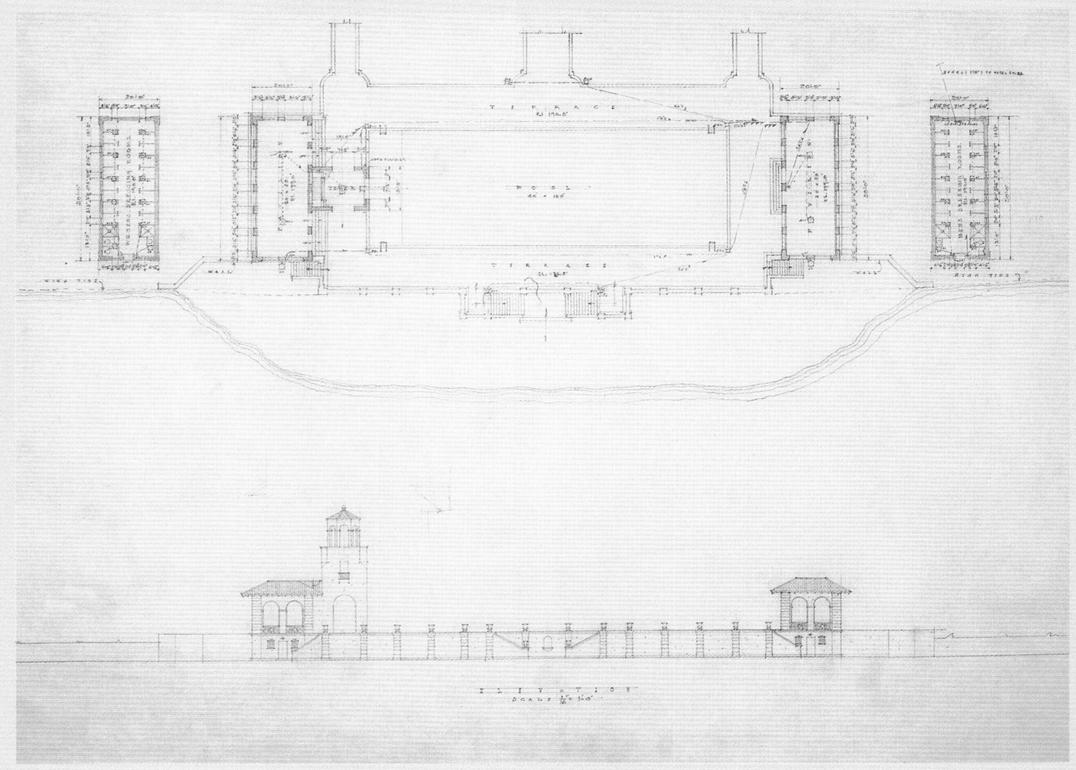

opposite:
Lounge (top) and dining room (bottom), from *The Savannah-Oglethorpe* (ca. 1927)
Because the hotel's service core was located between the two wings that housed the dining room and lounge, the architects maintained symmetry in their interior designs for these rooms by matching the high arched windows on the exterior walls with blind arches fitted with small clerestory windows on the walls that faced the service facility.

SHERRY-NETHERLAND HOTEL

New York, New York, 1926–27

Commissioned by the Fifty-ninth Street and Fifth Avenue Corp.

Purchased by the Sherry-Netherland Company, a subsidiary of Boomer-DuPont Properties Corporation, during construction

Constructed by the Schroeder-Koppel Company

Opened to the public in November 1927

Currently operated by Sherry-Netherland, Inc.

Located on the northeast corner of Fifth Avenue and Fifty-ninth Street, the Sherry-Netherland Hotel occupied the site where William Waldorf Astor's Hotel New Netherland (William H. Hume, 1893) once stood. When it opened on November 1, 1927, the $10 million, thirty-eight story building was twice the size of its predecessor; at 570 feet, it was the tallest apartment building in the world and was four feet taller than the Washington Monument. The hotel's high-peaked roof with gilded, minaret-like ornamental lantern was a noted addition to the New York City skyline. This distinctive flèche—an adaptation of a French Renaissance form—paid homage to the venerable Plaza Hotel across Fifth Avenue.

Designed by Schultze & Weaver, together with another firm, Buchman and Kahn, in a variation on the Italian Renaissance style, the building was set on a four-story travertine-clad base. Three monumental arches faced Fifth Avenue, the northernmost arch serving as the main entrance portal to the hotel. Catering to a wealthy and sophisticated clientele, accommodations ranged from one room with a bath to six rooms with four baths. All of the apartments had service pantries with heating and refrigeration equipment so that food from the hotel's kitchen could be served at home. Large apartments also had a room for a valet or maid. Bathrooms were modern and luxurious, with cream and black marble and silver-plated fixtures.

The building's setbacks allowed for several spacious private terraces beginning on the eighteenth floor. On floors twenty-four through thirty-five of the tower, a single apartment occupied the entire story; floors thirty-six and thirty-seven housed a single duplex apartment. *The New York Times* reported on November 1, 1927, that the average rent for the newly opened apartments ranged from $20,000 to $80,000 per year.

Under the management of Louis Sherry, Inc., the hotel spared no expense in appealing to New York's wealthiest patrons. According to a 1920s promotional brochure, Sherry went "a step further to meet the new social conditions and created a new type of residence apartment, staffed in a new way," employing, training, managing, and paying all service staff: Sherry maids cleaned apartments, and Sherry butlers served food prepared by the main dining room in a tenant's private apartment. Renowned for luxury service, Sherry employees operated, according to the brochure, under one dictum: "Never disappoint a patron."

above:
Sherry-Netherland Hotel logo, from an early brochure cover (ca. 1927)

opposite:
Presentation drawing for the Sherry-Netherland Hotel, rendered by Chester Price, 1926

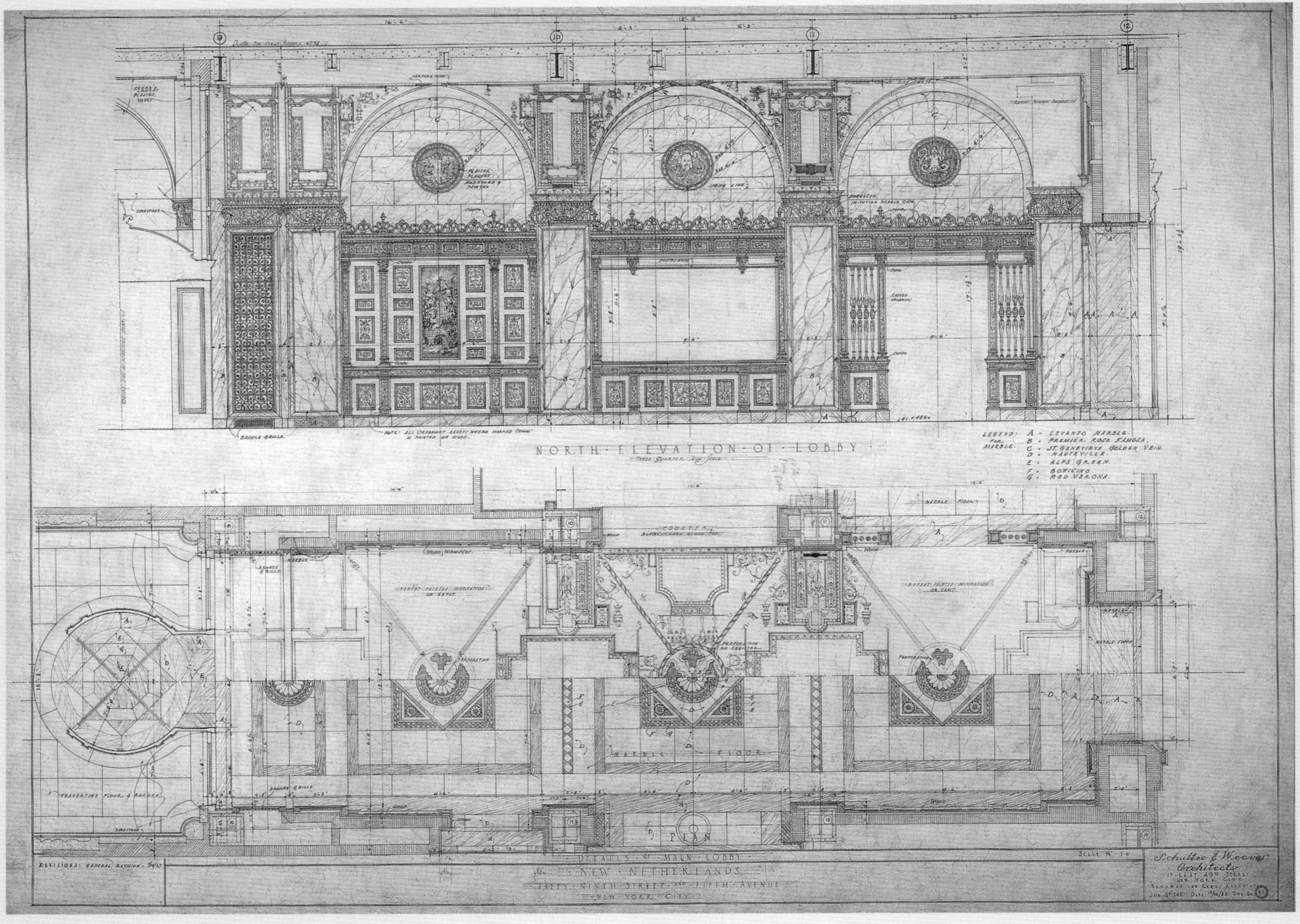

above:
Details of the main lobby, 1926

opposite:
Details of the tower cupola, 1926
The gilt minaret of the Sherry's tower rose out of the hotel's green copper roof and, according to *The New York Times*, pierced "the sky like a gold needle."

The jewel-like entrance vestibule and lobby were elaborately decorated with multicolored marbles, ornamental screens, and a delicately painted, vaulted ceiling. Entered through a gallery at the end of the lobby was a grand staircase leading down to the dining floor. The richly decorated room had classical balustrades, decorative tapestries, and a lavish chandelier. The grill room—a smaller restaurant on a level below the dining room—had a coffered ceiling and walls decorated with panels in faience depicting fables.

—M.L.

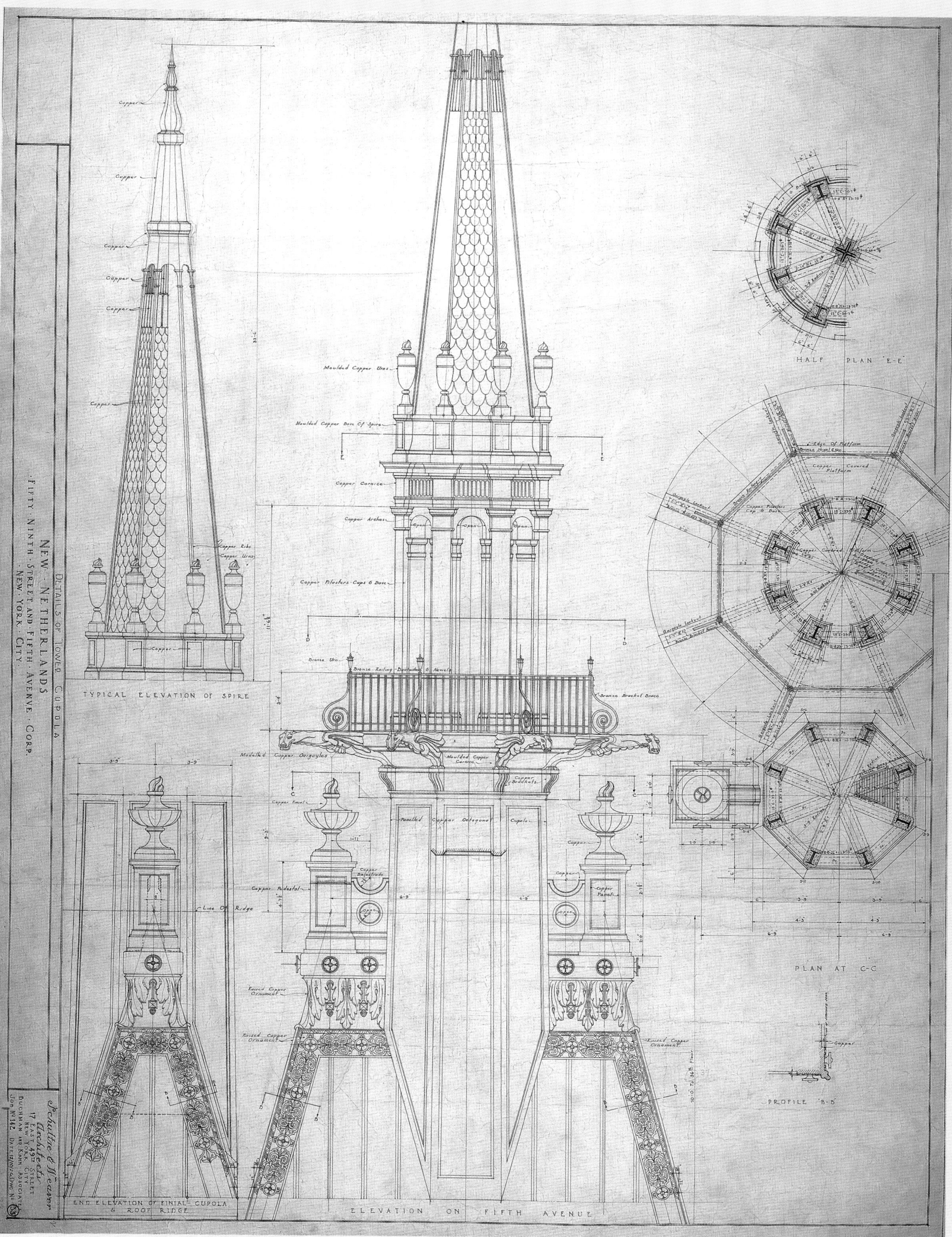
Details of Tower Cupola
New Netherlands
Fifty Ninth Street and Fifth Avenue Corp.
New York City
Copper
Copper Ribs
Copper Urns
Typical Elevation of Spire
Moulded Copper Urns
Moulded Copper Base of Spire
Copper Cornice
Copper Arches
Copper Pilasters Caps & Base
Bronze Urn
Bronze Railing Balusters & Newels
Bronze Bracket Brace
Moulded Copper Gargoyles
Moulded Copper Cornice
Copper Brackets
Copper Panel
Panelled Copper Octagonal Cupola
Copper Balustrade
Copper Pedestal
Line of Ridge
Raised Copper Ornament
End Elevation of Finial Cupola & Roof Ridge
Elevation on Fifth Avenue
Half Plan E-E
Edge of Platform
Copper Covered Platform
Plan at C-C
Profile B-B
Schultze & Weaver
Architects
17 East 49th Street
New York City

above:
Detail of the ceiling in the main lobby, from *Architecture* LVI, no. 6 (December 1927)

opposite:
Lobby of the hotel, ca. 1927
Aside from the relatively small lobby, dining room gallery, and dining room, the Sherry-Netherland had very limited public space on the ground floor, most of which was taken up by shops.

above:
Grill, from *Architecture* LVI, no. 6 (December 1927)

opposite top and bottom:
Views of the dining room, from *Architecture* LVI, no. 6 (December 1927)

top:
Bathroom in a typical hotel apartment, from *Architecture* LVI, no. 6 (December 1927)

bottom:
Interior treatment of an elevator cab, from *Architecture* LVI, no. 6 (December 1927)

opposite:
A postcard showing the hotel from Central Park, after 1927
To the right of the Sherry-Netherland is McKim, Mead & White's Savoy-Plaza Hotel (1927).

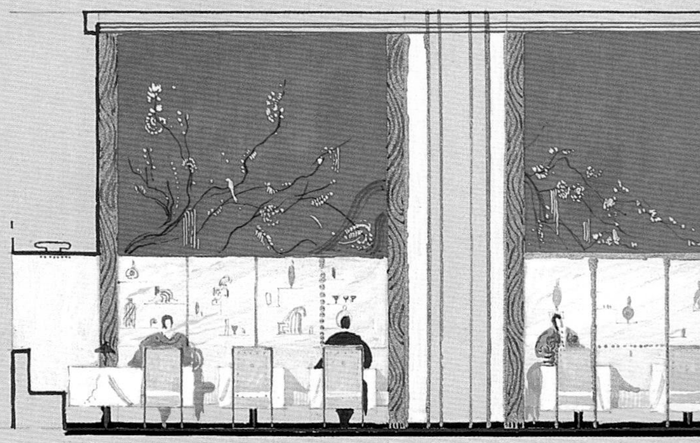

top:
Proposed café, ca. 1934

bottom:
Proposal for a sweet shop, ca. 1934
This sketch for a candy shop was most likely done in the early 1930s, around the same time that the café and bar were proposed.

opposite:
Proposed café, ca. 1934
Most likely a sketch for a new café/bar that opened at the Sherry-Netherland Hotel in 1934, this drawing and the one directly above show a spare, modern elegance that is in marked contrast to the highly ornate, Renaissance-inspired interiors of the hotel's original public rooms.

CAFÉ
RLAND HOTEL

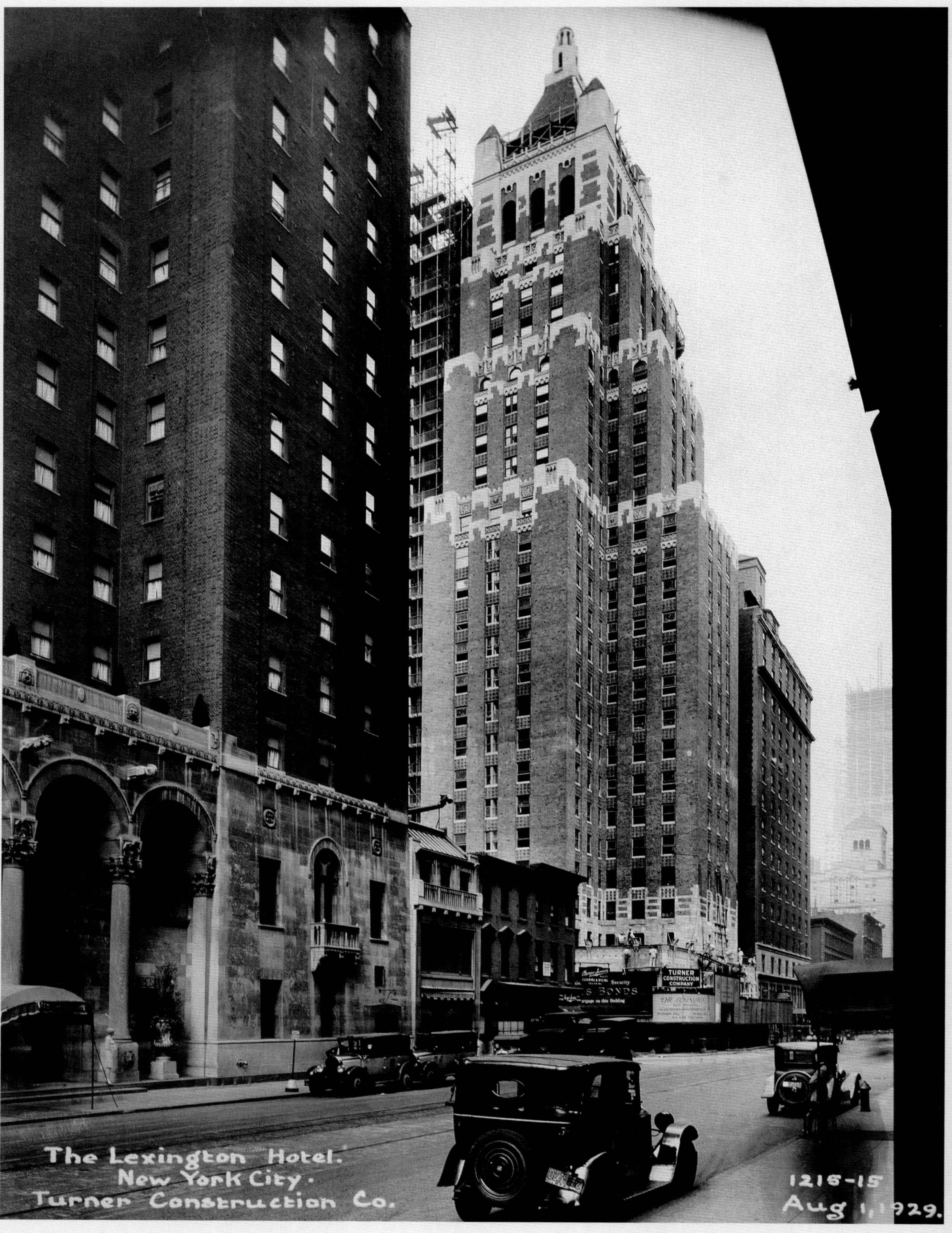
TURNER
CONSTRUCTION
COMPANY
The Lexington Hotel.
New York City.
Turner Construction Co.
1215-15
Aug 1, 1929.

HOTEL LEXINGTON

New York, New York, 1928–29

Commissioned by the American Hotels Corporation

Constructed by the Turner Construction Company

Opened to the public on October 15, 1929

Currently operated as a Radisson Hotel

The Hotel Lexington was built in the Grand Central Terminal area, on the southeast corner of Lexington Avenue and Forty-eighth Street. The hotel's brick and stone facade with terra-cotta trim had a combination of Romanesque and Gothic details, such as pointed arches, projecting piers, pinnacles, turrets, and gargoyles. The hotel's modernity was expressed in its height: the building rose over 300 feet, in twenty-four stories above a two-story base, its verticality emphasized by the brick piers between its windows. Deep setbacks at the top of the building created open courts that provided all rooms with good ventilation and light as well as views of the city's magnificent skyscrapers. An advertisement on the eve of the hotel's opening suggested that, for long-term guests, the setbacks could be developed into private terraces adjacent to suites of rooms.

The Hotel Lexington catered to a clientele of reasonably modest means, with its 801 rooms available for $4 to $7 per night. Amenities included a barber shop, a beauty salon, and large telephone booths fitted with comfortable swivel chairs and French-style telephones, a late 1920s innovation in which the handset contained both transmitter and receiver. Public rooms were limited to two lounges, a dining room, and a grill room. In keeping with the exterior decoration, the two-story lobby with a gallery at the mezzanine level had a quasi-Romanesque atmosphere, with pointed and double-rounded arches, shallow capitals, and a beamed ceiling. Like many of the Schultze & Weaver hotels designed in the Italian manner, the wall treatments included rough plaster, travertine, and marble.

Both the two-level dining room off the main lobby and the grill on the lower level were distinctly modern in appearance. The dining room decor was in the latest fashion—a modified contemporary neoclassicism. Jade walls were set off by gold and black marble; hand-wrought iron stair railings had graceful, curvilinear forms set within a geometric frame; and the painted, coffered ceiling featured delicate mythological figures. The jade and silver grill room was embellished with hand-painted dancing figures on decorative paneling. The room featured a sunken dance floor where the house orchestra entertained guests. An elaborate lighting system and mirrored panels contributed to the grill's modern appearance.

—M.L.

above:
Presentation drawing for the Hotel Lexington, ca. 1928
This early sketch for the hotel emphasizes the verticality of the towers, showing an even more strikingly Gothic design than what was finally executed.

opposite:
A view down Lexington Avenue with the Hotel Lexington nearing completion, August 1929
At the far left is the Shelton Towers Hotel (Arthur Loomis Harmon, 1924). Both hotels featured decorative motifs inspired by Romanesque architecture, such as niches with carved statuary and projecting gargoyles.

Presentation drawing for the Hotel Lexington, ca. 1928
The hotel's base was built from Indiana limestone, while the upper walls were a dark Harvard brick with terra-cotta trim.

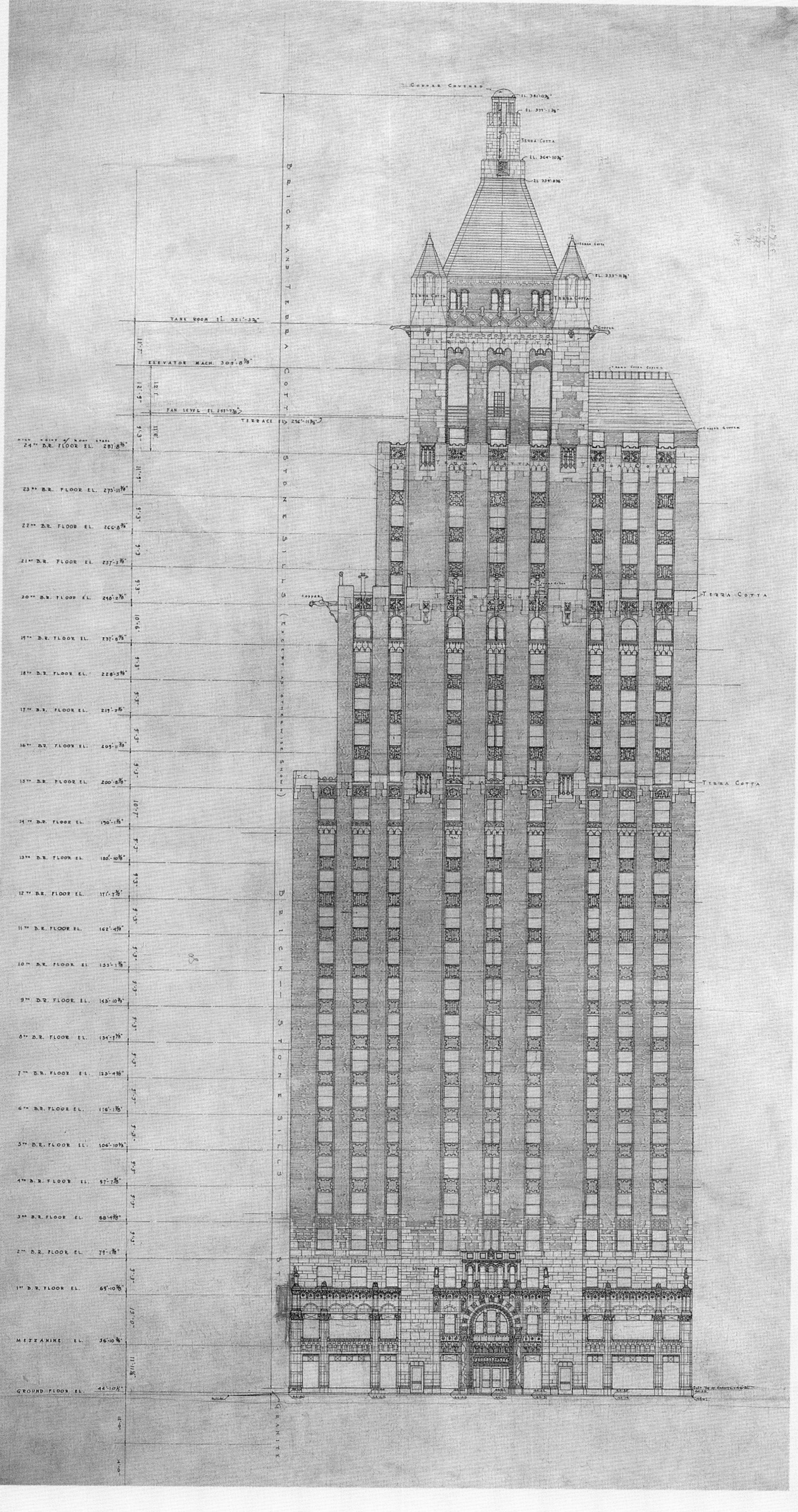

Lexington Avenue elevation (detail), 1928

top:

Brochure for the hotel, ca. 1930

The map emphasizes the hotel's central location in New York City, convenient to transportation, shopping, and entertainment.

bottom:

Entrance, from *The Architect*, 13 (January 1930)

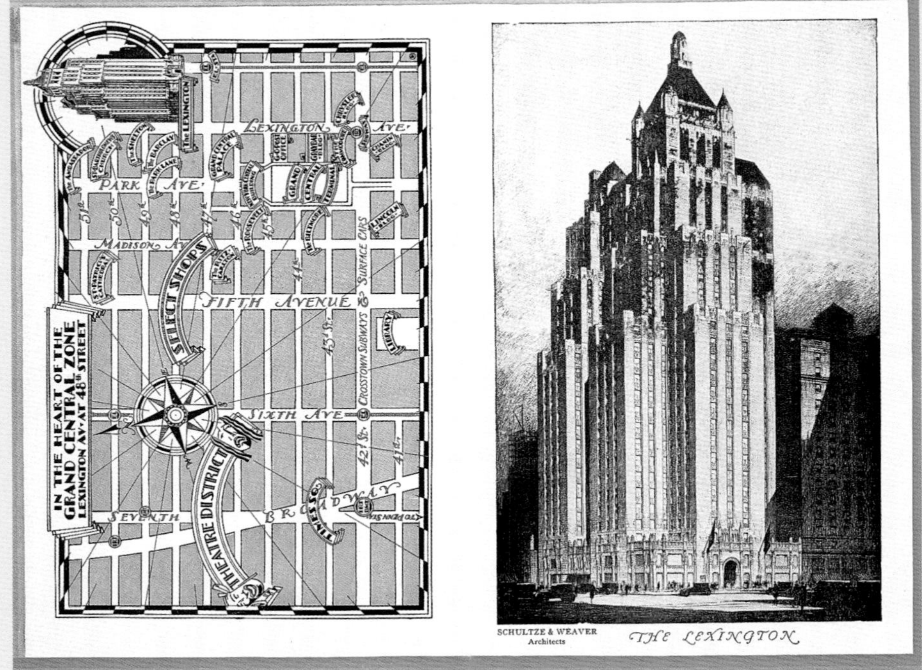

Lexington Avenue entrance (detail), 1928

top:
Postcard for the Revere Room, ca. 1937
With six murals by Anton Refregier about the life of Paul Revere, the Revere Room opened in the Lexington in 1937.

bottom:
Roof details, from *The Architect*, 13 (January 1930)

opposite:
Hotel lobby looking toward the dining room, from *The Architect* 13 (January 1930)

Perspective
Schultze & Weaver
Architects
18 East 48th St.
New York City

HOTEL PIERRE

New York, New York, 1929–30

Commissioned by Hotel Pierre, Inc.

Constructed by the George A. Fuller Company

Opened to the public in October 1930

Currently operated as a Four Seasons Hotel

The blocks around Grand Army Plaza, at the southeast corner of Central Park, became a magnet for high-rise hotel construction in the late 1920s. Schultze & Weaver made their first mark in this neighborhood with the Sherry-Netherland in 1927 and returned several years later to design a new, and much larger, hotel—the Pierre. Named after its president and managing director, Charles Pierre Casalasco, who had long operated a fashionable restaurant on Park Avenue, the hotel became an equally fashionable hub for upscale guests, who leased apartments in the building long term. The architects began designing the forty-two-story brick tower, set on a stone base, no later than early 1929. Built on a long lot facing Sixty-first Street at the corner of Fifth Avenue, the Pierre opened in October 1930.

The hotel was both a place of residence and a busy entertainment center, and its design reflects those disparate uses. The ground floor was divided into two areas, each with its own entrance on Sixty-first Street. At the western end was a dining room that overlooked Central Park, entered through an elegant oval foyer. The eastern end of the ground floor was occupied by the main lobby and a lounge and writing room. In between these two areas, connected only by a corridor and elevator lobby running along the back of the building, was the upper part of the hotel kitchen—a space inaccessible to guests. This separation of spaces allowed hotel guests to enjoy the peace and quiet of the lobby and lounge without disturbance from the comings and goings of people visiting the hotel for entertainment.

Because it was located in a neighborhood zoned for residential use, the Pierre, unlike most other large luxury hotels, had no ground-level shops. The lack of revenue from rental trade might have been a financial handicap, especially in combination with Prohibition, which made it impossible for the hotel to reap profits from a bar. The Pierre found a different source of revenue by creating one of the city's most lavish entertainment complexes. In addition to the dining room and—directly beneath it, in the basement—a grill room, the hotel also included several banquet rooms, two small ballrooms, and the 100- by 45-foot main ballroom. Almost all of the second floor was given over to these rooms, appointed, as was the ground floor, in variants of the neo-Georgian style derived from eighteenth-century English forms. Guests arriving for functions entered through a separate door on Sixty-first Street, between those leading to the lobby and to the dining room.

above:
Matchbook cover for the hotel, after 1930

opposite:
Study for the Hotel Pierre, 1928
This early study shows some slight differences (especially near the top of the building) from the final form.

Hotel Pierre and Sherry-Netherland Hotel, after 1930

PIERRE HOTEL
SHERRY NETHERLAND HOTEL
NEW YORK CITY
1930 - 1928

Above the third story, which was devoted to various house functions, were the bedroom floors. The roughly seven hundred apartments varied in configuration, from single rooms to suites of up to ten rooms. All were decorated in a style similar to that used on the public floors. The suites had small serving pantries, equipped with metal cupboards and shelves, a refrigerator, a plate warmer, and a sink. Often these pantries opened directly onto the service elevator lobby.

At the top and bottom of the building were those parts of the hotel that guests did not see. Under the hotel's copper mansard roof was a water tank room and, below that, the machinery that powered the hotel's eleven elevators. Beneath the ground level were floors housing the hotel kitchen and laundry; employees' showers, cafeterias and locker rooms; garbage refrigeration; a transformer room; storage; and facilities for a host of other purposes. Employees accessed these lower stories via an unobtrusive entrance at the eastern end of the Sixty-first Street facade.

—J.M.

Perspective view of the Hotel Pierre, rendered by Chester Price, 1929

right:
Fifth Avenue elevation, 1928

opposite:
Sixty-first Street elevation, 1928

· Sixty · First · Street · Elevation ·
Architects

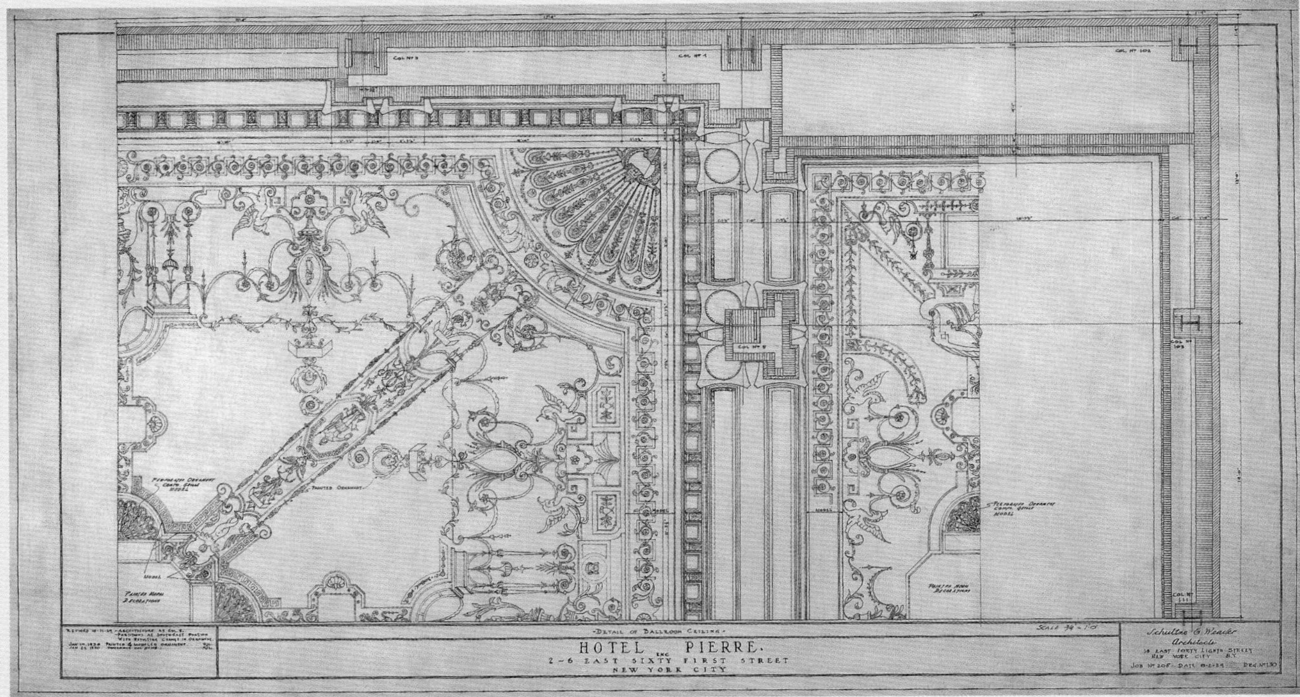

top:
Detailed plan for the grill room ceiling, 1929

bottom:
Detailed plan for the ballroom ceiling, 1929
The ballroom's ceiling had ornament painted in the style of Robert Adam, a popular eighteenth-century Scottish architect who designed elegant country houses.

top:
Grill room, ca. 1930
The Neptune Grill, with its painted aquatic panels lining the walls, was decorated in a blue-green, ivory, and gold color scheme.

bottom:
Ballroom of the Hotel Pierre, ca. 1930

MODELED PLASTER CEILING
AND PAINTED ORN. - SEE 3/4" DETAIL OF CEILING.
CORNICE TO BE PLASTER ORN.
(MODEL)
ORN. COMPO. GRILLE
ORN. COMPO. GRILLE
MIRRORS
MIRROR
MIRROR
MIRROR
MODELED PLASTER ORN.
ORN. CAST. I. GRILLE
ORN. CAST IRON GRILLE
PLASTER
RED VERONA MARBLE BASE
COL. No 3
BLDG. LINE
SECTION THRU SMALL WINDOWS
NORTH ELEVATION OF BALL ROOM.
REVISED 10-11-29 - BEAMS AT 3rd FLOOR LEVEL
JAN 10 1930 - COMPO. & C.I. GRILLES & SECTION
THRU SMALL WINDOWS
R.L.
JAN 28 1930 DIMENSIONS BETW. COLS. #5-#103 ELEC. OUTLETS
MARCH 19, 1930 - REGISTER SIZES, BASE AND CHAIR RAIL.
3/4" DETAILS OF MA
HOTEL
2 ~ 6 EAST SIX
NEW Y

Details of the main ballroom, 1929

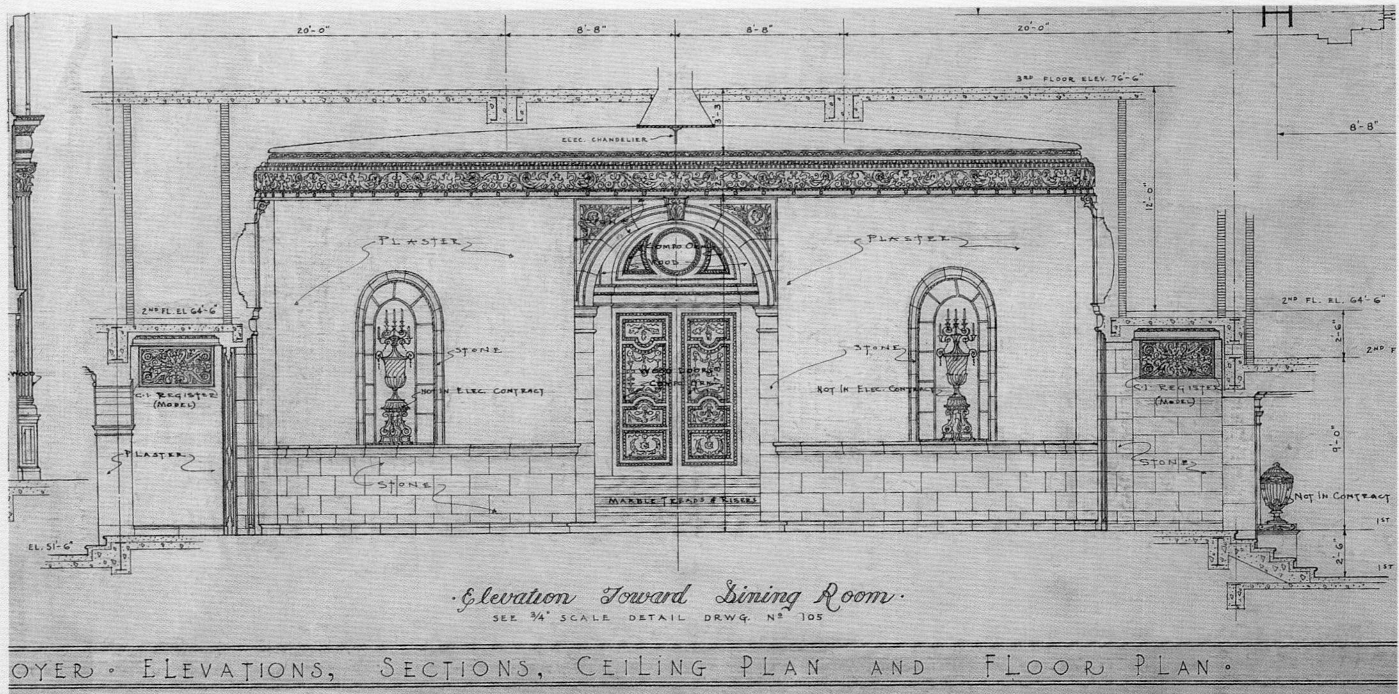

above:
Plan for the dining room foyer showing the elevation toward the dining room (detail), ca. 1929

right:
Lounge, ca. 1930
The wood-paneled walls, marble hearth, and mulberry carpet of the Pierre's lounge, wrote a critic for *The New York Times*, presented "the quiet richness of a great mansion."

Dining room foyer, ca. 1930

WALDORF-ASTORIA HOTEL

New York, New York, 1929–31

Commissioned by Boomer-DuPont Properties Corporation

Constructed by the Thompson-Starrett Company

Opened to the public on September 30, 1931

Currently in operation as a Hilton Hotel

The Waldorf-Astoria is a venerable name in hotel circles. The original establishment consisted of two joined buildings—the Waldorf (1893) and the Astoria (1897)—located at Fifth Avenue and Thirty-fourth Street. In its prime, the hotel was both a renowned destination for out-of-towners and an important business and social gathering place for New Yorkers. It struggled in the 1920s, however: high society had moved further up Fifth Avenue, while Prohibition undermined one of the hotel's main sources of revenue—its bars. Boomer-DuPont Properties sold the hotel at the end of 1928, and it was torn down the following year to make room for the Empire State Building.

Even before the hotel closed its doors, Lucius Boomer, its president, invited Schultze & Weaver to submit plans for a new, larger Waldorf-Astoria. The new hotel, on a block of land leased from the New York Central Railroad between Forty-ninth and Fiftieth streets and Park and Lexington avenues, would occupy the same spot at the apex of the New York hotel world as had its predecessor. During the planning phase, Boomer, Leonard Schultze, and Lloyd Morgan, the firm's chief designer, traversed Europe and Britain, viewing hotels, hunting for antiques and other furnishings, and meeting with artists who would provide decoration for the hotel. Demolition of existing buildings on the site began in mid-1929, and construction began early the next year. The site, located directly over New York Central Railroad tracks, presented special engineering and construction challenges: the building had to rest on steel columns placed at intervals between the tracks, and the work had to take place without interrupting the schedules of the trains. Neverthe-less, the building opened on time, on October 1, 1931.

Although nowhere near as tall as its contemporaries, the Empire State Building and the Chrysler Building, the Waldorf-Astoria shared with them a striking, modernistic profile on the skyline. Faced in gray limestone and a specially produced, matching gray brick, the Waldorf-Astoria lacked the historicist ornament of earlier Schultze & Weaver towers. Facing Park and Lexington avenues were two simple, twenty-story slabs. In between was a forty-two-story tower, on top of which were two turrets that housed elevator machinery, fans, and tank rooms. In terms of size and style, the hotel seemed to belong to a different era than

above:
Brochure for the Waldorf-Astoria (1938)

opposite:
View of the Waldorf-Astoria Hotel from the north, ca. 1931

the thirteen-story Park Lane, designed by Schultze & Weaver less than a decade earlier, which stood directly to its south.

The lower floors of the Waldorf-Astoria housed an enormous complex of public rooms and connected service areas. The main entrance foyer on Park Avenue was flanked by two raised terraces and, beyond, by two dining rooms—the Sert Room and the Empire Room. Proceeding through the foyer, a visitor would have crossed Peacock Alley (a corridor-like lounge named after a passageway in the old Waldorf-Astoria) to enter the windowless main lobby in the very center of the building. The lobby was flanked by the north and south lounges. Beyond the lobby, at the Lexington Avenue end of the building, were an informal restaurant and a barbershop. Lining much of the perimeter of this floor were shops, accessible both from the street and from the interior spaces.

Much of what would have been the second floor was taken up by the high-ceilinged rooms of the ground floor; what remained was given over to service spaces including the very large hotel kitchen. One floor above was perhaps the largest group of ballrooms in the country, consisting of the three-story main ballroom (which could accommodate two thousand people) as well as a number of smaller ballrooms, foyers, and galleries. The fourth floor (or, the part that was not taken up by the upper levels of the ballrooms) accommodated a large number of dining rooms and suites for private entertaining.

The Waldorf-Astoria had roughly two thousand guest rooms. The tower section of the building was exclusively for long-term tenants and even had its own entrance on Fiftieth Street with a private elevator lobby. Rooms for transient guests were located in the two wings on Park and Lexington avenues. Also on the upper stories were a number of private clubs, such as the Double Six Club, the Canadian Club, and the Junior League Club.

Schultze & Weaver and the many decorators they hired—including Arthur S. Vernay, Inc., Barton, Price and Wilson, Inc., W. & J. Sloane, and L. Alavoine & Co.—did not try to impose any uniform style on this huge and varied assemblage of spaces. There was a rough division, in terms of interior architecture and decoration, between the more private and more public parts of the hotel. Guest living quarters and the private entertainment rooms on the fourth floor were decorated in manners that conformed with conservative "good taste" (most notably, eighteenth-century French and English styles). This was also true of a few of the larger rooms on the lower floors, such as the Basildon Room, which was modeled after (and contained original pieces from) the main salon of the eighteenth-century English country home Basildon Park. But most of the larger public rooms—like the main ballroom, the entrance foyer, the hotel lobby, and adjoining lounges and passages—displayed more contemporary taste, with their indirect lighting, ample use of metal, and art moderne–influenced ornament. Still other rooms fell outside these categories. The Norse Grill, with its plank walls and carved wooden ceiling beams, was meant to evoke traditional Scandinavian style.

—J.M.

Photographic reproduction of an exterior perspective, rendered by Lloyd Morgan, ca. 1930

Presentation drawing for the main ballroom, rendered by Lloyd Morgan, 1930
The main ballroom, with a gray, silver, and gold scheme, had a floor measuring 135 by 130 feet. The grilles at the back of the stage masked a large pipe organ.

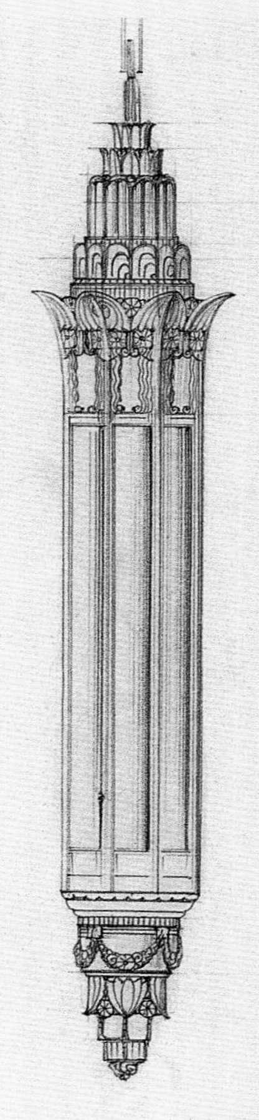

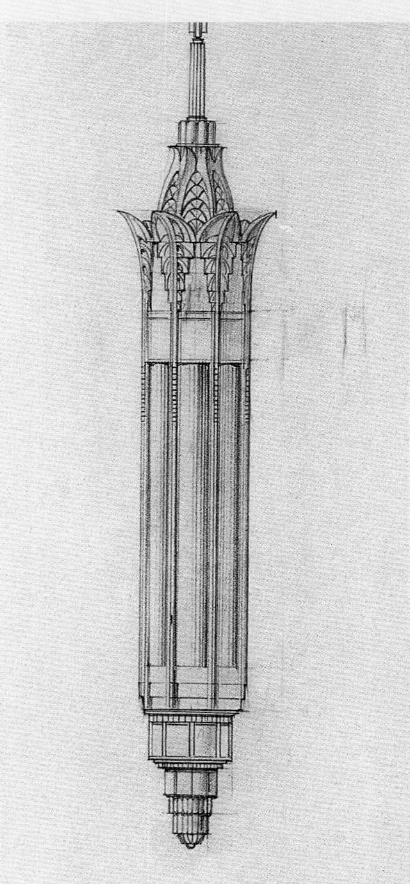

above:
Designs for lanterns for the hotel entrance on Park Avenue, ca. 1930

opposite:
Design for the Park Avenue entrance, ca. 1930

right:
Mirror in the Starlight Roof, ca. 1931
Victor White's designs for the Starlight Roof's mirrors were painted in green on gold-tinted mirrors. White also designed glass mosaics for the room's walls.

opposite:
Main foyer and stairs leading to the Empire Room, ca. 1931
A frieze of panels by the French artist Louis Rigal depicting music, dancing, and the pleasures of the table lined the walls of the foyer. Lamps inside the metal urns threw light onto the ceiling, stone walls, and pilasters.

above:
Presentation drawing for the men's restaurant, rendered by Lloyd Morgan, 1930

right:
Norse Grill, ca. 1931

opposite:
View of the Sert Room, ca. 1931
These are two of the fifteen panels painted by José Maria Sert for the ground-floor dining room that was named after him. The panels, inspired by scenes in Cervantes's *Don Quixote*, were meant to convey an atmosphere of high spirits and comedy.

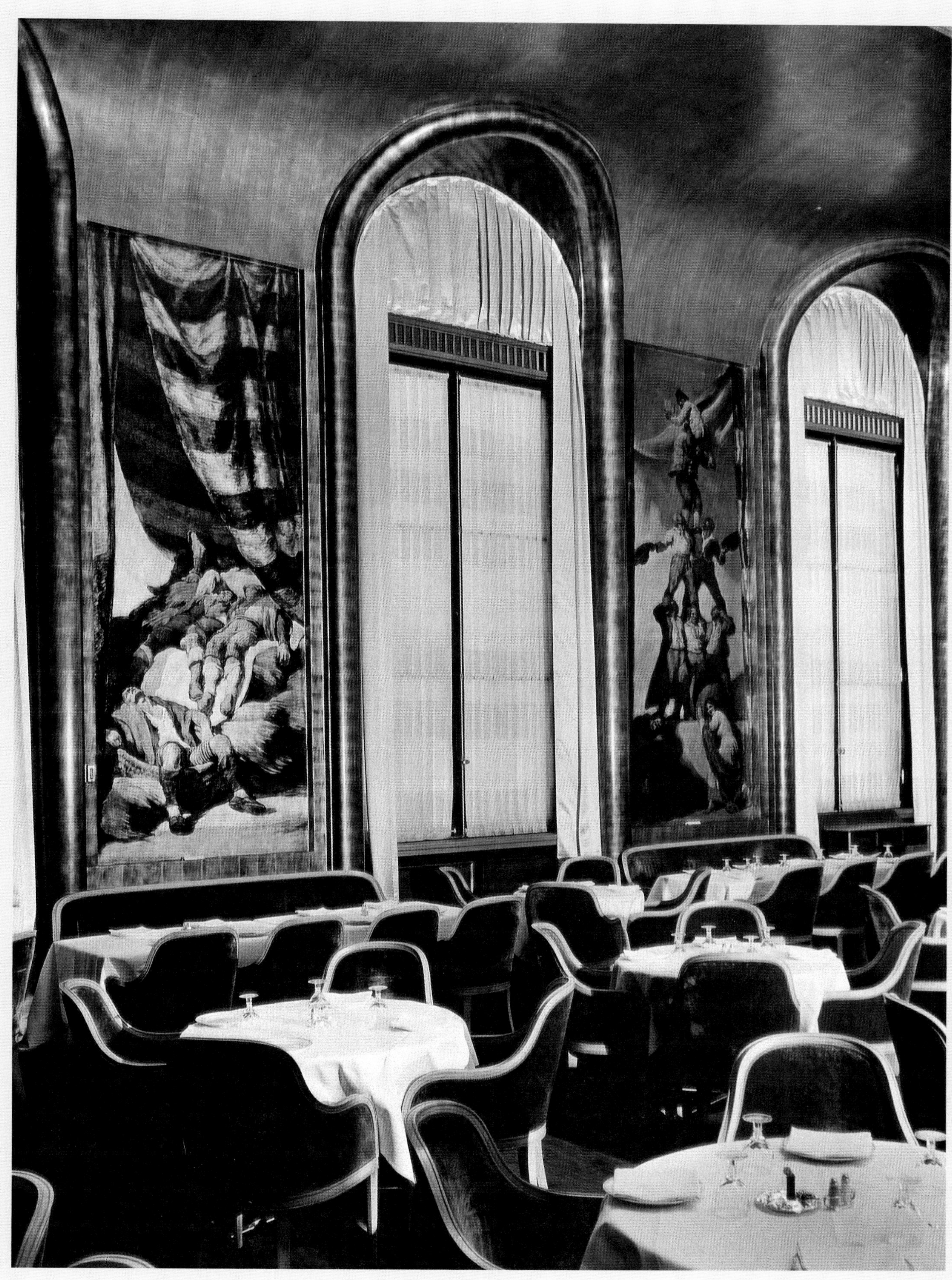

Living room in a tower suite, decorated in eighteenth-century French taste by Jacques Bodart, Inc., ca. 1931

top:
Living room in a tower suite, ca. 1931
This living room for one of the suites in the Waldorf's tower featured one of many antique mantels that were purchased abroad under the guidance of Ralph Edwards of London's Victoria and Albert Museum. The room was decorated by Mrs. Charles H. Sabin.

bottom:
Bedroom in a tower suite, decorated in eighteenth-century English taste, ca. 1931

Proposed mural for the Rose room, ca. 1930
This unrealized mural study shows that the plans for the decoration of the Rose Room, one of two large dining rooms on the ground floor, initially called for *chinoiserie* decoration. The final plan featured modernist murals by José Maria Sert (see page 239).

SELECTED BIBLIOGRAPHY
The Hotel Architecture of Schultze & Weaver

American Architect, August 27, 1923, pls. 66–72. Photos of the Atlanta Biltmore Hotel.

The Architect 5 (January 1926): 372–78. Chester P. Price drawings of the Miami Biltmore Hotel.

Architectural Forum XXXIX, no. 5 (November 1923): 198–204, pls. 73–79. Photos and drawings of the Los Angeles Biltmore Hotel.

Architectural Forum LI, no. 6 (December 1929): 594–98. Photos and plans of the Atlanta Biltmore Hotel.

Architectural Forum LI, no. 6 (December 1929): 599–602. Photos and plans of the Miami Biltmore Hotel.

Architecture LVI, no. 6 (December 1927): 326–32. Photos of the Sherry-Netherland Hotel.

Boomer, Lucius. "The Project." *Building Investment* VII, no. 5 (January 1932): 21–26.

Braden, Susan. *The Architecture of Leisure: The Florida Resort Hotels of Henry Flagler and Henry Plant*. Gainesville: University Press of Florida, 2002.

"The Breakers Hotel, Palm Beach, Fla." *American Architect* 135 (April 5, 1927): 453–62.

"The Breakers, Palm Beach." *Architectural Forum* XXXXVI, no. 5 (May 1927): 453–71.

Crowninshield, Frank, ed. *The Unofficial Palace of New York: A Tribute to the Waldorf-Astoria*. New York: Hotel Waldorf-Astoria Corporation, 1939.

Cullum, R. L. "How the New Breakers Was Built." *Turner Constructor* IV, no. 1 (February 1927): 26–30.

Davidson, Lisa Pfueller. "Early Twentieth-Century Hotel Architects and the Origins of Standardization." *The Journal of Decorative and Propaganda Arts* 25 (2005): 73–103.

Dolkart, Andrew S. "Millionaires' Elysiums: The Luxury Apartment Hotels of Schultze & Weaver." *The Journal of Decorative and Propaganda Arts* 25 (2005): 11–45.

Farrell, Frank. *The Greatest of Them All*. New York: K. S. Giniger Company, 1982.

Horowitz, Louis J. "The Process." *Building Investment* VII, no. 5 (January 1932): 28–29.

"Hotel Biltmore, Los Angeles, Calif." *Architecture and Building* LV, no. 12 (December 1923): 119, pls. 234–38.

"Hotel Lexington, New York City." *Architecture and Building* LXII, no. 2 (February 1930): 35, 39–40.

"Hotel Pierre, New York City." *Architecture* LXIII, no. 1 (January 1931): 23–32.

"Hotel Pierre, New York City." *Architecture and Building* LXII, no. 11 (November 1930): 310–11, 319–23.

LaRoue, Jr., Samuel D., and Ellen Uguccioni. *The Biltmore Hotel: An Enduring Legacy.* Miami: Arva Parks & Company and Centennial Press, 2002.

Lejeune, Jean-François, and Allan T. Shulman. *The Making of Miami Beach, 1933–1942: The Architecture of Lawrence Murray Dixon*. Miami Beach: Bass Museum of Art, 2000.

Lent, Henry B. *The Waldorf-Astoria: A Brief Chronicle of a Unique Institution Now Entering its Fifth Decade*. New York: Hotel Waldorf-Astoria Corporation, 1934.

Lockwood, Charles. *The Breakers: A Century of Grand Traditions*. Palm Beach: The Breakers, 1996.

"Los Angeles-Biltmore Hotel, Los Angeles." *Architectural Forum* XXXIX, no. 5 (November 1923): pls. 73–79.

Murchison, Kenneth. "The Drawings for the New Waldorf-Astoria." *American Architect* 139 (January 1931): 28–35.

Price, Matlack. "Great Modern Hotels of America: The Atlanta Biltmore." *Arts & Decoration* 22 (December 1924): 48–49, 76.

——. "Great Modern Hotels of America, Their Leadership in Architecture and Interior Decoration: The Los Angeles-Biltmore." *Arts & Decoration* 21 (June 1924): 25–28.

Ross, Michael Franklin. "A Comeback with Kudos." *Progressive Architecture* 59, no. 11 (November 1978): 66–71.

Schultze, Leonard. "The Architecture of the Modern Hotel." *Architectural Forum* XXXIX, no. 5 (November 1923): 199–204.

——. "The Plan." *Building Investment* VII, no. 5 (January 1932): 26–28.

——. "The Waldorf-Astoria Hotel." *Architecture* LXIV, no. 5 (November 1931): 251–309.

Stern, Robert A. M., Gregory Gilmartin, and Thomas Mellins. *New York 1930: Architecture and Urbanism Between the Two World Wars*. New York: Rizzoli, 1987.

Sutton, Horace. *Confessions of a Grand Hotel: The Waldorf-Astoria*. New York: Harry Holt and Company, 1951.

Weaver, S. Fullerton. "Planning the Modern Apartment Hotel." *Architectural Forum* XLI, no. 5 (November 1924): 205–12.

Wharton, Annabel. "Two Waldorf-Astorias: Spatial Economies as Totem and Fetish." *Art Bulletin* LXXXV, no. 3 (September 2003): 523–43.

Wilson, R. C. "The New Breakers Hotel, Palm Beach, Florida." *Turner Constructor* IV, no. 1 (February 1927): 4–10.

Yee, Roger. "Phyllis Lambert and Gene Summers: Biltmore Hotel Los Angeles." *Interiors* 136, no. 12 (July 1977): 60–65.

INDEX

IMAGE CREDITS

The editors would like to thank the many generous individuals and institutions that supplied images for this book. Sources are listed alphabetically, with photographer, copyright holder, and detailed collection information given in parentheses following the page number upon which the image appears. Unless otherwise noted, all Wolfsonian–FIU collection photography was taken by Silvia Ros.

Arva Parks & Company: 154; 156 top; 160; 161 (photographer G. W. Romer; © Romer Collection, Miami-Dade Public Library)

The Athenaeum of Philadelphia: 39 fig. 1

Chicago Historical Society: 41 fig. 2 (neg. no. ICHi–31506)

© Flagler Museum: 170; 171; 173 bottom; 178 (photographer E. F. Foley); 179 (photographer E. F. Foley)

© Flagler Museum Archives: 182; 183

Florida State Archives: 17, figs. 6, 7 (photographer W. A. Fishbaugh); 18 fig. 8; 22 fig. 15 (photographer W. A. Fishbaugh); 56 fig. 18 (photographer G. W. Romer; © Romer Collection, Miami-Dade Public Library); 158 (photographer W. A. Fishbaugh); 162; 166

Historical Museum of Southern Florida, Miami, Florida: 16 fig. 5 (photographer Fairchild Aerial Camera Corp.); 61 fig. 22; 65 fig. 24; 126; 127 top; 127 bottom (photographer J. N. Chamberlain); 128 (photographer J. N. Chamberlain); 164; 165 top and bottom

Kyushu University Design Library, Lloyd Morgan Architectural Collection: 27 fig. 20 (photographer Amemya); 30 fig. 23 (photographer Amemya); 31 fig. 25 (photographer Amemya); 72 fig. 7 (photographer Amemya); 124 (photographer Edgar Orr); 130 top (photographer Edgar Orr); 133 top and bottom (photos: Edgar Orr); 141; 145 bottom (photographer Edgar Orr); 146 top (photographer Edgar Orr); 147 (photographer Edgar Orr); 157 (photographer W. A. Fishbaugh); 159 (photographer W. A. Fishbaugh); 168 top and bottom; 169; 201 (photographer Amemya); 223 top and bottom (photographer Amemya); 226 bottom (photographer Amemya); 227 (photographer Amemya)

Los Angeles Public Library, Security Pacific Collection: 115; 116 left

Montauk Library: 184; 187 bottom (photographer Frank Turgeon); 188 top; 189

Millennium Biltmore Hotel, Los Angeles: 114 (photographer Keystone Photo); 116 right (photographer Keystone Photo); 119 top (photographer Keystone Photo); 121

Museum of the City of New York: 26 fig. 19; 205

Museum of the City of New York, The Byron Collection: 93 fig. 8 (acc. no. 93.1.1.6063; photographer The Byron Company); 94 fig. 11 (acc. no. 93.1.1.5787; photographer The Byron Company); 96 fig. 13 (acc. no. 93.1.1.6678; photographer The Byron Company)

Museum of the City of New York, The Wurts Collection: 93 fig. 9 (acc. no. 802260; photographer Wurts Brothers); 94 fig. 10 (acc. no. 802253; photographer Wurts Brothers)

Myrna and Seth Bramson Collection, Miami Shores, Florida: 51 fig. 13; 53 fig. 15; 57 fig. 19; 153

The New-York Historical Society: 42 fig. 4 (neg. no. 77588d); 70 fig. 4 (neg. no. 77497d); 74 fig. 11 (neg. no. 77496d); 103 fig. 20 (neg. no. 76630d/T); 212 top (neg. no. 77512T); 214 top (neg. no. 77513T); 229 (neg. no. 76630d/T)

The New York Public Library, Astor, Lenox and Tilden Foundations, General Research Division: 83 fig. 21 (photographer Wm. M. Rittase); 212 bottom; 214 bottom; 215

The New York Public Library, Astor, Lenox and Tilden Foundations, Map Division: 77 fig. 15

University of Miami, Coral Gables, Florida, Otto G. Richter Library: 24 fig. 18 (photographer Drix Duryea); 68 fig. 1 (photographer Amemya); 69 fig. 2; 70 fig. 3; 75 fig. 12; 142 (photographer Amemya); 145 top (photographer Amemya); 146 bottom (photographer Amemya); 148; 149 (photographer Amemya); 151 top and bottom (photographer Amemya); 200 (photographer Amemya); 202 (photographer Amemya); 203 top and bottom (photogrpher Amemya); 204 top and bottom (photographer Amemya)

University of Miami Libraries, Coral Gables, Florida, Cuban Heritage Collection: 138; 139 and 140 bottom

V. & J. Duncan Antique Maps & Prints, Savannah, Ga.: 190; 191; 193 bottom; 195

Vicki Gold Levi Collection: 44 fig. 5; 45 fig. 6; 46 figs. 7, 8; 47 figs. 9, 10; 49 fig. 11

The Wolfsonian–FIU, Miami Beach, Florida: 41 fig. 3; 62 fig. 23; 97 fig. 15; 101 fig. 19; 118; 143; 144; 193 top

The Wolfsonian–FIU, Miami Beach, Florida, The Mitchell Wolfson, Jr. Collection: 20 fig. 10 (photographer Keystone Photo); 21 figs. 12–14; 34 fig. 30; 50 fig. 12; 52 fig. 14; 55 fig. 17; 58 fig. 20; 59 fig. 21; 72 fig. 8; 74 fig. 10; 87 fig. 1; 90 figs. 4, 5; 94 fig. 12; 98 fig. 16; 100 fig. 18; 117; 119 bottom; 120 top and bottom (photographer Keystone Photo); 122 (photographer Keystone Photo); 123 (photographer Keystone photo); 125; 130 bottom; 136 right; 150; 152; 156 bottom; 163; 185; 188 bottom; 217

The Wolfsonian–FIU, Miami Beach, Florida, The Mitchell Wolfson, Jr. Collection [Schultze & Weaver collection]: cover; frontispiece; 11 fig. 1; 12 fig. 2 (photographer Kaiden-Keystone Studios); 13 fig. 3 (photographer Park Lane Studio); 19 fig. 9; 20 fig. 11; 23 fig. 16 (photographer Virgil R. Boozer Studios); 23 fig. 17; 27 fig. 21; 29 fig. 22; 30 fig. 24; 30 fig. 26; 32 fig. 27; 33 fig. 28; 34 fig. 29 (photographer Richard Averill Smith); 34 fig. 31 (photographer Guild Photography); 35 fig. 32 (photographer F. M. Demarest); 36 fig. 33 (photographer Richard Averill Smith); 37 fig. 34 (photographer Blackstone-Shelburne); 54 fig. 16; 70 fig. 5; 72 fig. 6; 73 fig. 9; 75 fig. 13; 76 fig. 14; 78 fig. 16; 79 fig. 17; 81 fig. 18; 82 fig. 19; 83 fig. 20; 85 fig. 22; 88 fig. 2; 89 fig. 3; 91 fig. 6; 92 fig. 7; 96 fig. 14; 99 fig. 17; 129 top and bottom; 131; 132; 137 top and bottom; 167 top and bottom; 172–73 top; 174; 175; 176; 177 top and bottom; 180–181 (photographer Virgil R. Boozer Studios); 186; 187 top; 192; 194 top and bottom; 196; 197; 198; 199; 206–07 top; 206 bottom; 207 bottom; 208; 209; 210; 211; 213; 216; 218; 219; 220; 221; 222 top and bottom; 224–25; 226 top; 228; 231; 232–33; 234; 235; 236 (photographer Richard Averill Smith); 237 (photographer Richard Averill Smith); 238 top; 238 bottom (photographer Richard Averill Smith); 239 (photographer Richard Averill Smith); 240 (photographer F. M. Demarest); 241 top and bottom (photographer Mattie Edwards Hewitt); 242–43

The Wolfsonian–FIU, Miami Beach, Florida, Long-term loan, The Mitchell Wolfson, Jr. Private Collection, Miami, Florida: 15 fig. 4; 155

The Wolfsonian–FIU, Miami Beach, Florida, The Vicki Gold Levi Collection: 134; 135; 136 left